BEAUMARCHAIS
AND
THE WAR OF
AMERICAN INDEPENDENCE
(VOLUME II)

LECTOR HOUSE PUBLIC DOMAIN WORKS

This book is a result of an effort made by Lector House towards making a contribution to the preservation and repair of original classic literature. The original text is in the public domain in the United States of America, and possibly other countries depending upon their specific copyright laws.

In an attempt to preserve, improve and recreate the original content, certain conventional norms with regard to typographical mistakes, hyphenations, punctuations and/or other related subject matters, have been corrected upon our consideration. However, few such imperfections might not have been rectified as they were inherited and preserved from the original content to maintain the authenticity and construct, relevant to the work. The work might contain a few prior copyright references as well as page references which have been retained, wherever considered relevant to the part of the construct. We believe that this work holds historical, cultural and/or intellectual importance in the literary works community, therefore despite the oddities, we accounted the work for print as a part of our continuing effort towards preservation of literary work and our contribution towards the development of the society as a whole, driven by our beliefs.

We are grateful to our readers for putting their faith in us and accepting our imperfections with regard to preservation of the historical content. We shall strive hard to meet up to the expectations to improve further to provide an enriching reading experience.

Though, we conduct extensive research in ascertaining the status of copyright before redeveloping a version of the content, in rare cases, a classic work might be incorrectly marked as not-in-copyright. In such cases, if you are the copyright holder, then kindly contact us or write to us, and we shall get back to you with an immediate course of action.

HAPPY READING!

BEAUMARCHAIS
AND THE WAR OF AMERICAN INDEPENDENCE
(VOLUME II)

ELIZABETH SARAH KITE,
JAMES M. BECK

ISBN: 978-93-90314-03-4

Published: -

© 2020
LECTOR HOUSE LLP

LECTOR HOUSE LLP
E-MAIL: lectorpublishing@gmail.com

P. A. CARON DE BEAUMARCHAIS

BEAUMARCHAIS AND THE WAR OF AMERICAN INDEPENDENCE (VOLUME II)

BY

ELIZABETH S. KITE

Diplôme d'instruction Primaire-Supérieure, Paris, 1905 Member of the Staff of the Vineland Research Laboratory

WITH A FOREWORD BY JAMES M. BECK

Author of "The Evidence in the Case"

IN TWO VOLUMES,
VOL. II.

ILLUSTRATED

"The faith of a believer is a spring to which uncertain convictions yield; this was the case of Beaumarchais with the King in the cause of American Independence."

Gaillardet, in Le Chevalier d'Eon.

CONTENTS

Chapter *Page*

XV. Curious History of the Chevalier d'Eon—Secret Agent of Louis XV—The Chevalier Feigns to Be a Woman—Curiosity of London Aroused—Necessity for the French Government to Obtain Possession of State Papers in d'Eon's Hands—Beaumarchais Accepts Mission—Obtains Possession of the Famous Chest. 1

XVI. Beaumarchais's Earliest Activities in the Cause of American Independence—First Steps of the Government of France—Bonvouloir—Discord Among Parties in England—Beaumarchais's Memoirs to the King—Meets Arthur Lee—Lee's Letter to Congress—King Still Undecided—Curious Letter of Beaumarchais, with Replies Traced in the Handwriting of the King. 12

XVII. Beaumarchais's English connections—With Lord Rochford—With Wilkes—Meets Arthur Lee—Sends Memoir to the King—His Commission to Buy Portuguese Coin—Called to Account by Lord Rochford—Vergennes's Acceptance of his Ideas—Article in *The Morning Chronicle*. 27

XVIII. Memoir Explaining to the King the Plan of His Commercial House—Roderigue Hortalès et Cie.—The Doctor Du Bourg—Silas Deane's Arrival—His Contract with Beaumarchais—Lee's Anger—His Misrepresentations to Congress—Beaumarchais Obtains His Rehabilitation. 39

XIX. Suspicions of English Aroused Through Indiscretions of Friends of America—Treachery of du Coudray—Counter Order Issued Against Shipments of Beaumarchais—Franklin's Arrival—England's Attempt to Make Peace Stirs France—Counter Order Recalled—Ten Ships Start Out—Beaumarchais Cleared by Vergennes. . . 56

XX. The Declaration of Independence and Its Effect in Europe—Beaumarchais's Activity in Getting Supplies to America—Difficulties Arise About Sailing—Treachery of du Coudray—Lafayette's Contract with Deane—His Escape to America—Beaumarchais's

Losses—Baron von Steuben Sails for America in Beaumarchais's Vessel, Taking the Latter's Nephew, des Epinières, and His Agent, Theveneau de Francy—The Surrender of Burgoyne—Beaumarchais Finds Himself Set Aside While Others Take His Place—Faces Bankruptcy—Vergennes Comes to His Assistance.. 69

XXI. De Francy Sails for America—His Disappointment in the New World—Beaumarchais Recounts His Grievances against the Deputies at Passy—Rejoices Over American Victories—Manœuvers to Insure Safety to his Ships—The Depreciation of Paper Money in America—De Francy Comes to the Aid of Lafayette—Contract between Congress and De Francy Acting for Roderigue et Cie.—Letters of Lee to Congress—Bad Faith of that Body—Deane's Signature to Documents Drawn up by Franklin and Lee—Beaumarchais's Triumph at Aix—Gudin Seeks Refuge at the Temple—Letters of Mlle. Ninon. 86

XXII. Deane's Recall—Beaumarchais's Activity in Obtaining for Him Honorable Escort—Letters to Congress—Reception of Deane—Preoccupation of Congress at the Moment of His Return—Arnold and Deane in Philadelphia the Summer of 1778—Deane's Subsequent Conduct—Letters of Carmichaël and Beaumarchais—Le Fier Roderigue—Silas Deane Returns to Settle Accounts—Debate Over the "Lost Million"—True Story of the "Lost Million"—Mr. Tucker's Speech—Final Settlement of the Claim of the Heirs of Beaumarchais. 104

XXIII. The *Mariage de Figaro*—Its Composition—Difficulties Encountered in Getting it Produced—It is Played at Grennevilliers—The First Representation—Its Success—*Institut des mères nourrices*—Beaumarchais at Saint Lazare. 121

XXIV. The Marine of Beaumarchais—Success of His Business Undertakings—His Wealth—Ringing Plea of Self-Justification in the Cause of America, Addressed to the Commune of Paris, 1789—The Beautiful House Which He Built in Paris—His Liberality—His Friends—His Home Life—Madame de Beaumarchais—His Daughter, Eugénie. 135

XXV. House of Beaumarchais Searched—The 10th of August—Letter to his Family in Havre—Letter of Eugénie to her Father—Commissioned to Buy Guns for the Government—Goes to Holland as Agent of *Comité de Salut Public*—Declared an Emigré—Confiscation of his Goods—Imprisonment of his Family—The Ninth Thermidor Comes to Save Them—Life During the Terror—Julie again in Evidence—Beaumarchais's Name Erased From List of Emigrés—Returns to France. 148

XXVI. Beaumarchais After His Return from Exile—Takes Up All His Business Activities—Marriage of Eugénie—Her Portrait Drawn by Julie—Beaumarchais's Varied Interests—Correspondence with Bonaparte—Pleads for Lafayette Imprisoned—Death of Beaumarchais—Conclusion. 160

Bibliography 170

Index 172

LIST OF ILLUSTRATIONS

Page

I. P. A. Caron de Beaumarchais. iv

II. Charles de Beaumont 9

III. Charles Gravier — Comte de Vergennes 25

IV. Silas Deane 40

V. William Carmichael 55

VI. Lafayette 68

VII. General John Schuyler. 72

VIII. General Baron von Steuben. 85

IX. Robert Morris 93

X. The Temple 103

XI. Cæsar Augustus Rodney — Attorney General of the U. S. 113

XII. John Jay 126

XIII. D'Estaing 134

XIV. The Bastille 140

XV. House of Beaumarchais 147

XVI. Madame de Beaumarchais 158

CHAPTER XV

> Figaro-"Feindre d'ignorer ce qu'on sait, de savoir tout ce qu'on ignore; d'entendre ce qu'on ne comprend pas, de ne point ouïr ce qu'on entend; surtout de pouvoir au delà de ses forces; avoir souvent pour grand secret de cacher qu'il n'y en a point; s'enfermer pour tailler des plumes, et paraître profond, quand on n'est, comme on dit, que vide et creux; jouer bien ou mal un personage; répandre des espions et pensionner des traîtres; amollir des cachets, intercepter des lettres, et tâcher d'ennoblir la pauvreté des moyens par l'importance des objets; voilà toute la politique ou je meure."
>
> Le Comte—"Eh! c'est l'intrigue que tu définis!"
>
> Figaro—"La politique, l'intrigue, volontiers; mais, comme je les crois un peu germaines, en fasse qui voudra!"
>
> Le Mariage de Figaro, Act III, Scene V.

Curious History of the Chevalier d'Eon—Secret Agent of Louis XV—The Chevalier Feigns to Be a Woman—Curiosity of London Aroused—Necessity for the French Government to Obtain Possession of State Papers in d'Eon's Hands—Beaumarchais Accepts Mission—Obtains Possession of the Famous Chest.

IT was the summer of 1775. The moment was approaching when the attention of Europe would be directed towards the events transpiring on the other side of the Atlantic, in that New World, of which the old was as yet scarcely conscious. The stand for freedom, for individual rights, for the liberty of expansion which was there made, was destined to rouse the warmest sympathies amongst all classes, especially in France. The enthusiasm which greeted the resistance of the colonies rapidly became a national sentiment which the French government was unable to suppress or even to keep within bounds. To direct this enthusiasm into a practical channel that should lead to immediate and efficient support of the insurged colonies whilst awaiting the active intervention of the government, was to be primarily the work of one man, and that man was Beaumarchais.

But in starting for London on the present occasion, he was unconscious of the historic importance which this journey was destined to assume. The mission with which he was charged was one of the most singular with which any government ever seriously commissioned one of its agents.

There was living at this time in London the Chevalier d'Eon de Beaumont, who was a former agent of the occult diplomacy of Louis XV, and who at this time was an exile from his country, to which he had been forbidden to return in consequence of the scandalous and disgraceful quarrel that had occurred between him and the French Ambassador, the Comte de Guerchy, years before. Although publicly disgraced, he retained the secret confidence of the old King, who allowed him an annual income of 12,000 francs. The present government was willing to continue this pension, but on condition that the chevalier give up the secret correspondence of the late King, which remained in his possession, and of which it was very important that the French government should obtain control. It was to negotiate the remittance of this correspondence that Beaumarchais was commissioned the summer of 1775. The oddity of the character with which he had to deal, rather than the actual nature of the mission, was what made the negotiation so difficult and the proceedings so unusual.

Several years previous, about 1771, a rumor began to circulate in England that the Chevalier in question was really a woman disguised. Although one of the most belligerent of characters, who "smoked, drank and swore like a German trooper," it appears that "the rarity of his blond beard and the smallness of his form (Gaillardet)," "a certain feminine roundness of the face, joined to a voice equally feminine, contributed to give credit to the fable (note of M. de Loménie, *sur le* Chevalier d'Eon)." There were also certain facts in the life of the chevalier which supported this theory; among others it was known that as a very young man he had been sent by Louis XV in the guise of a woman to the court of St. Petersburg, where he had succeeded in being admitted as reader to the Empress Elizabeth.

As the Chevalier d'Eon was a widely known personage in English society, the matter took on great proportions and became a subject of betting according to the *manière anglaise*. D'Eon, who seems to have cared primarily for one thing, namely, notoriety of whatever sort, secretly encouraged the dispute, although he wrote at the same time to the Comte de Broglie: "It is not my fault if the court of Russia during my sojourn here, has assured the court of England that I am a woman.... It is not my fault if the fury of betting upon all sorts of things is such a national malady among the English that they often risk more than their fortunes upon a single horse.... I have proved to them, and I will prove it as often as they wish, that I am not only a man, but a captain of dragoons, with his arms in his hands." And yet he was able to keep the world in a state of complete mystification as to his true sex, up to the time of his death in 1810.

Voltaire says of him: "The whole adventure confounds me. I cannot understand either d'Eon, or the ministers of his time, or the measures of Louis XV, or those being made at present. I understand nothing of the whole affair." In his *Memoires sur le Chevalier d'Eon de Beaumont*, M. Gaillardet says: "The history of the Chevalier d'Eon was one of the most singular and most controverted enigmas of the 18th century. That century finished without its being known what was the veritable sex of that mysterious being, who after being successively doctor of law, advocate in the Parliament of Paris, censor of belles-lettres, secretary of embassy at St. Petersburg, captain of dragoons, Chevalier de Saint Louis, minister plenipotentiary to London, suddenly, at the age of 46 years announced himself to be a woman, assumed the costume of his new rôle, and conserved it until the time of his death in 1810."

As we shall presently see, and for reasons wholly justifiable, it is Beaumarchais who works this transformation in the life of d'Eon. Nothing in relation to his strange character is so passing strange as the fact that the King and his minister, and above all that Beaumarchais himself, the cleverest of men—should have been completely duped by the Chevalier as to the matter of his sex. It even went so far as to be generally believed that the *demoiselle* d'Eon was seriously in love with Beaumarchais, and the latter himself believed it. In the most skillful way the chevalier endeavored to make use of this deceit to further his own ends. Failing in this, and having made the fatal avowal and received the King's orders to assume the garb of a woman, the fury of d'Eon knew no bounds. Powerless to wreak his vengeance in any other way, he endeavored by calumny and abuse to thwart the career of the man upon whom he had been able to impose only in the matter of his sex. Beaumarchais readily excused all the insults cast at him, believing as he did, that this is the manner of revenge of the strange creature, "his amazon"—(as d'Eon is familiarly called in the correspondence between himself and the minister Vergennes)—for finding that her love is not requited.

But to return to the facts of the case: D'Eon, at the time of the death of Louis XV was living in constant hope of being restored to favor and allowed to return to France. His pension of 12,000 francs had proved all too small for his support and he was heavily in debt. No sooner had the young king, Louis XVI, mounted the throne than the Chevalier sent word to Vergennes, minister of foreign affairs, announcing that he had in his possession important letters which were of such a nature that should they fall into the hands of the English, it might precipitate a war between the two nations. An agent was therefore dispatched to enter into negotiations. "Understanding," says Gaillardet, "that if he did not profit by this occasion, he would have little to expect from the new reign, d'Eon resolved to put a high price on the papers in his possession. He demanded: first, that he be solemnly justified of the imputations directed against him by his enemies—especially the family of the Comte de Guerchy; second, that all the sums, indemnities, advances, etc., due him for the past 26 years, be paid, amounting in all to 318,477 livres, 16 sous."

Unable to come to any reasonable terms, the negotiations were broken off and the agent returned to France. He was replaced by another who was equally unsuccessful, and for a time the matter was dropped.

In the meantime noise of the affair reached the English government, and d'Eon soon had the satisfaction of receiving large offers from that quarter if he would consent to give up the papers. The Chevalier, whatever his faults, or the violence of his character, was not a traitor; he had no intention of giving the papers in his possession to the English at any price, but he was well satisfied that their value should be thus enhanced.

In the meantime, his pension was suspended and finding himself without funds, "he borrowed 5,000 pounds from his devoted friend and protector, the

Lord Ferrers, giving him as security a sealed chest, which, Ferrers supposed, contained the famous correspondence. He took care, however," says Gaillardet, "to withdraw from that deposit precisely the personal documents of the late King, which were the most important for the court of France and for himself. These papers contained a plan for the restitution of the Stuarts, a descent upon England, and other dreams, constituting what d'Eon called *le grand projet* of Louis XV."

At this juncture Beaumarchais appeared on the scene. "To interest the latter in his cause, and give him a mark of confidence (Gaillardet) d'Eon avows with tears that he is a woman, and this avowal was made with so much art that Beaumarchais did not conceive the least doubt."

D'Eon recounted the history of the papers in his possession, and the offers which he had resisted. Charmed to oblige a woman so interesting by her sorrows, her courage, her *esprit*, Beaumarchais addressed at once touching letters to the King in favor of his new friend. "When one thinks," he writes, "that this creature, so much persecuted, belongs to a sex to which one forgives everything, the heart is touched with a sweet compassion." "I do assure you, Sire," he writes elsewhere, "that in taking this astonishing creature with dexterity and gentleness, although she is embittered by twelve years of misfortune, she can yet be brought to enter under the yoke, and to give up all the papers of the late King on reasonable conditions."

As to the motives which could have induced le chevalier d'Eon to avow himself a woman, his biographer, already quoted, gives the following explanation:

"His military and diplomatic career was about finished; disgraced, he would disappear from the scene of the world and fall into obscurity. But precisely shadow and silence were a horror to him. If there was a mystery in his existence, if they learned that he was a woman, he would become the hero of the day and of the century; his services would then appear extraordinary. This metamorphosis would attract to him the attention of Europe, and enable him more easily to obtain satisfaction from the French government, who would no longer refuse a woman the price of blood shed and services rendered."

Both Gaillardet and Loménie, after a careful examination of all the correspondence in relation to the affair between the Chevalier d'Eon and Beaumarchais, assure us that not a line exists which does not prove that the latter was completely deceived as to the matter of the sex of the Chevalier.

Lintilhac, however, thinks that he has found proofs to the contrary in a letter which begins, "Ma pauvre Chevalière, or whatever it pleases you to be with me...." London, Dec. 31, 1775. Gudin, in his life of Beaumarchais, says, "It was at a dinner of the Lord Mayor Wilkes that I encountered d'Eon for the first time. Struck to see the cross of St. Louis shining on his breast, I asked Mlle. Wilkes who that chevalier was; she named him to me. 'He has,' I said, 'the voice of a woman.' It is probably from that fact that the talk has all come. At that time I knew nothing more about him; I was still ignorant of his relations with Beaumarchais. I soon learned them from herself. She avowed to me with tears (it appears to have been the manner of d'Eon—note of Loménie) that she was a woman, and showed me her scars, remains of wounds which she had received, when, her horse killed under her, a squadron of cavalry passed over her body and left her dying on the plain."

"No one," says Loménie, "could be more naïvely mystified than is Gudin. In the first period of the negotiation, d'Eon is full of attentions for Beaumarchais; he calls him his 'guardian angel' and sends him his complete works in fourteen volumes; for this curious being, this dragoon, woman and diplomat, was at the same time a most fruitful scribbler of paper. He has characterised himself very well in the following letter: 'If you wish to know me, Monsieur the Duke, I will tell you frankly that I am only good to think, imagine, question, reflect, compare, read, write, to run from the rising to the setting sun, from the south to the north, and to fight on the plain or in the mountains ... or I will use up all the revenues of France in a year, and after that give you an excellent treatise on economy. If you wish to have the proof, see all I have written in my history of finance, upon the distribution of public taxes.'"

This, then, was the strange being with whom Beaumarchais had to deal. On the 21st of June, 1775, he received from Vergennes the following letter, which shows in the best possible light the credit which the secret agent of the government had already acquired. He wrote:

"I have under my eyes, Monsieur, the report which you have given M. de Sartine of our conversation, touching M. d'Eon; it is of the greatest exactitude; I have taken in consequence the orders of the King. His Majesty authorizes you to assure to M. d'Eon the regular payment of the pension of 12,000 francs.... The article of the payment of his debts is more difficult; the pretensions of d'Eon are very high in that respect; they must be considerably reduced if we are to come to any arrangement.... M. d'Eon has a violent character, but I do him the justice to believe that his soul is honest, and that he is incapable of treason.... It is impossible that M. d'Eon takes leave of the English King; the revelation of his sex does not permit it; it would be ridiculous for both courts.... You are wise and prudent, you know mankind, and I have no doubt but that you will be able to arrange the affair with d'Eon, if it can be done. Should the enterprise fail in your hands, we shall be forced to consider that it cannot succeed and resolve to accept whatever may come from it.... I am very sensible, Monsieur, of the praises which you have been so good as to give me in your letter to M. de Sartine. I aspire to merit them, and accept them as a gage of your esteem, which will always be flattering to me. Count, I beg you, upon my own, and upon the sentiments with which I have the honor to be very sincerely, Monsieur, etc.

"De Vergennes.

"A Versailles, June 21st, 1775."

July 14, 1775, Beaumarchais wrote to M. de Vergennes announcing that he had obtained possession of the keys of the famous chest, which he had sealed with his own seal and which was deposited in a safe place. "Whatever happens, M. le Comte, I believe that I have at least cut off one head of the English hydra ... the king and you may be quite certain that everything will rest in *statu quo* in England, and that no one can abuse us from now to the end of the negotiation which I believe about finished." But in the meantime, while undertaking the settlement of the affair with d'Eon, the active mind of Beaumarchais had become enflamed with an ardent zeal for the cause of liberty, as it was being then defended on the other side of the Atlantic. "One of the first," says Gaillardet, "he had embraced the cause of the Americans, had espoused it with a sort of love that partook of idolatry.... He followed every phase with an interest which nothing discouraged, not ceasing to hope in the midst of reverses, triumphing and clapping his hands at every victory.... He excused their faults, exalted their virtues, plead for them with all the faculties of his *esprit* and of his soul, before those whom he wished to interest in their fate."

Every voyage back to Paris, which the interests of his mission necessitated, every letter which it occasioned, was made to subserve itself to this one end which transcended all others; namely, to rouse the young King from that state of indecision and indifference to which he was born, and where he seemed likely to remain.

In the next chapter this subject will be taken up in all its detail; for the present it is necessary only to remind the reader that the matter of which we are now treating is all the while secondary in the mind of Beaumarchais. It is, however, of vital importance in that, at the beginning, it offers the avenue of approach to the King and his ministers which might otherwise have been wanting. Through the masterly way in which he settled the affair with d'Eon, the confidence of the King and of his minister was secured. Before the affair was terminated, an open channel had been established which permitted the whole current of the genius of Beaumarchais to flow direct to its goal.

It will be remembered that the Chevalier d'Eon had borrowed five thousand pounds of his friend the English Admiral, Lord Ferrers, and had left him as security the chest containing the famous correspondence of the late King. Before it could be delivered to Beaumarchais there were many difficult questions to settle, the chief one being the Chevalier's return to France, owing to the resentment still felt by the family of the Comte de Guerchy towards the Chevalier, and the latter's well known violence of temper. The King and M. de Vergennes demanded absolute oblivion of the past and a guarantee that no further scandals should arise. This was difficult to assure, owing to the fiery nature of the Chevalier. Already, as we have seen, the latter had avowed "with tears" that he was a woman.

August 7th, 1775, M. de Vergennes wrote to the King, "If your Majesty deigns to approve the propositions of the Sieur de Beaumarchais to withdraw from the hands of the Sieur d'Eon the papers which it would be dangerous to leave there, I will authorize him to terminate the affair. *If M. d'Eon wishes to take the costume of his sex*, there will be no objection to allowing him to return to France, but under any other form he should not even desire it."

In a letter to Beaumarchais, the 26th of the same month, M. de Vergennes wrote: "Whatever desire I may have to see, to know, and to hear M. d'Eon, I cannot hide from you a serious uneasiness which haunts me. His enemies watch, and will not pardon easily all that he has said of them.... If M. d'Eon would change his costume everything would be said.... You will make of this observation the use which you shall judge suitable."

The idea appeared not only good to Beaumarchais, but to offer, perhaps, the only solution to the difficulty. He therefore made this the condition of settlement of the debts of d'Eon, the continuation of his pension, as well as of his being allowed to return to France. The same motives which had actuated the Chevalier to declare himself a woman worked now in favor of what Beaumarchais, endowed with full power in his regard, demanded of him. Realizing, as M. de Vergennes had done, that if the matter were not now adjusted, it would never be again taken up; realizing too that his notoriety would be increased tenfold by this metamorphosis, he decided to submit to what was imposed upon him.

Early in October, Beaumarchais wrote to M. de Vergennes: "Written promises to be good are not sufficient to arrest a head which enflames itself always at the simple name of Guerchy; the positive declaration of his sex and the engagement to live hereafter in the costume of a woman is the only barrier which can prevent scandal and misfortunes. I have required this and have obtained it."

As a matter of fact, on the 5th of October, the Chevalier signed the famous contract, in which he promised to deliver the entire correspondence of the late King, declared himself a woman and engaged to "retake and wear the costume of that sex to the time of his death;" and he added with his own hand, "which I have already worn on divers occasions known to his Majesty." The agent of the French Government on his side agreed to deliver a contract or pension of 12,000 francs, as well as "more considerable sums which shall be remitted for the acquittal of the debts of the Chevalier in England." "Each of the contractants," said Loménie, "reserved thus a back door; if the more considerable sums did not seem considerable enough, the Chevalier intended to keep a portion of the papers, so as to obtain still more funds. Beaumarchais, on his side, had no intention of paying all the debts which it should please the Chevalier to declare, and had demanded of the King the faculty to *batailler* to employ his own expression — with the demoiselle d'Eon, from 100,000 to 150,000 francs, reserving the right to give him the money in fractional parts, and to extend or retract the sum according to the confidence which that cunning personage should inspire."

After the contract was signed, Beaumarchais still holding the money in reserve, demanded the papers of which it was questioned. The chest was produced. Suddenly realizing, however, that he had no authority to open the chest and to examine the contents, and having but small confidence in the veracity of the chevalier, he hastened back to Versailles, obtained the desired permission, and reappeared in London with his new commission. On opening the chest he found indeed that papers of but small importance were contained therein. D'Eon, blushing, confessed that the letters of which the French government desired to obtain possession were hidden under the floor of his room in London.

"She conducted me to her room," wrote Beaumarchais, "and drew from under the floor five boxes, well sealed and marked, 'Secret Papers to remit to the King alone', which she assured me contained all the secret correspondence, and the entire mass of the papers which she had in her possession. I began by making an inventory, and marking them all so that none could be withdrawn; but, better to assure myself that the entire sequence was there contained, I rapidly ran over them, while she made the inventory."

This want of honor in the Chevalier, whose security left with the Lord Ferrers had been proved of comparatively little value, dispensed Beaumarchais, so he considered, from the necessity of acquitting the full debt contracted by d'Eon. This was afterwards most bitterly reproached to him by the Chevalier. In a letter to Lord Ferrers, Beaumarchais wrote: "I have lived too long and know mankind too well to count upon the gratitude of anyone, or to feel the least annoyance when I see those fail whom I have the most obliged." (From a letter dated Jan. 8, 1776, to Lord Ferrers,—Gaillardet.)

The note of 13,933 pounds sterling first addressed to M. de Vergennes had since been increased by 8,223 pounds sterling, of which d'Eon demanded the payment. Beaumarchais, however, true to the interest of the King and his minister, to their great satisfaction, terminated the transaction for a little less than 5,000 pounds sterling. From the determined refusal of Beaumarchais to increase the sum arose the wild fury of d'Eon, who saw his last hope escape him. His invectives against Beaumarchais, his abuse, all had their origin here.

"I assured this demoiselle," wrote Beaumarchais to Vergennes, "that if she was prudent, modest and silent, and if she conducted herself well, I would render so good an account of her to the minister of the King, and even to His Majesty, that I hoped to obtain for her new advantages. I did this the more willingly because I had still in my possession nearly 41,000 francs, from which I expected to recompense every act of submission and of sobriety on her part, by acts of generosity approved successively by the King and by you, Monsieur le Comte, but only as favors, and not as acquittals. It was in this way that I hoped still to dominate and bring into subjection this fiery and deceitful creature."

Early in December, Beaumarchais appeared in Versailles with his famous chest, containing at last the entire mass of papers, the negotiation of which had occupied the minister of Louis XVI since the time of the latter's accession to the throne. Overjoyed at the successful termination of the affair, the King and his minister testified their satisfaction with warmth.

A very honorable discharge was given their agent with a certificate which terminated thus: "I declare that the King has been very well satisfied with the zeal which he has shown on this occasion, as well as with the intelligence and dexterity with which he has acquitted himself of the commission which his Majesty has confided to him. The King has therefore ordered me to deliver the present attestation to serve him at all times and in all places where it may be necessary.

"Made at Versailles, the 18th of December, 1775.

"Signed: Gravier de Vergennes."

CHAPTER XV

CHARLES DE BEAUMONT

dit Mademoiselle le Chevalier D'Eon
1728 - 1810

The matter of the papers was indeed settled; they were safe in the hands of the government, and all uneasiness in regard to them was at an end; not so Beaumarchais with his *amazone intéressante*. Furious to find that his exorbitant demands upon the French government had miscarried, d'Eon thought only of wreaking his vengeance upon Beaumarchais. After exhausting himself with very "masculine abuse" upon his "austere friend" (Loménie), he suddenly, with the same art with which he had avowed himself a woman, set about convincing Beaumarchais that he was in love with him, uttering bitter reproaches for the cruelty, hardness and injustice with which he had treated an unhappy woman, who in a moment of weakness had revealed herself to him. "Why," cried this disguised dragoon, "why did I not remember that men are good for nothing upon this earth but to deceive the credulity of women, young and old?... I still thought that I was only rendering justice to your merits, admiring your talents, your generosity; I loved you already no doubt; but this situation was still so new for me that I was very far from realizing that love could be born in the midst of trouble and sorrow."

In a note, M. de Loménie remarked that what there was specially *piquant* in this correspondence of d'Eon and Beaumarchais is that the former, while posing as a woman, "often gives an enigmatic turn to his phrases, as though he wished to establish for the day when the fraud would be unveiled, that he had been able to dupe a man as clever as the author of the *Barbier de Séville*, and that he duped him in mocking at him to his very face, without being suspected. Beaumarchais, for his part, amused himself at the expense of that *vieille Dragonne* in love, and confirmed himself more and more in the error as d'Eon more adroitly simulated the anger of an offended old maid."

Beaumarchais wrote to M. de Vergennes: "Everyone tells me that this crazy woman is crazy over me. She thinks that I undervalue her, and women never forgive similar offenses. I am very far from doing so; but who could ever have imagined that to serve the King well in this affair, I should have been forced to become gallant cavalier to a *capitaine de dragons*? The adventure appears to me so ridiculous that I have all the trouble in the world to regain my seriousness so as suitably to finish this memoir."

If d'Eon had the satisfaction of duping Beaumarchais in a certain sense, he failed utterly in inducing him to loosen the strings of the royal purse which he carried, and without which nothing was accomplished. Finding that Beaumarchais was inexorable on this point, all the pent-up fury of the chevalier blazed forth. He began at once addressing interminable memoirs to the minister Vergennes, full of accusations against his agent, couched in the coarsest and most violent language, attributing to the latter all the epithets that fall so glibly from his pen, "the insolence of a watchmaker's boy, who by chance had discovered perpetual motion."

"Beaumarchais," said Loménie, "received these broadsides of abuse with the calm of a perfect gentleman: 'She is a woman,' he wrote to M. de Vergennes, 'and a woman so frightfully surrounded that I pardon her with all my heart; she is a woman—that word says everything.'"

But exactly this was what the chevalier did not want; he did not want to be pardoned by Beaumarchais; he wanted a quarrel with him, and to have his accusations credited by the minister. He succeeded in neither of his objects, although his resentment and his desire for revenge augmented rather than diminished with time. Returned to France, he openly accused Beaumarchais of having retained for himself money that was destined for him. His abuse was so violent that in self-defense the accused man appealed for justification to the minister, and received the following letter, which bears date of January 10th, 1778:

"I have received, Monsieur, your letter of the 3rd of this month, and I have not been able to see without surprise that the demoiselle d'Eon imputes to you having appropriated to yourself to her prejudice the funds which she supposes to have been destined for her. I have difficulty in believing, Monsieur, that this demoiselle has been guilty of an accusation so calumnious; but if she has done so, you should not have the slightest disquietude or be in the least affected; you have the gage and the guarantee of your innocence in the account which you have given of your management of the affair, in the most approved form, founded upon the most authentic titles, and in the discharge which I have given you of the approval of the King. Far from the possibility of your disinterestedness being suspected, I have not forgotten, Monsieur, that you made no account of your personal expenses, and that you never allowed me to perceive any other interest than to facilitate to the demoiselle d'Eon the means of returning to her native land.

"I am very perfectly, Monsieur, your very humble and very obedient servitor,

"De Vergennes."

Beaumarchais was at this time far too deeply engaged in his gigantic mercantile operations to be seriously disturbed by the accusations of the Chevalier d'Eon. Far greater difficulties were to overwhelm him, and still more signal ingratitude was to be his portion. He will accept that too, in very much the same spirit in which he has accepted all the rest.

CHAPTER XVI

"Vor der Ankunft Dean's und Franklin's, Beaumarchais war ohne Frage, der bestunterrichtete Kenner Englands und der Vereinigten Staaten auf dem continent."

Bettelheim, *"Beaumarchais: Eine Biographie."*

Beaumarchais's Earliest Activities in the Cause of American Independence—First Steps of the Government of France—Bonvouloir—Discord Among Parties in England—Beaumarchais's Memoirs to the King—Meets Arthur Lee—Lee's Letter to Congress—King Still Undecided—Curious Letter of Beaumarchais, with Replies Traced in the Handwriting of the King.

No record of the actual awakening of Beaumarchais's interest in the War of American Independence has ever been brought to light, but certain it is that for nearly a year before the date of any document contained in the French Archives, Beaumarchais was the "real, though secret, agent of the Minister Vergennes in London."

The earliest written allusion to any definite commission from the government in regard to this matter is found in the letter of Beaumarchais to Vergennes, written July 14, 1775, a part of which, relating to the Chevalier d'Eon, is given in the previous chapter. After announcing exultantly the possession of the keys to the famous chest of which it had just been questioned, he continued: "I would return at once to give the details of what I have accomplished if I were only charged with one object; but I am charged with four, and find myself obliged to leave for Flanders with milord Ferrers and in his vessel. It would not be just that the *King and M. de Sartine* were less content than the *King and M. de Vergennes*....

"In politics, it is not sufficient to work, one must succeed....

"I shall take no repose until I have informed you in regard to the veritable state of things in England, a knowledge of which becomes more important from day to day. As soon as I shall be as tranquil over the objects of M. de Sartine as I am now over '*notre amazone*' (the Chevalier d'Eon) I shall return to Versailles....

"I profit by the first sure occasion of dropping a letter into the post at Calais, to tell you, without its being known in London, that I have just put into the hands of the King, the papers and the creature that they have wished to use against him at any price.

"I say, 'without its being discovered in London,' because it is a great question to find out what my object is, but what can be gotten from a man who neither speaks nor writes?

"I am with the most respectful devotion, M. de Comte ... etc.... Beaumarchais" (letter given by Gaillardet in his *Mémoires sur le Chevalier d'Eon*).

Beaumarchais's mission to Flanders is alluded to in another place by Gaillardet, without, however, giving any authority for the statement which he made. He said, "The court of Louis XVI still hesitated to follow Beaumarchais in the adventurous career whither he was drawing it, so to speak, with a tow-line,... although Holland and Spain were already engaged by his efforts to embrace the cause of France and the United States against England."

Doniol in his *Histoire de la Participation de la France dans l'Etablissement des Etats-Unis,* said: "Franklin before returning to America had treated with armorers and merchants of England, Holland and France for the furnishing and transmitting of munitions of war to the colonies. These operations were centralized in London, and Beaumarchais did not remain ignorant of them.... He knew, heard, and prepared many things."

Although "no special memoir, no private archive has up to the present revealed the intimate details (Doniol, II, 31)," it seems certain that the plans of Beaumarchais centered in the dispatching of funds, or if possible, of ammunitions of war, to the insurged colonies, and that the head of these operations was to be in the Low Countries. To further these projects, the most profound secrecy was necessary, not only to ensure their success, but to prevent the government from being compromised. This fact accounts sufficiently for the almost total lack of documents relative to these negotiations. What facilitated them was the profound discord which existed at this time in England itself, and especially the diversity of opinion in relation to the uprising among the colonists. No one realized the deep significance of this fact for the interest of France and of America better than Beaumarchais, and no one knew so well how to turn it to the advantage of both these countries. It goes without saying that had England been united in her desire to crush America and united in her attempts to prevent foreign interference, the history of the war would have been very different from what it was.

As a matter of fact in England "a party, small indeed in numbers, but powerful from its traditions, its connections, and its abilities, had identified itself completely with the cause of the insurgents, opposed and embarrassed the Government in every effort to augment its forces and to subsidize allies, openly rejoiced in the victories of the Americans, and exerted all its eloquence to justify and encourage them." (Lecky, III, 545.)

"This glorious spirit of Whiggism," said Chatham in a speech delivered in January, 1775, "animates three millions in America, who prefer poverty with liberty, to gilded chains and sordid affluence, who will die in defence of their rights as freemen.... All attempts to impose servitude upon such men, to establish despotism over such a mighty continental nation, must be vain, must be fatal. We shall be forced ultimately to retreat. Let us retreat while we can, not when we must."

From the beginning, the members of the Opposition had emphasized the danger to Great Britain that would arise from a prolonged struggle with the colonies, foreseeing that they later would be forced into an alliance with France. (Walpole's last Journal, 11-182.)

At this time the Americans had no sympathy for the French and no desire to incur any debt of gratitude towards them. "France had hitherto been regarded in America, even more than in England, as a natural enemy. Her expulsion from America had been for generations one of the first objects of American patriots, and if she again mixed in American affairs it was naturally thought that she would seek to regain the province she had lost." (Lecky, 111, 453.) To ask aid of her was at first an intolerable thought to the greater number among the Revolutionary party—necessity alone finally drove them to the step. Even then, it was with no intention of accepting the help with gratitude, as subsequent events proved: It was a means to an end, and the less said about it, the sooner it was obliterated or forgotten, the better for all concerned.

The attitude of France towards America was of a totally different nature. There was never any feeling of animosity against Americans engendered by those wars which finally terminated so disastrously for the French in the peace of 1763. As these wars had all been of European origin, the resentment of the French fell upon the English alone. The very name America had a wild, sweet charm for every Frenchman's ear. For him the red man was no savage foe, but a friend and brother. Side by side they penetrated together the dense fastnesses of the primeval forests, ascended the rivers, climbed the mountains, shot the cataracts; at night they lay down under the same tent, shared the same meals and smoked together the pipe of peace. The dread which kept the English settlers hovering near the coast was unknown to the French. Thus they were able to explore and claim for the great Sun-King the vast central region, part of which bears his name to the present day. Not only was the thought of these great possessions alluring to adventurers and traders; philosophers and thinkers as well looked into the future and saw the part that they were to play in the development of the race. In 1750 Turgot had uttered the following words, "Vast regions of America! Equality keeps them from both luxury and want, and preserves to them purity and simplicity with freedom. Europe herself will find there the perfection of her political societies, and the surest support of her well-being." But since 1763 the fruit of French explorations on the continent of America had been in the hands of the English; a few sugar islands among the West Indies alone remained to them. Their foot-hold in America was gone, but not their love for America. More than this a generosity of nature, joined to a tolerance of, and admiration for qualities not of the same type as their own, has always been a marked characteristic of the French. It was therefore in the very nature of things that the nation should have been roused to enthusiasm by the news of the heroic resistance of the colonies, especially when it is taken into consideration that every blow dealt by the defenders of liberty, was aimed directly at the "triumphant political rival of France."

But the people of the nation were not its government, and at the time of the uprising in America, France was ruled by a king, weak indeed in character yet absolute in power, in whose divine right to rule, his ministers as well as himself, believed. It was not, therefore, to be expected that the French government would look with favor upon the rebellious subjects of any nation, whether friend or foe. It was in the nature of things that they should hesitate before encouraging measures that were intended to aid revolt. As late as March 5, 1775, M. de Vergennes had written to the French ambassador in London bidding him quiet the fears of the English government in regard to the probable interference of France. "The maintenance of peace with England," he wrote, "is our unique object."

The French government, however, could not wholly resist the tide of public sentiment or remain altogether unmoved by considerations of interest. It was thought well to send some prudent and sagacious agent to the New World to try the public temper and to see if the interference of France actually was desired. A man admirably fitted for the task recently had arrived in London from the French West Indies, who in returning, had passed through the colonies, and who knew them well, leaving many acquaintances there. This man was Bonvouloir. The 7th of August, 1775, M. de Vergennes wrote to the French Ambassador, "The King very much approves the mission of Bonvouloir." (Bancroft—IV—360) "His instructions," he wrote to the ambassador a little later, "should be verbal and confined to the two most essential objects: the one to make a faithful report to you of the events and of the prevailing disposition of the public mind; the other to secure the Americans against jealousy of us. Canada is for them *le point jaloux*: they must be made to understand that we do not think of it in the least." (Quoted from J. Durand's *New Materials for the History of the American Revolution*, 1889, p. 1-16, Bonvouloir.)

On the 8th of September he set sail. The result of his mission, although it promised nothing to the colonies, was to them at least an encouragement. Already in the Summer of 1775 a motion had been made in Congress and strongly supported by John Adams, to send an ambassador to France. "But Congress still shrank from so formidable a step, though it agreed, after long debates and hesitation, to form a secret committee to correspond with friends in Great Britain, Ireland, and other parts of the world." (Adams's Life, I, 200-202.) It was with this secret committee, of which the celebrated Dr. Franklin was a prominent member, that Bonvouloir came in touch.

Although the French government had taken this one preliminary step, she remained to all appearances as indifferent to the cause of the colonists as she was to the condition of affairs in England. Beaumarchais began deluging her with such volumes of information on both these subjects, that almost in spite of herself, her own interest was aroused. "The energy of a believer is a force to which undecided convictions yield—and this was the case with the King in regard to the schemes of Beaumarchais." (Gaillardet.)

But before entering into a consideration of those schemes, it would be well to glance at the actual condition of England herself. We already have spoken of the division existing in her midst, but the greatest difficulty which the English government had to encounter was the one that she has had to face in 1914 when she found herself suddenly plunged into war with another country, namely that of raising a formidable army. Then as now, the hatred of conscription was so deep rooted in the English people that even the government of Lord North did not dare to resort to it. "To raise the required troops on short notice was very difficult.... The land tax was raised to four shillings in the pound. New duties were imposed; new bounties were offered. Recruiting agents traversed the country.... Recruits, however, came very slowly. There was no enthusiasm for a war with English settlers. No measure short of conscription could raise at once the necessary army in England and to propose conscription would be fatal to any government." (Lecky, III, 455.)

In her dilemma, England found herself reduced to the infamous measure of hiring German soldiers to fight for her against her own subjects. The shameful conduct of the Landgrave of Hesse, the Duke of Brunswick and the Prince of Waldeck, has been immortalized by Germany's great poet, Schiller, in his *Kabale und Liebe*; "In England they excited only contempt and indignation." (Lecky) Moreover, the disorders arising from the press-gang service ran high, while "after three expulsions, the famous demagogue Wilkes" still retained his seat in Parliament, and in 1774 had been made Lord-Mayor of London. At a public dinner he had been heard to exclaim insolently, "For a long time the King of England has done me the honor of hating me. On my side, I have always rendered him the justice of despising him; the time has come to decide which has the better judged the other, and to which side the wind will make the heads fall." This divided condition among the people themselves justified the assertion of Beaumarchais, made in his memoir to the King: "Open war in America is less pernicious to England than the intestine war which seems likely to break out before long in London; the bitterness between the parties has risen to the highest excesses since the proclamation of the King, declaring the Americans rebels." Beaumarchais in this was only voicing the general opinion. But "The English People," says Loménie, "with that national sentiment and good sense which often has characterized them in great crises, baffled these previsions. The defeat of the English troops weakened the opposition more than the ministry. Everything became subordinate to the necessity of combatting with energy; and the irritation, instead of augmenting, cooled down considerably."

As the war progressed, party-feeling disappeared while the actual entry of France into the struggle developed a unity of purpose among the English which would have been very disastrous to the new nation, had it existed in the beginning.

The summer of 1775 was passed by Beaumarchais, ostensibly in negotiations with the chevalier d'Eon, in reality with plans and arrangements made with other European powers to join France in the secret support of the colonies. No word written or spoken of these negotiations escaped him, so that we can judge of their nature only from the results. "The middle of September," says Doniol (p. 134, I) "having arranged his combinations, he returned to Versailles to emphasize the necessity of France's conducting herself as the future ally of the Americans, that is, to come to an understanding with them in regard to the aid necessary for the development of their revolt."

M. de Vergennes seems to have been his first confidant. It was decided to act on the mind of the King. A memoir was to be drawn up and given to M. de Sartine

CHAPTER XVI 17

who should believe himself the unique confidant. This plan was disclosed in the following letter which Beaumarchais wrote to Vergennes:

"Sept. 22, 1775

"Pour vous seul;

"M. le comte: M. de Sartine gave me back the paper yesterday, but said nothing to me of the affair. Now in relation to the secret which I let him think I was guarding from you, relative to my memoir to the King, I thought it better that I wrote to you an ostensible letter which you could carry or send to His Majesty and if you were not charged by him with a reply, at least I should receive one from your bounty to console me for having taken useless pains. Send, I beg you, a blank passport, if you think I should await the orders of the King in London, in case he has not the time now, to decide the matter well. Of all this, please be kind enough to inform me. Everything being understood thus between us, it will be to your advantage to write to me so obscurely that no one but myself can divine the object of your letter, if you should send it to me by way of the ambassador." ...

The "ostensible" letter, which was written at the same time for the purpose of making an impression upon the King, was sent to the latter the next day by Vergennes with the following note:

"I see, Sire, by the letter of the Sieur de Beaumarchais which I have the honor to join to this, that he himself already has had that of reporting to Your Majesty the notions he collected in London, and what profit he thinks can be drawn from them."... After asking for the King's orders, he continued, "I requested M. de Beaumarchais, who was to leave to-night for London, to defer starting until to-morrow at noon....

"De Vergennes.

"A Versailles, le 23 Septembre 1775."

(Quoted from Doniol I, 133.)

The "ostensible" letter is addressed to Vergennes but is really a second appeal to the King. In it Beaumarchais dared to state forcefully the embarrassment into which the King's silence plunged him. He says:

"Monsieur le Comte,

"When zeal is indiscreet, it should be reprimanded; when it is agreeable, it should be encouraged; but all the sagacity in the world, would not enable him to whom nothing is replied, to divine what conduct it is expected he should maintain.

"I sent yesterday to the King through M. de Sartine, a short memoir which is the resumé of the long conference which you accorded me the day before; it is the exact state of men and things in England; it is terminated by the offer which I made you to suppress for the time necessary for our preparations for war, everything which by its noise, or its silence could hasten or retard the moment. There must have been question of all this in the council yesterday, and this morning you have sent me no word. The most mortal thing to affairs of any kind is uncertainty or loss of time.

"Should I await your reply or must I leave without having received any? Have I done well or ill to penetrate the sentiments of those minds whose dispositions are becoming so important for us? Shall I allow in the future these confidences to come to nothing and repel them instead of welcoming them—these overtures which should have a direct influence upon the actual resolution? In a word, am I an agent useful to his country, or only a traveller deaf and dumb? I ask no new commission. I have too serious work for my own personal affairs to finish in France for that, but I would have felt that I had failed in my duty to the King, to you, to my country, if I allowed all the good I might bring about and all the evil which I might prevent to remain unknown.

"I wait your reply to this letter before starting. If you have no answer to make me, I shall regard this voyage as blank and nul; and without regretting my pains, I will return instantly to terminate in four days what remains to do with d'Eon and come back without seeing anyone; they will indeed be very much astonished, but another can do better perhaps; I wish it with my whole heart."

The memoir which had been sent to the King by way of M. de Sartine, the 21st September, 1775, shows in its first sentence that another memoir had preceded it. Beaumarchais wrote:

"Au Roi:

"Sire,

"In the firm confidence which I hold, that these extracts which I address to Your Majesty are for you alone, I will continue, Sire, to present to you the truth in all points known to me, which seem to me to be of interest to your service, without having regard to the interests of anyone else whomsoever. I left London under pretext of going to the country and have come running from London to Paris, to confer with MM. de Vergennes and de Sartine upon objects too important and too delicate to be confided to the care of any courier.

"Sire, England is in such a crisis, such a disorder within and without, that she would touch almost upon her ruin if her rivals were in a state seriously to occupy themselves with her condition. Here is the faithful exposition of the situation of the English in America; I hold these details from an inhabitant of Philadelphia arrived from the colonies, after a conference with the English ministers, whom his recital has thrown into the greatest trouble and petrified with fear. The Americans, resolved to suffer everything rather than yield, and full of that enthusiasm of liberty which has often rendered the little nation of Corsica so redoubtable to the Genoese, have thirty-eight thousand men, effectively armed and determined, under the walls of Boston; they have reduced the English army to the necessity of dying of hunger in that city, or of going elsewhere to find winter quarters, something which it will do immediately. Nearly eight thousand men well armed and equally determined, defend the rest of the country without a single cultivator having been taken from the land, or a workman from the manufactories. Every one who was employed in the fisheries, which the English have destroyed, has become a soldier and wishes to revenge the ruin of his family and the liberty of his country; all who followed maritime commerce, which the English have stopped, have joined the fishermen to make war upon their common persecutors; all those working in the ports have served to augment this army of furious men, whose every action is animated by vengeance and rage.

"I say, Sire, that such a nation must be invincible, especially having behind her sufficient country for a retreat, even if the English were to become masters of the coast, which is far from being said. All sensible people are convinced in England that the English colonies are lost for the metropolis, and that is also my opinion."

Then follows an account of the discord prevailing within the country itself, as well as an account of the secret negotiations being carried on by members with Spain and Portugal. He concluded thus:

"Résumé. America escapes from the English in spite of their efforts; the war is more vividly illuminated in London than in Boston.... Our ministry, uninformed and stagnant, remains passive while events are occurring which touch us most closely....

"A superior and vigilant man would be indispensable in London to-day....

"Here, Sire, are the motives of my trip to France, whatever use Your Majesty may make of this memoir I count upon the virtue, the goodness of my Master, trusting that he will not allow these proofs of my zeal to turn against me, in confiding them to anyone, which would only augment the number of my enemies. They will, however, never hinder me from serving you so long as I am certain of the protection of Your Majesty.

"Caron de Beaumarchais."

Of the secret deliberations of the council and the resolutions arrived at we can judge only from the letter of Beaumarchais addressed to Vergennes the night of the 23rd of September. The King had read the "ostensible" letter, and as Beaumarchais hoped, had been more stirred by it. He had conferred with his minister and had given his orders. Vergennes hastened to communicate them to Beaumarchais who left the same night for London. Later he wrote:

"Paris the 23rd of September, 1775.

"Monsieur le Comte:

"I start, well informed as to the intention of the King and of yourself. Let your Excellency have no fears; it would be an unpardonable blunder in me to compromise in such an affair the dignity of my master, or of his minister: to do one's best is nothing in politics; the first man who offers himself can do as much. Do the best that can possibly be done under the circumstances is what should distinguish from the common servitor, him whom His Majesty and yourself Monsieur le Comte, honor with your confidence in so delicate a matter. I am, etc.

"Beaumarchais."

But the French government was slow to move. They were willing to make use of the indefatigable zeal of their secret agent in collecting information, but they were in no haste to commit themselves by any act that might bring them prematurely into conflict with England. Rightly enough, they wished to wait until the colonists themselves had arrived at a decision. "France," says Lecky, "had no possible interest in the constitutional liberties of Americans. She had a vital interest in their independence." No one realized this fact better than Beaumarchais, and for exactly this reason he continued to urge, with unabated ardor that France should consent to give the colonists the secret, yet absolutely indispensable aid, which he had been preparing; the fear which tormented him was that through lack of means of effective resistance they should reconcile themselves with the mother country. Still apparently occupied with the affair of d'Eon, late in November he appeared again at Versailles. On the 24th in a letter to Vergennes relating to the change of costume decided upon for the Chevalier, Beaumarchais wrote: "Instead of awaiting the reply, which should bear a definite decision, do you approve that I write the King again that I am here, that you have seen me trembling lest in a thing as easy as it is necessary, and perhaps the most important that he will ever have to decide, his Majesty should choose the negative?

"Whatever else happens I implore the favor of being allowed an audience for a quarter of an hour, before he comes to any decision, so that I may respectfully demonstrate to him the necessity of undertaking, the facility of doing, the certainty of succeeding, and the immense harvest of glory and repose which this little sowing will yield to his reign.... In case you have orders for me, I am at the hotel of Jouy rue des Recollets."

The "seed" which Beaumarchais demanded, which should bring such a harvest of prosperity and glory to France was a sum of money, 2,000,000 francs perhaps, which he proposed to send as specie, or converted into munitions of war through such channels as he had prepared in other countries. During the first period of Beaumarchais's activity in our cause, no idea of his personal intervention except as transmitter of the funds of the government, appeared to have entered his mind. The icy coldness with which his advances were met did not in the least chill his ardor—he only looked about for some new avenue of approach. His plans had been disapproved, not to say rejected.—The 7th of December he addressed another memoir to the King, couched in such respectful language, so warm and glowing from his inmost heart, that its daring boldness was almost forgotten. (In his *New Materials for the History of the American Revolution*, Durand gives the Memoir in full.—The selections here given are taken from his translation of the original.)

"Au Roi

"Sire: Your Majesty's disapproval of a plan is, in general, a law for its rejection by all who are interested in it. There are plans, however, of such supreme importance to the welfare of your Kingdom, that a zealous servant may deem it right to present them more than once, for fear that they may not have been understood from the most favorable point of view.

"The project which I do not mention here, but of which Your Majesty is aware through M. de Vergennes, is of this number; I rely wholly upon the strength of my reasons to secure its adoption. I entreat you, Sire, to weigh them with all the attention which such an important affair demands.

CHAPTER XVI   21

"When this paper is read by you, my duty is done. We propose, Sire, and you judge. Yours is the more important task, for we are responsible to you, while you, Sire, are responsible to God, to yourself, and to the great people to whom good or ill may ensue according to your decision.

"M. de Vergennes informs me that Your Majesty does not deem it just to adopt the proposed expedient. The objection, then, has no bearing on the immense utility of the project, nor on the danger of carrying it out, but solely on the delicate conscientiousness of Your Majesty.

"A refusal due to such honorable motives would condemn one to silence, did not the extreme importance of the proposed object make one examine whether the *justice* of the King of France is not really interested in adopting such an expedient. In general it is certain that any idea, any project opposed to justice should be discarded by every honest man.

"But, Sire, the policy of governments is not the moral law of its citizens.... A kingdom is a vast isolated body, farther removed from its neighbors by a diversity of interests, than by the sea, the citadels, and the barriers which bound it. There is no common law between them which ensures its safety.... The welfare and the prosperity of each impose upon each, relations which are variously modified under the name of international law, the principle of which, even according to Montesquieu, is to do the best for one's self as the first law, with the least possible wrong to other governments as the second.'...

"The justice and protection which a king owes to his subjects is a strict and rigorous duty; while that which he may offer to other states is never other than conventional. Hence it follows that the national policy which preserves states, differs in almost every respect from the civil morality which governs individuals....

"It is the English, Sire, which it concerns you to humiliate and to weaken, if you do not wish to be humiliated and weakened yourself on every occasion. Have the usurpations and outrages of that people ever had any limit but that of its strength? Have they not always waged war against you without declaring it? Did they not begin the last one in a time of peace, by a sudden capture of five hundred of your vessels? Did they not humble you by forcing you to destroy your finest seaport?... humiliation which would have made Louis XIV *plutôt manger ses bras* than not atone for? A humiliation that makes the heart of every true Frenchman bleed.... Your Majesty is no longer ignorant that the late king, forced by events to accept the shameful treaty of 1763, swore to avenge these indignities.... The very singularity of his plan only the better discloses his indignation....

"Without the intestine commotions which worry the English they already would have profited by the state of weakness and disorder under which the late king transmitted the kingdom to you, to deprive you of the pitiful remains of your possessions in America, Africa, and India, nearly all of them in their hands, and yet Your Majesty is so delicate and conscientious as to hesitate!

"An indefatigable, zealous servant succeeds in putting the most formidable weapon in your hand, one you can use without committing yourself and without striking a blow, so as to abase your natural enemies and render them incapable of injuring you for a long while....

"Ah, Sire, if you believe you owe so much to that proud English people, do you owe nothing to your own good people in France, in America, in India? But if your scruples are so delicate that you have no desire to favor what may injure your enemies, how, Sire, can you allow your subjects to contend with other European powers, in conquering countries belonging to the poor Indians, the African Savages or the Caribs who have never wronged you? How can you allow your vessels to take by force and bind suffering black men whom nature made free and who are only miserable because you are powerful? How can you suffer three rival powers to seize iniquitously upon and divide Poland under your very eyes?...

"Were men angels, political ways might undoubtedly be disdained. But if men were angels there would be no need of religion to enlighten them, of laws to govern them, of magistrates to restrain them, of soldiers to subdue them; and the earth instead of being a faithful image of hell, would be indeed a celestial abode. All we can do is to take men as they are, and the wisest king can go no farther than the legislator Solon, who said: 'I do not give the Athenians the best laws, but only those adapted for the place, the time and the people for whom I make them.'...

"I entreat you, Sire, in the name of your subjects, to whom you owe your best efforts; in the name of that inward repose which your Majesty so properly cherishes; in the name of the glory and prosperity of a reign begun under such happy auspices; I entreat you, Sire, not to be deceived ceived by the brilliant sophism of a false sensibility. *Summum jus summa injuria.* This deplorable excess of equity towards your enemies would be the most signal injustice towards your subjects who soon suffer the penalty of scruples out of place.

"I have treated the gravest questions summarily, for fear of weakening my arguments by giving them greater extension, and especially through fear of wearying the attention of Your Majesty. If any doubts still remain, Sire, after reading what I have presented to you, efface my signature, and have this attempt copied by another hand, in order that the feebleness of the reasoner may not diminish the force of the argument, and lay this discussion before any man instructed by experience and knowledge of worldly affairs; and if there is one, beginning with M. de Vergennes, who does not agree with me, I close my mouth;...

"Finally, Sire, I must confess to being so confounded by your Majesty's refusal, that, unable to find a better reason for it, I conjecture that the negotiator is an obstacle to the success of this important affair in the mind of Your Majesty. Sire, my own interest is nothing, that of serving you is everything. Select any man of probity, intelligence and discretion, who can be relied upon; I will take him to England and make such efforts as I hope will attain for him the same confidence that has been awarded to myself. He shall conduct the affair to a successful issue, while I will return and fall back into the quiet obscurity from which I emerged, rejoicing in having at least begun an affair of the greatest utility that any negotiator was ever honored with.

"Caron de Beaumarchais."

Post Scriptum.

CHAPTER XVI

"It is absolutely impossible to give in writing all that relates to this affair at bottom on account of the profound secrecy which it requires, although it is extremely easy for me to demonstrate the safety of the undertaking, the facility of doing, the certainty of success, and the immense harvest of glory and tranquillity which, Sire, this small grain of seed, sowed in time, must give to your reign.

"May the guardian angel of this government incline the mind of Your Majesty. Should he award us this first success, the rest will take care of itself. I answer for it."

Consider for a moment that the loyal subject who dared to write thus to an absolute king, his master, was a civilly degraded man, incapable in the eyes of the law of fulfilling any public function. It is the same man to whom had been addressed several years previously, the famous letter from some English admirer, which was inscribed "To Beaumarchais, the only free man in France," and it was delivered to him.

No special attention seems to have been paid to this memoir. At least no outward sign was given; and Beaumarchais after waiting several days, resorted to another measure. He addressed a letter to the King upon the very inconsequent subject of the costume which the Chevalier D'Eon should assume and the disposition that should be made of his man's attire. To such questions, at least, Louis XVI would not fear to give a definite answer—perhaps he might be induced to take an additional step and half unconsciously to decide weightier matters. The expedient was worth a trial and Beaumarchais resorted to it. In writing the letter he left a wide margin and humbly begged the King to write the answer opposite each question.

"The autograph," said Loménie, "is interesting. The body of the piece is written in the hand of Beaumarchais and signed by him; the replies to each question are traced in the margin, in a handwriting fine, but uneven, weak, undecided, where the v's and t's are scarcely indicated. It is the hand of the good, though weak and unhappy sovereign whom the revolution was to devour seventeen years later.... Below is written and signed in the hand of Vergennes, 'All the additions are in the handwriting of the King.'"

"Essential points which I implore M. de Vergennes to present for the decision of the King to be replied to on the margin:

"Does the King accord the demoiselle d'Eon permission to wear her cross of St. Louis on her woman's attire?	In the provinces only.
"Does His Majesty approve the gratification of 2000 pounds which I allowed that demoiselle for her Trousseau?	Yes.
"Does His Majesty allow her the entire disposition of her man's attire?	She must sell it.

. . . .
. . . .

"The King not being able to refuse a recognition in good form of the papers which I have brought back from England, I have begged M. de Vergennes, to implore His Majesty to add with his own hand, several words showing his approval of the way in which I have filled my mission. That recompense, the dearest to my heart, may one day be of great utility to me....

> Good.

"As the first person whom I will see in England is milord Rochford, and as he is likely to ask me in secret the reply of the King of France to the prayer which the King of England made through me, what shall I reply?

> That you received none.

"If that lord wishes secretly to engage me to see the monarch shall I accept or not?

> Perhaps.

"If that minister ... wishes to bring me into connection with other ministers, or if the occasion in any way arises shall I accept or not?"

> It is useless.

....
....

Finally Beaumarchais brought forward the demand for which the rest of the letter is but a cloak, the one burning question for the answer of which he had waited so long and in vain and to which Louis XVI still made no reply:

"And now I ask before starting, the positive response to my last memoir; but if ever question was important, it must be admitted that it is this one. I answer on my head, after having well reflected, for the most glorious success of this operation for the entire reign of my master, without his person, or of that of his ministers, or his interests being in the least compromised. Can anyone of those who influence His Majesty against this measure answer on his head to the King for the evil which will infallibly come to France if it is rejected?

"In the case that we shall be so unhappy as that the King should constantly refuse to adopt a plan so simple and so wise, I implore His Majesty to permit me to take note for him of the date when I arranged this superb resource, in order that one day he may render me the justice due to my views, when it will only be left to us bitterly to regret not having followed them.

"Caron de Beaumarchais."

"The temerity of the secret agent," says M. de Loménie, "in the end prevailed over the prudence of the King; but for the moment ... Beaumarchais was obliged to start for London knowing only that d'Eon must sell his old clothes."

For the moment the hopes of Beaumarchais seemed wholly shattered. "Intrigues of the court," said Doniol, "controlled the actions of M. de Vergennes, and made him feel the danger. The minister was visibly the butt of serious attacks, Beaumarchais was in consequence held at a distance. Everything seemed to be compromised. He seized the occasion of the new year to write to M. de Vergennes.

CHAPTER XVI

CHARLES GRAVIER — COMTE DE VERGENNES

"January 1, 1776.

"Monsieur le comte:

"It is impossible to be so deeply touched as I am with your favors without being very much so by your apparent coldness. I have examined myself well, and I feel that I do not merit it. How could you know that I had carried my zeal too far, if you do not first enter with me into the details of what I have done or ought to have done?

"Great experience with men, and the habit of misfortune, have given me that watchful prudence, which makes me think of everything and direct things according to the timid or courageous character of those for whom I do them."

Thus the year 1775 ended and the new year began with but little encouragement for the agent of the King in the cause of America; but his was a heart that did not easily lose courage. More than this, matters were really advancing; the timid policy of the King and the objections of the ministers began to give way to "the quiet and uniform influence of M. de Vergennes, which imperceptibly overcame the scruples of the inexperienced Prince, who never comprehended the far reaching influence of the question." (Bancroft—History of America, IV, p. 363.)

CHAPTER XVII

> *It was absolutely necessary to the existence and prosperity of France that the great commercial power and assumed preponderance of Great Britain and her attempted monopoly of the seas should be broken. The revolt of the American Colonies was her opportunity."*
>
> George Clinton Genet in Magazine of American History, Nov., 1878.

Beaumarchais's English connections—With Lord Rochford—With Wilkes—Meets Arthur Lee—Sends Memoir to the King—His Commission to Buy Portuguese Coin—Called to Account by Lord Rochford—Vergennes's Acceptance of his Ideas—Article in *The Morning Chronicle.*

As has been stated already, Beaumarchais during his stay in London came in touch with all classes. It was Lord Rochford whom he had known intimately at Madrid who introduced him at the court of St. James. It was d'Eon and Morande who brought him into touch with the brilliant, daring Wilkes, then Lord Mayor of London.

Around the latter's table the most pronounced members of the opposition, as well as the leading Americans then in London, were wont to assemble. It was here that Beaumarchais met the young and gifted representative of America, Arthur Lee, who was destined to bring so much discord into all continental relations with America. The bitterness which subsequent developments brought out in his character had not then shown itself.

During the winter of 1776, Lee was replacing Franklin in London. Ardent and intelligent, with decided personal charm he captivated Beaumarchais. In fact it was primarily through Lee that Beaumarchais came in touch with the pulse of American life and from him that he acquired that ardent sympathy with the sons of the new world, which never left him.

Both Beaumarchais and the Count de Lauragais, another agent of France in London, urged the French minister to permit Lee to appear before him, to plead in person the cause of his country. But on this point Vergennes was inexorable, and Arthur Lee was not permitted to come to Versailles.

Most of the correspondence which passed between Beaumarchais and the

French ministers during the early part of 1776 is lacking, but the following memoir addressed to the king, February 29, 1776, shows that a decided advance had been made:

"La Paix ou la Guerre

"To the King alone:

"The famous quarrel between America and England which is soon going to divide the world and change the system of Europe, imposes upon every power the necessity of examining well how the event of this separation will influence it, either to serve its ends or to thwart them.

"But the most interested of all is certainly France, whose sugar islands have been, since the peace of 1763, the constant object of regret and of hope to the king of England....

"In the first memoir placed before Your Majesty three months ago by M. de Vergennes, I tried to prove that the sense of justice of Your Majesty could not be offended in taking wise precautions against this enemy who never has shown herself delicate in those which she has taken against us.

"To-day when a violent crisis is advancing upon us with great strides, I am obliged to warn Your Majesty that the conservation of our American possessions and the peace which you so desire depends solely upon this one proposition—*We must aid the Americans!*

"This is what I will prove to you.... The King of England, the ministers, the parliament, the opposition, the nation, the English people, parties, in a word, which tear the state to pieces, all agree that it is not to be hoped that they can bring back the Americans, even if the great efforts which they now put forth should be able to subdue them. From this, Sire, the violent debates between the ministry and the opposition, the action and reaction of opinions admitted or rejected, do not in the least advance matters, they serve, however, to throw much light upon the subject....

"The fear exists in England that the Americans, encouraged by their successes and perhaps emboldened by some secret treaty with France and Spain, will refuse the same conditions of peace to-day which they demanded with clasped hands two years ago. On the other hand the Sieur L. (Lee) secret deputy of the colonies at London, absolutely discouraged at the uselessness of the efforts which he has made through me to obtain from the French Ministry aid of powder and munitions of war—said to me to-day,

"'For the last time, is France absolutely decided to refuse us all aid and has she become the victim of England and the laughing stock of Europe, by this unbelievable torpor?'

"Obliged myself to reply positively, I await your last reply to his offer before I give my own.

"'We offer,' he says, 'to France as a price of her secret aid, a secret treaty of commerce which will enable her to reap during a certain number of years after the peace, all the benefits with which we have for the last century enriched England, besides a guarantee of her West Indian Possessions according to our power.

"'If this is rejected, Congress immediately will make a public proclamation and will offer to all nations of the world what I secretly offer to you to-day.... The Americans, exasperated, will join their forces to those of England and will fall upon your sugar islands—of which you will be deprived forever.'...

"Here, Sire, is the striking picture of our position. Your Majesty sincerely wishes to maintain peace. The means to conserve peace, Sire, will make the *résumé* of this memoir.

"Admit all the foregoing hypotheses and let us reason. *This which follows is very important.*

"Either England will have the most complete success in the campaign over the Americans; or the Americans will repel the English with loss; or England will adopt the plan of abandoning the colonies to themselves and separating in a friendly manner; or the opposition taking possession of the ministry, will bring about the submission of the colonies on condition of their being reinstated as in 1763.

"Here are all the possibilities brought together. Is there a single one which does not instantly bring upon us the war which you desire to avoid? Sire, in the name of Heaven, deign to examine the matter with me.

"First, if England should triumph over America, it can only be at an enormous expense of men and money, now the only indemnity which England will propose to make on her return, will be the capture of our sugar islands.... Thus Sire, it will only remain for you, the choice of beginning too late an unfruitful war, or to sacrifice to the most disgraceful inactivity your American colonies and to lose two hundred and eighty millions of capital and more than thirty millions of revenue.

"Second, if the Americans win, the moment they are free from the English, the latter in despair at seeing their possessions diminished by three fourths, will be still more anxious to indemnify themselves by the easy capture of our islands, and one may be sure that they will not fail in attempting it.

"Third, if the English imagine themselves forced to abandon the colonies to themselves, which is the secret desire of the king, their loss being the same and their commerce equally ruined the result remains the same for us.

"Fourth, if the opposition comes into power and concludes a treaty with the American colonies, the Americans, outraged against the French whose refusal to aid alone forces them to submit to England, menace us from to-day forth, to take away the islands by joining forces with the English....

"What shall we do in this extremity to win peace and to save our islands?

"*Sire the only means is to give help to the Americans,* so as to make their forces equal to those of England.... Believe me Sire, the saving of a few millions to-day soon may cause a great deal of blood to flow, and money to be lost to France....

"If it is replied that we cannot aid the Americans without drawing upon us a storm, I reply that this danger can be averted if the plan be adopted which I have so often proposed, to aid the Americans secretly....

"If your Majesty has no more skillful man to employ, I am ready to take the matter in charge and will be responsible for the treaty without compromising anyone, persuaded that my zeal will better supplement my lack of dexterity, than the dexterity of another could replace my zeal.... Your Majesty knows better than anyone that secrecy is the soul of action and that in politics a project made known, is a project lost.

"Since I have served you sire, I have never asked for any favor. Permit, O my master, that no one be allowed to prevent my working for you and my whole existence is consecrated to you.

"Caron de Beaumarchais."

Under the outward show of indifference the French government had been steadily moving toward the point aimed at by its secret agent. Early in March Vergennes had placed a list of considerations before the king in which the future actions of the government were outlined. Beaumarchais had been recalled in order to deliberate with the ministers, and when all was arranged, he returned to London to continue the work there.

But the enemies of the cause of America were not slumbering and in spite of his precautions he found that he was being watched. "Beaumarchais," says Doniol, "already under the suspicion of the police of the foreign office, of being employed with that with which he was really occupied, had been furnished with a letter by M. de Sartine, which gave him a mission in the name of the king to buy up ancient Portuguese coin, to be used in the islands."

Beaumarchais wrote to Vergennes, April 12, 1776, "I wrote yesterday to M. de Sartine thanking him as well as the king for having furnished me with the means of sleeping tranquilly in London. Certain that you will deliver him my dispatch I lay down my pen, because for eight hours I have been writing and making copies, and I am exhausted.

"Deign to remember sometimes, M. le Comte, a man who respects you and who even dares in his heart to add a more tender sentiment.

Beaumarchais."

The following letter bears the date, April 12th, 1776; but as Beaumarchais later explains, it really was written on the 16th. It shows the intimate relation which existed between him and Lord Rochford, as well as the skill and address of Beaumarchais in extricating himself from a very difficult situation.

"Monsieur le Comte:

"While England assembled at Westminster Hall is judging the Duchess of Kingston, I will give you an account of a serious conversation which took place between Lord Rochford and myself." ...

The lord, after informing Beaumarchais of a letter he had just received from King George of England appointing him to the vice-royalty in Ireland, continued:

CHAPTER XVII

"But I must not omit to read you the last phrase of the letter of the King, M. de Beaumarchais, because it regards you particularly.

"'A vessel from Boston, charged with letters and merchandise from Congress for a merchant of Nantes, with orders to exchange for munitions of war, has been brought to Bristol. This circumstance, joined to that of two French gentlemen, secretly in communication with Congress, and having, it is said, hidden relations with persons in London, has singularly alarmed our council....

"'Several evilly informed persons have endeavored to cause suspicions of this connivance to fall upon you. What do you think of all this? I know very well that you are here to finish with d'Eon; on this point I wish to trust your word alone, as I have already said to the king.'

"'Before replying, Milord,' I said, 'to that which regards me, permit me to speak first of the vessel from America. Not that I have orders from our ministers, but following my own light. I have learned already of the arrival of the American vessel at Bristol, but I was no more astonished that it was charged for a merchant of Nantes, than if it had been one for Amsterdam, or Cadiz, or Hamburg. The insurgents have need of munitions, and have no money to buy them, they are forced, then, to hazard their raw materials in order to exchange them, and any port whatever where they can find munitions is naturally as good as any other.'

"'But, Monsieur, has not France given orders in her ports in regard to this? Have we not the right to expect the merchants of Nantes to be punished?'

"'Milord, you have permitted me the right to speak frankly. I will do it all the more freely since I have no commission and what I say will compromise no one. Indeed, Milord, do you wish our administration to deal harshly with the people of Nantes? Are we at war with anyone? Before asking this question of me, let me ask a preliminary one of you. Because England has a private quarrel with someone, what right has she to restrict our commerce? What treaty obliges us to open or close our ports according to the wish of the British nation? Certainly, Milord, I scarcely can believe that anyone would dare to raise so unbelievable a question, the solution of which might have consequences which England has great interest not to provoke....

"'Nothing prevents you from chasing the Americans as much as you like, seizing them whenever you can,—except under the cannon of our forts, by the way! But require of us to disturb our merchants because they have dealings with people with whom we are at peace, whether we regard them as your subjects or a people become free, ... in truth that is asking too much! I do not know what the administration would think of such a demand, but I know very well that it seems to me decidedly more than out of place.'

"'I see, Monsieur, that you are crimson with anger.' (In truth M. le Comte, the fire had mounted to my face, and if you disapprove, that I have shown so much heat, I ask your pardon.)

"'Milord,' I replied, with gentleness and modesty, 'you who are English and patriotic, you should not think evil that *un bon Français* should have pride for his country.'

"'Therefore, I am not in the least offended.'"

The conversation now turned on the delicate matter of Beaumarchais's mission. After showing his credentials for the buying up of Portuguese coin and frankly affirming that the affair with d'Eon was settled so far as he was concerned, he continued, "'If there should be any pretended French agents in England, I am sure that if they could be captured, the government would disavow them, and even punish them....

"'And now, Milord, I offer you my sincere compliments for that which the king destines for you. If you accept the Vice-Royalty, I hope you will remember your ancient friendship for M. Duflos whom I recommend to you afresh. I hope you will charge him with the details of your house in Ireland as you have in France. He promised me this.' (This Duflos, M. le Comte, is a Frenchman whom I long ago secured for Lord Rochford; he is absolutely devoted to me, and through him you will always have certain news of the most intimate interior of the vice-royalty. I am a little like Figaro, M. le Comte, I do not lose my head for a little noise.)

"By the way, the Hessian troops have started. They took the oath of allegiance to England the 22nd of March.

"The Americans have actually twelve vessels of from twenty-two to forty-four pieces of cannon, and twelve or fifteen of twenty pieces, and more than thirty of twelve pieces, which gives them a navy almost as respectable as that of the English, and for the last two and a half months the insurgents have lost only one vessel brought into Bristol, which is indeed worthy of remark.

"I count upon your goodness to hope that my recommendations for Aix are not forgotten. [In allusion to his suit with the count de La Blache, still pending.] It is not just that I be judged in the South when I am nine hundred miles away in the North.

"Receive my respects, my homage, and the assurance of my perfect devotion.

"Caron de Beaumarchais."

(Doniol I, 407.)

On the 26th of the same month, M. de Vergennes wrote to his secret agent, "almost as though he spoke to an ambassador." (Doniol.)

"I have the satisfaction of announcing to you that His Majesty very much approves the noble and frank manner with which you repelled the attack made upon you by Lord Rochford in relation to the American vessel destined for Nantes and conducted to Bristol. You have said nothing which His Majesty would not have prescribed you to say if he had foreseen that you would be obliged to answer in regard to a matter so far removed from the business with which you are charged. Receive my compliments, Monsieur. After having assured you of the approbation of the king, mine cannot seem very interesting to you; nevertheless, I cannot refuse myself the satisfaction of applauding the wisdom and firmness of your conduct and renewing the assurances of my entire esteem. I have not neglected your

CHAPTER XVII 33

commission for Aix. M. le Garde des Sceaux assured me that it would remain in suspense till your return.

"I am very perfectly
"de Vergennes.

"Versailles, April 26th, 1776."

Post Scriptum.

"The king approves, that you do not refuse the overtures the Lord Rochford may make to you. You are prudent and discreet. I should be without uneasiness even if you had a more important commission than that which M. de Sartine has given you. It was well, however, that you had it, since it served to disperse the suspicions aroused by your frequent voyages to London. It must be admitted that the English whom we believe to be men are really far less than women, if they are so easily frightened.... Nothing equals the sincere attachment with which I have the honor to be, Monsieur, your very humble, etc.

"de Vergennes."

The same day Beaumarchais addressed the count with a letter from London which runs as follows:

"M. le Comte:

"I profit by this occasion to entertain you with freedom upon the only really important matter at present, America and all that pertains to it. I reasoned a long time, day before yesterday, with the man you thought best to prevent coming to France. (Arthur Lee.) He incessantly asks if we are going to do absolutely nothing for them. And without wasting time in repeating to me how very important their success is to France because he does us the honor of believing that we agree with him on that point, he tells me simply, 'We need arms, powder, and above all engineers: only you can help us, and it is to your interest to do so.'

"The Americans are as well placed as possible; army, fleet provisions, courage, everything is excellent, but without powder and engineers how can they conquer or even defend themselves? Are we going to let them perish rather than loan them one or two millions? Are we afraid of losing the money?

"Weakness and fear is all that one sees here....

"It is clear that the ministry is silent because it has nothing to reply. Fear and anger on one side, weakness and embarrassment on the other, this is the real condition. You would be still more convinced of this truth if you will recall the nature of their treaties with Germany and if you examine the rate of the new loan.... And when this is well proved, is it really true, M. le Comte, that you will do nothing for the Americans?

"Will you not have the goodness to show once more to the King how much he can gain, without striking a blow, in this one campaign? And will you not attempt to convince His Majesty that this miserable pittance which they demand, and over which we have been disputing for more than a year, will bring to us all the fruits of a great victory without undergoing the dangers of a combat? That this help can give to us while we sleep, all that the disgraceful treaty of 1763 made us lose? What greater view can occupy the council of the king and what force your pleading will take on if you show the reverse of the picture and count what the defeat of the Americans will cost us. Three hundred millions—our men—our vessels, our islands, etc. ... because their forces once united against us, their audacity augmented by their great success, it is only certain that they will force these same Frenchmen to support a fatal war which two millions now would avert.

"In spite of the danger which I run in writing these daring things from London, I feel myself twice as much French in London as at Paris. The patriotism of this people stirs my own...."

As may be seen from this letter, Arthur Lee still inspired complete confidence in the agent of the French government, so much indeed that Beaumarchais gladly disclosed to him the plans which he had formed for coming to the aid of the Americans.

So certain was he that France would ultimately yield to the necessity of giving them secret support that he no doubt spoke with indiscreet assurance on the subject. Exactly what passed between the two men will never be known, but what is certain is, that during the spring of 1776, Arthur Lee addressed to the secret committee of Congress a letter in which he says:

"In consequence of active measures taken with the French Embassy in London, *M. de Vergennes has sent me a secret agent to inform me that the French court cannot think of making war on England but that she is ready to send five million worth of arms and ammunition to Cap Français to be thence sent to the colonies.*"

A careful analysis of this important missive will at once make clear the profound misunderstanding which arose in the mind of the secret committee of Congress regarding the true state of affairs in France. So completely was every statement perverted that though the whole bears a semblance of truth yet in reality nothing could be further removed from it.

For instead of sending an agent to confer with Arthur Lee, M. de Vergennes had steadily refused to enter into any relation whatever with him. Instead of promising munitions of war for which Beaumarchais had been pleading so long and so ardently, the government continued to refuse to compromise itself by making any statement regarding them.

And yet in judging Arthur Lee, whether he intentionally distorted the truth or only indulged in what he considered a harmless exaggeration, we must not forget that this letter with its assurances of help, arriving at the moment which it did, had a profound influence in shaping men's minds for independence.

As regards Lee himself, the letter had the effect of greatly augmenting his credit with Congress. Silas Deane was already on his way to France, charged with an express commission to secure munitions of war on credit, so it was determined to join Arthur Lee to the commission as soon as it could be brought about.

But to return to the French court. The first intimation of anything like an avowed approval of the plans of Beaumarchais is to be found in a letter of M. de

CHAPTER XVII

Vergennes under date of May 2, 1776. He wrote:

"I have received the first of this month, Monsieur, the letter with which you honored me, written the 26th of last month."

Then follows a lengthy preamble in which the count, speaking as an observer of men and one used to dealing with them, continues:

"This preface is not destined to refute your foresight, which on the contrary I praise and approve. But do not suppose that because your plans are not immediately acted on, that they are rejected. Although the method which I employ is sure, I am forced to curb the desire which I feel to express to you all my thoughts, therefore, I rely upon your sagacity to divine them. Think well and you will find that I am nearer to you than you imagine.... A thousand thanks, Monsieur, for the news items which you communicate to me, they have been seen and relished.... I have delivered the letter which you recommended to me; if an answer comes I will forward it to you. I flatter you that you know my friendship and attachment for you.

"de Vergennes."

In fact the hindrances were gradually disappearing from the path of the minister. In a résumé, in all probability drawn up by Vergennes himself, entitled, *"Réflexions sur la nécessité de secourir les Américains et de se préparer à la guerre avec l'Angleterre,"* without date, but placed by Doniol the first of May, 1776, the following passages occur:

"There is no obstacle, and it is even necessary to aid the insurgents indirectly by means of munitions or of money....

"We are to make no agreement with them until their independence is established. The aid must be veiled and hidden, and appear to come from commerce so that we can always deny it.

"It would be sufficient for an intelligent merchant, faithful and discreet, to be stationed in each one of the ports, where the American vessels would come to land their cargoes—he would treat directly with their captains and would mask the shipments to prevent the reproach of the court of England."—Doniol.

This was not at all what Beaumarchais had been planning and preparing. In the next chapter we shall see him with his usual flexibility abandon his own ideas and adopt those of the ministry, since they tended to the same end. In the meantime he was addressing the following letters to Vergennes:

"Monsieur le Comte:

"There is nothing very important here but the news of the evacuation of Boston, which arrived three days ago....

"The government assumes an air of approbation, of mystery, of intelligence even. It wishes to have it considered as a ruse of the ministry, but that does not take. It is too certain that the impossibility to hold Boston from lack of provisions has driven the English away....

"All this confirms what I announced in my last dispatch, that the Americans are in good condition everywhere, engineers and powder excepted. I thank you for your obliging goodness in regard to my affair at Aix. I thank you also for the honorable encouragement which the approbation of the king and your own gives to my enterprise.... Say what you will, M. le Comte, a little exaltation in the heart of an honest man, far from spoiling him for action vivifies everything he touches, and enables him to do more than he would have dared to promise from his natural capacity. I feel this exaltation, it remains for my prudence to direct it in a way that turns to the good of the affairs of the king. Conserve for me his esteem, Monsieur le Comte.

"Ah, Monsieur le Comte, as a favor ... some powder and engineers! It seems to me that I never wanted anything so much...."

(Given by Gaillardet.)

Five days later; London, May 8, 1776.

... "I say then, the time approaches when the Americans will be masters at home.... If they have the upper hand, as everything seems to point to that end, will we not have infinitely to regret, Monsieur le Comte, not to have ceded to their prayers? If, far from having acquired the right to their gratitude, as we could easily do at small cost and without risk, we will have alienated them forever? As they will have conquered without us, they will revenge themselves for our hardness to them. What are two or three millions advanced without compromising ourselves? Because I can engage my sacred faith to make any sum you wish reach them at second hand by way of Holland, without risk or other authorization than that which exists between us. A small effort will perhaps suffice, because I know that the Virginians have now an abundant manufacture of saltpeter, and that the Congress has decided that powder shall be made in every place instead of at Philadelphia as formerly. Beside this, Virginia has seven thousand regular troops, and seventy thousand militia, iron in abundance, and she makes almost as many arms as all the rest of America together.

"But engineers, engineers and powder! Or the money to buy them!"

(Gaillardet.)

Three days later, London, May 11, 1776.... "All the quarrels for the last eight days are in relation to the *quomodo* of the evacuation of Boston. The opposition and the ministry are openly tearing out each other's eyes about it. The whole affair consists of the doctors deciding how the sick man died. Let them dispute over that great coffin. The couriers arrive at every moment.... To-morrow all the news of the American papers will be printed in the English ones. The whole affair begins to clear up. You were certainly very near me as you said, when I imagined you very very far."

(Gaillardet.)

"London, May 17, 1776.

"... Eight days ago a pack boat from Virginia sent by Lord Dunmore brought news to the government, but it was so bad that it was thought advisable to say that the chest containing the mail was washed overboard in a storm. Admirable ruse!

CHAPTER XVII

Effort of superior genius! Yesterday another vessel arrived from Canada. A man jumped into a boat and the vessel pushed out again. That man hurried straight to London without stopping. No one can find out his errand. From these incidents comes the refrain; the news must be very black since it is kept such a mystery."

(Gaillardet.)

Thus ended the first phase of the activity of Beaumarchais in the cause of the Americans. In a few more days he was back in France ready to turn the force of his mind, the power of his intellect and all the energy of his being into the development of that vast mercantile establishment which was for a time to supply the colonies with munitions of war and other necessities.

As a proof that no one ever was able to pass from grave to gay with more facility than Beaumarchais, we will close the present chapter with a rather lengthy extract from an article which appeared in the London *Morning Chronicle* shortly before his return to France:

From the *Morning Chronicle*, London, May 6, 1776.

"Monsieur, the Editor:

"I am a stranger, full of honor. If it is not to inform you absolutely who I am, it is at least to tell you in more than one sense who I am not.

"Day before yesterday, at the Pantheon, after the concert and during the dance, I found under my feet a lady's mantle of black taffeta, lined with the same and bordered with lace. I am ignorant to whom this mantle belongs, never having seen, even at the Pantheon, her who wore it and all my investigations since have not enabled me to learn anything in relation to her.

"I therefore beg you, M. the Editor, to announce in your paper this lost mantle so that it may be returned faithfully to whomever shall reclaim it.

"But that there may be no error in relation to it, I have the honor to announce to you that the person who lost it wore a pink plume that day in her hair; I think she had diamond pendants in her ears, but I am not so sure of that as of the rest. She is tall and well formed, her hair is a silvery blonde; her complexion dazzlingly white; her neck is fine and gracefully set; her form slender, and the prettiest little foot in the world. I have even remarked that she is very young. She is lively and distracted; her step is light and she has a decided taste for the dance.

"If you ask me, M. the Editor, why, having noted her so well, I did not at once return her mantle, I shall have the honor to repeat what I said to you before, that I have never seen this person; that I do not know either her features, or her eyes, or her costume, or her carriage, and do not know who she is, or what she is like.

"But if you insist upon knowing how I am able to so well define her, never having seen her, I in turn will be astonished that so exact an observer as you do not know that the simple examination of a lady's mantle is sufficient to give of her all the notions by which she could be recognized.

"Now suppose, Monsieur, that on examining this mantle, I found in the hood some stray hair of a beautiful blonde attached to the stuff, also some bits of down escaped from the feathers, you will admit that a great effort of genius would not be needed to conclude that the hair and the plume of that blonde must in every way resemble the samples which have detached themselves. You feel that perfectly. And since similar hair never grew from skin of uncertain whiteness, analogy will have taught you as it has taught me, that this beautiful silvery hair must have a dazzling complexion, something which no observer can dispute with us without dishonoring his judgment.

"It is thus that a slightly worn spot in the taffeta on the two lateral parts of the interior of the hood which could not have come from anything but a repeated rubbing of two small hard bodies in movement, showed me that, not that she wore the pendants on that particular day, but that she does so ordinarily; and that it is hardly probable between you and me, that she would have neglected this adornment on a day of conquest or of grand assembly, both which are one. If I reason badly do not spare me, I beg you. Rigor is not injustice.

"The rest goes without saying. It can easily be seen that it was sufficient for me to examine the ribbon which was attached to the mantle at the neck, and to knot it at the place rumpled by the ordinary usage to see that the space enclosed being small, the neck daily enclosed in that space must also be very fine and graceful. No difficulty there.

"Suppose again, Monsieur, if on examining the body of the mantle you should have found upon the taffeta the impression of a very pretty little foot, marked in gray dust, would you not have reflected as I did, that had any other woman stepped on the mantle since its fall, she would certainly have deprived me of the pleasure of picking it up? Therefore it would have been impossible that the impression of the shoe came from any other person than her who lost the mantle. It follows, you would have said that if the shoe was small the foot must be smaller still. There is no merit in my having recognized that; the most careless observer, a child would have found that out.

"But this impression made in passing and even without being felt, announces, besides an extreme vivacity of step, a strong preoccupation of mind to which grave, cold, or aged persons are little susceptible. I therefore very simply concluded that my charming blond is in the flower of her age, very lively and distracted. Would you not have thought the same, M. the Editor?

"The next day in recalling that I had been able to pick up the mantle in a place where so many people passed (which proves that it fell at the very instant) without having been able to see who lost it (which proves that she was already far away), I said to myself, 'Assuredly this person is the most alert beauty of England, Scotland and Ireland; and if I do not join America to the rest, it is only because they have become of late *diablement alerte* in that country.'

"In giving you this mantle, M. the Editor, permit me to envelop myself in my own and that I sign myself,

"*L'Amateur français.*"

CHAPTER XVIII

> *Look upon my house, gentlemen, from henceforward as the chief of all useful operations to you in Europe, and my person as one of the most zealous partisans of your cause, the soul of your success and a man most deeply impressed with the respectful esteem with which I have the honor to be....*
>
> "Roderigue Hortalès et Compagnie"
>
> Beaumarchais to the Secret Committee of Congress, Aug. 15, 1776.

Memoir Explaining to the King the Plan of His Commercial House—Roderigue Hortalès et Cie.—The Doctor Du Bourg—Silas Deane's Arrival—His Contract with Beaumarchais—Lee's Anger—His Misrepresentations to Congress—Beaumarchais Obtains His Rehabilitation.

ON the 24th of May, 1776, Beaumarchais returned to France. He wrote to the Count de Vergennes the same night:

"Monsieur le Comte,

"I arrive very tired, completely exhausted. My first care is to ask you for your orders and the hour when you will be so good as to give me audience. It is three o'clock in the morning. My negro will be at your levée, he will be back for mine. I hope he will bring me the news which I desire with the greatest impatience, which is to go in person, and assure you of the very respectful devotion with which, I am, M. le Comte, yor very humble and very obedient servitor, Beaumarchais."

(Doniol.)

No written statement was ever made of the exact arrangement arrived at between the minister and his confidential agent. What is certain is that as soon as the latter understood the new plan of procedure he brought at once to the aid of the undertaking the whole force of his powerful mind as well as the experience of those years passed under the tutelage of old Du Verney, and in his attempted enterprise at the court of Spain.

SILAS DEANE

A letter without date, published for the first time by George Clinton Genet in the *Magazine of American History*, 1878, written by Beaumarchais to the King, gives a clear statement of how he proposed to proceed in founding this new mercantile house which should hide from all the world and even from the Americans themselves the connivance of the Government in the operations:

"To the King Alone:

"While state reasons engage you to extend a helping hand to the Americans, policy requires that Your Majesty shall take abundant precaution to prevent the secret succor sent to America from becoming a firebrand between France and England in Europe.... On the other hand, prudence wills that you acquire a certainty

CHAPTER XVIII 41

that your funds may never fall into other hands than those for whom you destined them. Finally, the present condition of your finances does not permit you to make so great sacrifice at the moment as passing events seem to require.

"It becomes my duty, Sire, to present to you, and it is for your wisdom to examine the following plan, the chief object of which is to avoid, by a turn which is absolutely commercial, the suspicion that your majesty has any hand in the affair.

"The principal merit of this plan is to augment your aid so that a single million ... will produce the same results for the Americans as if your Majesty really had disbursed nine millions in their favor.... Your Majesty will begin by placing a million at the disposition of your agent, who will be named Roderigue Hortalès et Cie.; this is their commercial name and signature, under which I find it convenient that the whole operation shall be carried out.... One half million exchanged into Portuguese pieces, the only money current in America, will be promptly sent there, for there is an immediate necessity for the Americans to have a little gold at once to give life to their paper money, which without means of making it circulate already has become useless and stagnant in their hands. It is the little leaven that is necessary to put into the paste to raise it and make it ferment usefully.

"Upon that half million no benefit can be obtained except the return of it in Virginian tobacco, which Congress must furnish to the house of Hortalès, who will have made a sale in advance to the Farmers-General of France, by which they will take the tobacco from them at a good price; but that is of no great consequence.

"Roderigue Hortalès counts on employing the second half million in the purchase of cannon and powder, which he will forward at once to the Americans."

Here follows an exposition of the proceedings, with an explanation of how, supposing the king permits him to buy powder at actual cost price from the magazines, instead of buying it in the market of France, Holland, or elsewhere, the money invested by the king will increase not in double progression, 1-2-4-8, etc., but in triple progression, 1-3-9-27, etc.

"Your Majesty will not be frightened at the complicated air that this operation assumes under my pen, when you remember that no commercial speculation is carried on or succeeds by any more simple or more natural means than this.

"I have treated this affair in so far, Sire, in the spirit of a great trader, who wishes to make a successful speculation and I have developed to you the unique secret by which commerce in bulk augments the prosperity of all states that have the good sense to protect it....

"If the return in tobacco and the sale of the product take place as I have pointed out, Your Majesty soon will find yourself in a position to send back by the hands of Hortalès et Cie. the three millions provided for from the price and profits of these returns, to recommence operations on a larger scale."

Then follow considerations upon the advisability of employing Holland or French vessels for the transport of the munitions to Cape Francis, chosen by Hortalès et Cie. as the first depot of commerce.

"Holding to the choice of French vessel charged to the account of Roderigue

Hortalès et Cie., Congress, or rather Mr. Adams, Secretary of Congress, will be alone forewarned by the agent in England that a vessel is carrying to him at Cape Francis both goods and munitions, which are to be returned in Virginian tobacco, so that he may send to the Cape upon a vessel loaded with tobacco an agent who will bear his power to receive both and to send back by the captain of Hortalès et Cie. the entire return in tobacco or at all events a recognition that he owes Hortalès et Cie. the balance of the amount for which he may not have been able to furnish return."

So far in Beaumarchais's mind, the mercantile undertaking was to be for the king, only cloaked by the appearance of a mercantile house. But it seems that the French government, anxious to evade all possible risk and wishing to deny all connivance in the transactions, decided to remain entirely foreign to the operation.

"We will give you secretly," said the government, "a million. We will try to obtain the same amount from the court of Spain. ... with these two millions and the co-operation of private individuals, whom you will associate in your enterprise, you will found your house and at your own risk and perils you will provision the Americans with arms and munitions, and objects of equipment and whatever is necessary to support the war. Our arsenals will deliver to you these things, but you will replace them or pay for them. You shall not demand money of the Americans, because they have none, but you shall ask returns in commodities of their soil, the sale of which we will facilitate in our country.... In a word, the operation secretly sanctioned by us at the outset must grow and develop through its own support. But on the other hand, we reserve the right of favoring or opposing it according to political contingencies. You will render us an account of your profits and losses, while we will decide whether we should grant you new subsidies or discharge you of all obligations previously made." (Loménie, II, p. 109.)

In this transaction, the responsibility of the agent to the United States had no consideration. "The advances of the government were simply a guarantee to Beaumarchais against loss." (Durand, p. 90.)

The difficulties and dangers of this undertaking have been admirably summed up by M. de Loménie. "They were of a nature to cause any other man than Beaumarchais to hesitate.... He threw himself into this, however, with all his usual intrepidity, and the tenth of June, 1776, a month before the United States had published their Declaration of Independence, he signed the famous receipt which, kept secret under the monarchy, delivered to the United States in 1794, under the republic, occasioned a suit lasting fifty years, and to which we shall return. The receipt read thus:

"'I have received of M. Duvergier, conformably to the orders of M. de Vergennes, on the date of the 5th of this month, the sum of one million, for which I shall render count to my said Sieur Comte de Vergennes.

"'Caron de Beaumarchais.

"'Good for a million of *livres tournois*.

"'At Paris, this 10th of June, 1776.'

CHAPTER XVIII

"Two months later, Spain advanced the like sum, besides which Beaumarchais had associated with himself numerous private individuals in France and elsewhere, so that his first sending to the Americans surpassed in itself alone, three millions." (Loménie, II, p. 110.)

Early in June the vast mercantile house of Roderigue Hortalès et Cie. was established at Paris, while agents, clerks, and employees of every sort were installed at the center of operations, as well as at the various sources of supplies and in the seaports, Beaumarchais remaining the head and center of action, in every place.

It so happened at this time, that a complete change was being made in the equipment of the French army, so that the arsenals and forts were charged with munitions of war, which the government was willing to dispose of at a nominal price.

Before the arrival of Beaumarchais on the scene of action, the Comte de Vergennes had countenanced and furthered the operations begun by Franklin before he left London. Among the agents employed by the latter were the Brothers Mantaudoin of Nantes, who had undertaken the transportation of munitions of war to the Americans. (Doniol, I, p. 373.)

Another agent and intimate friend of Franklin was a certain Doctor Dubourg, a man more or less widely known as a scientist, but possessing as well a decided taste for mercantile operations. He had entered heartily into the cause of the Americans, and was very zealous in forwarding munitions of war to the insurgents. He seems at the beginning to have possessed to a considerable degree the confidence of the French minister, who deigned to correspond with him in person, and to consult him on several occasions. But as it became necessary "to act on a grander scale, the intervention of the friend of Franklin was no longer sufficient." (Doniol, p. 374.) The "faithful and discreet agent" spoken of in the *Réflexions* had long been fixed in the mind of the Minister of War. The good doctor who knew nothing of the relationship between the famous author of the *Barbier de Séville* and the French Government or of his interest and services in the cause of American Independence, all along had been secretly aspiring to a complete control of the transactions. What succeeded in convincing him that he was the man destined for the place was that early in June, 1776, Silas Deane, the agent of the Secret Committee of Congress, arrived in Paris charged with a letter from Franklin to his "dear good friend Barbeu Dubourg," with express instructions to regard this latter as "the best guide to seek after and to follow." (Doniol, V. I, p. 485.)

Elated at this mark of esteem shown him by the colonies, the good doctor undertook to fulfill then to the letter the instructions of Congress and to prevent Silas Deane from coming in contact with anyone but himself. Deane soon realized that though "inspired with the best intentions in the world," the doctor would be a "hindrance rather than the essential personage pointed out by Franklin." (Doniol.) He therefore insisted so strongly upon meeting the French minister that Dubourg was forced to yield. The meeting took place the 17th day of July, 1776.

"It must be said of Silas Deane at this important meeting that he fulfilled the intention of his mandate not only with intelligence, but with a fecundity of reasoning which could only come from a vigilant patriotism. All the impression which he could desire to produce and which was hoped from his mission flowed from his replies." (Doniol, V. I, p.491.)

The Comte de Vergennes appeared to refuse to give the aid asked, but he led Silas Deane to understand that a confidential agent would take the matter in charge. This confidential agent was no other than Beaumarchais.

Four days before this interview, the Doctor Dubourg had learned to his great disappointment where the confidence of the minister had been placed. Knowing nothing of the real situation, he thought to dissuade the latter from his choice by attacking the private character of the man who had usurped his place. The effect of his letter upon the Comte de Vergennes can be judged from the fact that the latter immediately communicated it to Beaumarchais himself, who was charged with the reply.

The Doctor wrote:

"Monseigneur:

"I have seen M. de Beaumarchais this morning and conferred with him without reserve. Everyone knows his wit, his talents, and no one renders more justice to his honesty, discretion and zeal for all that is good and grand; I believe him one of the most proper men in the world for political negotiations, but perhaps at the same time, the least proper for mercantile enterprises. He loves display, they say that he keeps women; he passes in a word for a spendthrift and there is not a merchant in France who has not this idea of him and who would not hesitate to enter into the smallest commercial dealings with him. Therefore, I was very much astonished when he informed me that you had charged him not only to aid you with his advice but had concentrated on him alone the *ensemble* and the details of all the commercial operations....

"I represented to him that in taking the immense traffic and excluding those who already had run so many dangers and endured so many fatigues ... it would be doing them a real wrong.... But I return to my first and principal reflection and implore you, Monseigneur, to weigh it well. Perhaps there are a hundred, perhaps a thousand persons in France with talents very inferior to those of M. de Beaumarchais, who would fill better your views, inspire more confidence, etc., etc...."

The reply of Beaumarchais, first published by M. de Loménie, and since become so famous, is in the former's most characteristic style. It had its part to play as we shall see, in the trouble which came to its author, and was partly responsible for the non-recognition of his services by the American people. The good doctor always retained a grudge against his brilliant and preferred rival. From him Doctor Franklin imbibed in the beginning such a prejudice against the indefatigable friend of the American cause, that he always avoided him as much as possible. From the reply, a copy of which Beaumarchais sent at the same time for the amusement of the ministers, we quote the following:

"Tuesday, June 16, 1776.

"Eh! What has that to do with our affairs, that I am a man widely known,

CHAPTER XVIII   45

extravagant, and who keeps women? The women that I keep for the last twenty years are your very humble servants. They were five, four sisters and one niece. For three years two of these women are dead, to my great regret. I keep now only three, two sisters and a niece, which is still extravagant for a private individual like myself. But what would you have thought if, knowing me better, you should have learned that I push scandal so far as to keep men as well; two nephews, very young and good looking, even the very unhappy father who brought into the world this scandalous voluptuary? As for my display, that is even worse. For three years, finding lace and embroidered garments too petty for my vanity, have I not affected the pride of having my wrists always garnished with the most beautiful fine muslin? The most superb black cloth is not too elegant for me, at times I have been known to push dandyism so far as to wear silk when it was very hot, but I beg you, Monsieur, do not write these things to M. the Comte de Vergennes; you will end in losing for me his good opinion.

"You have reasons for writing evil of me to him, without knowing me. I have mine for not being offended, although I have the honor of knowing you; you are, Monsieur, an honest man so inflamed with the desire to do a great good that you have thought you could permit yourself a little evil to arrive at it.

"This thought is not exactly the thought of the *évangile* but I have seen a good many persons accommodate themselves to it. But let us cease to speak lightly; I am not angry because M. de Vergennes is not a small man and I hold to his reply. That those to whom I apply for advances may distrust me I admit, but let those who are animated with true zeal for their common friends look twice before they alienate themselves from an honorable man who offers to render every service and to make every useful advance to those same friends. Do you understand me now, Monsieur?

"I will have the honor of meeting with you this afternoon. I have also that of being with the highest consideration, Monsieur, your very humble and very obedient servitor, well known under the name of Roderigue Hortalès et Compagnie."

It was on the 17th of July that Silas Deane and Beaumarchais met for the first time. Both men recognized at once in the other the man for whom each was looking. Both had warm, generous and unselfish natures; both had their minds fixed upon one object alone, the procuring and sending of aid as quickly as possible to the insurged colonies. In excusing himself to Congress for discarding the services of the "dear, good friend" of Franklin, Mr. Deane wrote: "I have been forced to discourage my friend on seeing where the confidence of M. de Vergennes was placed." At the same time he does ample justice to the kindness and interest manifested by Dubourg.

"M. Dubourg has continued," wrote Deane, "to render me every assistance in his power.... His abilities and connections are of the first class in this kingdom and his zeal for the cause of the colonies is to be described only by saying that at times they are in danger of urging him beyond both."

Beaumarchais, on his side, finding Silas Deane empowered by Congress to act directly, ceased to communicate with Arthur Lee.

Already a change had come in their relationship. Returned to France and finding the government bent upon another form of offering aid to the Americans, it had become necessary to break his connections with Lee. Unable to explain the true nature of the enterprise, being bound to absolute secrecy, Beaumarchais wrote the 12th of June, 1776: "The difficulties which I have found in my negotiations with the ministers have forced me to form a company which will cause aid to reach your friends immediately by the way of *Cap Français*."

Naturally enough this meager information was very unsatisfactory to Lee; more than this, he had hoped to play himself a principal rôle in the enterprise (Spark's *Life of Franklin*, p. 449).

From Beaumarchais he learned that Silas Deane had arrived from the colonies empowered to treat with the ministers who had refused steadily to permit his own appearance at Versailles; more than this, he learned that Beaumarchais had entered at once into negotiations with the agent of Congress and that he, Arthur Lee, was being consulted by no one. "Enraged and disappointed," continued Sparks, "Lee hurried to Paris, where he endeavored to bring about a quarrel between Deane and Beaumarchais. Failing in this, he returned to London, vexed in his disappointment and furious against Deane." To avenge himself he wrote to the committee in congress that the two men were agreed together to deceive at once the French Government and the Americans by changing what the former meant to be a gratuitous offering into a commercial speculation. (Silas Deane Papers.)

As can readily be seen, these letters arriving in Philadelphia before any report from Deane, predisposed Congress—two of whose members were brothers of Arthur Lee, against the measures Deane was taking with Beaumarchais. But for the moment, no one interfered with their operations and both men were too intent upon the all-important matter in hand to speculate upon the possible results of the irritation of Doctor Dubourg, or the anger and jealousy of Arthur Lee. Deane, however, fearing lest the noise of Lee's visit to Paris should offend the French Minister, addressed to the latter the following letter:

"Sir: I was informed this morning of the arrival of Arthur Lee. This was a surprise to me, as I know of no particular affair that might call him here, and considering the extreme jealousy of the British ministry at this time and that Mr. Lee was the agent of the colonies in Great Britain, and known to be such, I could wish unless he had received some particular orders from the United Colonies that he had suspended his visit, as I know not otherwise how he can serve me or my affairs—with profound gratitude I say it—now in as favorable a course as the situation of the times will admit. I have the honor to be,

"Silas Deane."

(From Spark's *Dip. Correspondence*, p. 40.)

Immediately after their first meeting, Beaumarchais had addressed a letter to Deane of which the following is an extract:

"Paris, July 18, 1776.

"I have the honor to inform you that for a long while I have formed the project

CHAPTER XVIII 47

of aiding the brave Americans to shake off the yoke of England.... I have spoken already of my plans with a gentleman in London (Arthur Lee), who says he is very much attached to America; but our correspondence since I left England has been followed with difficulty and in cipher; I have received no reply to my last letter, in which I fixed certain points of this great and important affair. Since you are clothed, Monsieur, with a character which permits me to have confidence in you, I shall be very well satisfied to recommence, in a more certain and regular manner, a negotiation which till now has been barely touched...."

Silas Deane replied:

"Paris, Hôtel Grand-Villars, July 20, 1776.

"Monsieur:

"Conformably with your demand in our interview yesterday, I enclose a copy of my commission and an extract of my instructions, which will give you the certitude that I am authorized to make the acquisitions for which I addressed myself to you....

"In regard to the credit which we demand and which I hope to obtain from you, I hope that a long one will not be necessary. A year is the most that my compatriots are in the habit of asking; and Congress having engaged a great quantity of tobacco in Virginia and Maryland which will be embarked as soon as ships can be procured, I do not doubt but considerable returns in nature will be made within six months, and the whole be paid for within the year. I shall press Congress for this in my letters. Nevertheless, events are uncertain, and our commerce is exposed to suffer; but I hope that whatever comes you will soon receive sufficient returns to be enabled to wait for the rest. In case that any sum whatever remains due after the expiration of the accepted credit, it is of course understood that the usual interest will be paid you for the sum.

"I am with all the respect and attachment possible, your, etc.

"Silas Deane."

In his reply to this letter Beaumarchais after accepting the conditions offered by the agent of Congress ends thus:

"As I believe I have to do with a virtuous people, it will suffice for me to keep an exact account of all my advances. Congress will be master to decide whether I shall be paid in merchandise at their usual value at the time of their arrival or to receive them at the buying price, the delays and assurances with a commission proportional to the pains and care, which is impossible to fix to-day. I intend to serve your country as though it were my own, and I hope to find in the friendship of a generous people the true recompense for my work which I consecrate to them with pleasure."

In a lengthy letter written the 24th of July, 1776, the agent of Congress set forth the difficulties of the enterprise in which they are engaged.

He manifested also with warmth his grateful recognition of the services of Beaumarchais. He wrote to him:

"Paris, July 24th, 1776.

"Monsieur:

"I have read with attention the letter which you have done me the favor to write the 22nd, and I think that your propositions for the regulation of the price of merchandise are just and equitable. The generous confidence which you place in the virtue and justice of my constituents inspires me with the greatest joy and gives me the most flattering hopes for the success of this enterprise, for their satisfaction as well as yours, and permit me to assure you again that the United Colonies will take the most effective measures to send you returns, and to justify in all respects the sentiments which animate you toward them.

"Silas Deane."

Nothing could be clearer and more explicit than the understanding arrived at between Beaumarchais and Deane. The latter possessed full power to act, and the former relied unreservedly upon the good faith of the American Congress. In the meantime Deane wrote, introducing his new friend to the Committee of Secret Correspondence.

"Paris, August 18, 1776.

"... I was directed to apply for arms, etc., for 25,000 men.... This I wished to get of the ministry direct, but they evaded it and I am now in treaty for procuring them through the Agency of M. Chaumont and M. Beaumarchais, on credit of eight months, from the time of their delivery. If I effect this as I undoubtedly shall, I must rely on the remittance being made this fall and winter, without fail, or the credit of the colonies will suffer...." (Spark's *Diplomatic Correspondence*, V. I, p. 28.)

Three days earlier he had written, "I find M. de Beaumarchais possessed of the entire confidence of the ministry; he is a man of wit and genius, and a considerable writer on comic and political subjects. All my supplies come through his hands, which at first greatly discouraged my friends...."

At the same time Beaumarchais, inflamed with zeal for the cause of liberty, and wholly unconscious of the effect which his sincere but fantastic letters would have upon the unexpansive nature of the men to whom they were addressed, wrote the following to Congress:

"Paris, August 18, 1776.

"Gentlemen:

"The respectful esteem which I bear towards that brave people who so well defend their liberty under your conduct has induced me to form a plan concurring in this great work by establishing an extensive commercial house ... to supply you with necessaries of every sort that can be useful for the honorable war in which you are engaged. Your deputies, gentlemen, will find in me a sure friend, an asylum in my home, money in my coffers, and every means of facilitating their operations whether of an open, or of a secret nature. I will, so far as possible, remove all obstacles that may oppose your wishes, from the politics of Europe.... The secrecy necessary in some parts of the operations which I have undertaken for your

CHAPTER XVIII

service, requires also on your part a formal resolution that all vessels and their demands should be directed constantly to our house alone, in order that there may be no idle chatting or loss of time, two things that are the ruin of affairs....

"... I shall facilitate your unloading, selling, or disposing of that which I do not wish.... For instance, five American vessels have just arrived in the port of Bordeaux laden with salt fish; though this merchandise coming from strangers is prohibited in our ports, yet as soon as your deputy had told me that these vessels were sent to him by you to raise money by the sale for aiding him in his purchases in Europe, I took such care that I secretly obtained from the government an order for the landing without notice being taken....

"I shall have a correspondent in each seaport town, who on the arrival of your vessels shall wait on the captain and offer every service in his power.... Everything which you wish to arrive safely in any country in Europe ... shall go with great punctuality through me, and this will save much anxiety and many delays. I request you, gentlemen, to send me next spring, if it is possible, ten or twelve thousand hogsheads or more if you can of tobacco of the best quality from Virginia.

"You will understand well that my commerce with you is carried on in Europe; that it is in the great ports of Europe that I make and take returns. However well founded my house may be and though I have appropriated many millions to your trade alone, yet it would be impossible for me to support it, if all the dangers of the sea, of exports and imports were not entirely at your risks....

"Your deputy shall receive as soon as possible full power and authority to accept what I shall deliver to him, to receive my accounts, examine them, make payments upon them or enter into engagements which you shall be bound to ratify as the head of the brave people to whom I am devoted. In short, you may always treat of your interests directly with me.

"Notwithstanding the open opposition which the King of France and his ministers show, and ought to show, to the violation of foreign treaties ... I dare promise you, gentlemen, that my indefatigable zeal shall never be wanting to clear up all difficulties, soften prohibitions, and, in short, facilitate all operations of commerce....

"One thing can never diminish; it is the avowed and ardent zeal which I have in serving you to the utmost of my power....

"Look upon my house, then, gentlemen, henceforth, as the chief of all useful operations to you in Europe and my person as one of the most zealous partisans of your cause, the soul of your success, and a man most deeply impressed with the respectful esteem with which I have the honor to be, etc.

"Roderigue Hortalès et Cie."

"It must be admitted," says Loménie, "that the letters of Beaumarchais were curious enough by their medley of patriotism and commercialism, both equally sincere with him, to inspire distrust in the minds already prejudiced. Imagine serious Yankees, who nearly all before having made war had been merchants, receiving masses of stuff, embarked often in secret, during the night, and whose bills presented in consequence certain irregularities, accompanied with letters in which Beaumarchais associated protestations of enthusiasm, offers of limitless services, political counsels and demands for tobacco, indigo, and salt fish.

"The calculating minds of the Yankees were naturally inclined to think that a being so ardent and fantastic, if he really existed, was playing a commercial comedy concurred in by the government and that one might with all security of conscience utilize his remittances, read his amplifications, and dispense with sending him tobacco," which, as we shall soon see, was exactly what happened.

Infinite difficulties and complications, however, were to arise before even the first shipments could leave the ports of France, and in August the cargoes were not yet collected.

The sixteenth of August Beaumarchais wrote to Vergennes:

"It is decided that all vessels coming from America shall be addressed to the house of Hortalès.... So many things must be carried on together without counting the manufacture of cloth and linen, that I am forced to take on more workers. This affair *politico-commerçante* is becoming so immense that I shall drown myself in details as well as the few aids which I have employed up to the present time, if I do not add more. Some will travel, some reside in the seaports, the manufactories, etc.

"I have promised tobacco to the Farmers-General, and I ask it of the Americans. Their hemp will be a good commodity. At last I begin to see the way clear for my business. The only thing which I do not see are those fatal letters-patent of which I have neither wind nor news.... M. de Maurepas tells me every time he sees me, 'It is attended to, it is finished.'... I should have had them Tuesday. Here it is Friday, but the letters have not come. At the end of the session of parliament this delay of three days makes me lose three months, because of vacation. I am not angry but distressed to see my condition so equivocal and my future uncertain." (Doniol, V. I, p. 513-14.)

As shown in the above letter, Beaumarchais while beginning his extraordinary operations for the Americans was not forgetful of his own interests. He was still a civilly degraded man with no solid basis upon which to build. Gudin, in his history of Beaumarchais, says: "Arriving from London, May, 1776, he presented a petition to the council in order to obtain letters of relief; that is, letters of the king by which it was permitted him to appeal from the judgment rendered against him, although the delay accorded by law had long expired.

"The development of his projects called him to the west coast of France; he did not wish to go until his request was admitted.

"'Go all the same,' M. de Maurepas said to him. 'The council will pronounce very well without you.'"

The projects alluded to by Gudin were, of course, his mercantile operations for supplying the Americans with munitions of war. But so well did Beaumarchais guard his secret, that his dearest friend knew as little of the real nature of his enterprise as the rest of the world. In his visit to the ports of France during the summer of 1776, Gudin accompanied him. Their reception at Bordeaux is described by the

CHAPTER XVIII

latter.

Here as elsewhere, Beaumarchais hid his real occupation under the show of seeking amusement.

"When it was known," says Gudin, "of our arrival, invitations poured in upon us from every side; the women received him as the most amiable of men, the merchants as the most intelligent, the crowds as the most extraordinary; we passed several days in the midst of festivities.... All the while Beaumarchais was preparing new commercial combinations.

"One evening, on entering, he found several letters from Paris; he read them while I was preparing for bed, hurried by fatigue to repose myself. I asked him if he was satisfied with his news.

"'Very well,' he said to me without the least emotion. I was soon asleep. In the morning I felt myself pulled by the arm; I wakened, recognized him and asked if he were ill.

"'No,' he replied, 'but in half an hour we leave for Paris.'

"'*Eh, pourquoi?* What has happened? Have you been sent for?'

"'The council has rejected my demands.'

"'*Ah, ciel!* and you said nothing to me last evening?'

"'No, my friend, I did not wish to disturb your night. It was enough that I did not sleep. I have been thinking all night of what there is for me to do. I have decided, my plan is formed and I go to execute it....'

"Sixty hours later we were in Paris.

"'Eh, what,' he said to M. de Maurepas, who was somewhat surprised to see him so promptly, 'while I was running to the extremities of France to look after the affairs of the king, you lose mine at Versailles.'

"'It is a blunder of Mormesnil (the minister of justice). Go find him, tell him that I want him, and come back together.'

"They explained themselves all three. The matter was taken up under another form, the council judged differently, the request was granted and letters of relief obtained the 12th of August, 1776."

This, however, was but the first step. The letters patent simply allowed Beaumarchais the privilege of having his case brought up a second time for judgment. At this juncture, a new difficulty presented itself. In the words of Loménie: "It was the end of August; the parliament was about to enter on its vacation and it did not wish to take up the matter until afterwards. But Beaumarchais did not adjourn so easily anything once begun. He went again to M. de Maurepas, and persuaded that one is never better served than by himself he did with the first minister what we have seen him do with the king. He drew a note for the first president of Parliament and for the solicitor-general, had M. de Maurepas to sign two copies of the note and send one to each of the above officials." The notes ran thus:

"Versailles, this 27th of August, 1776.

"That part of the affairs of the king with which M. de Beaumarchais is charged, requires, Monsieur, that he make several voyages very shortly. He fears to leave Paris before his case has been tried. He assures me that it can be done before vacation. I do not ask any favor as to the ground of the affair, but only celerity for the judgment; you will oblige him who has the honor to be, very truly yours, etc.

"Maurepas."

In the same way, Beaumarchais served himself through Monsieur de Vergennes, obtaining with the same facility the favor which he desired. He wrote:

"August 29th, 1776.

"I had the honor of seeing M. le Comte de St.-Germain yesterday.... I was very well received.... After two hours' conversation, he wished to keep me to dinner. But can a miserable unfortunate who is running after the solution of his lawsuit take time to dine? I left him, but I have hope that he will be an additional protector. If all is not well, at least all is not bad. I have drawn up a letter intended to correct the fault committed.

"It is your reply to his letter. Pardon, M. de Comte, if I have taken the liberty of acting as your secretary. For so long I have been attached to you by all possible titles, if you approve of the letter there is only a signature and an envelope necessary." (Doniol, V. I, p. 574.)

M. de Loménie continued: "This was still not sufficient for Beaumarchais. He wished the Attorney-General Seguier to speak and to be eloquent in his favor; for this he wrote a letter to Maurepas, accompanied by another note, rather more expressive, for M. Seguier, a note which the minister copied with the same docility as the preceding one." It runs as follows:

"Versailles, this 30th of August, 1776.

"I learn, Monsieur, by M. de Beaumarchais, that if you have not the goodness to speak on his affair it will be impossible for him to obtain a judgment before the 7th of September. That part of the affair of the king with which M. de Beaumarchais is entrusted requires that he make a voyage very soon; he fears to leave Paris before he is restored to his estate as citizen; it has been so long now that he suffers, and his desire in this respect is truly legitimate. I ask no favor as to the ground of the affair, but you will oblige me infinitely if you will contribute towards having him judged before vacation.

"I have the honor to be, etc. Maurepas."

The trial took place. Beaumarchais chose for his defense a lawyer, Target, who had remained firm during the entire existence of the parliament Maupeou, refusing to plead before it. "Beaumarchais," says Loménie, "always faithful to his taste for *mise en scène*, wrote him a letter which circulated everywhere and which commenced with the words, 'The Martyr Beaumarchais to the Virgin Target.'"

An immense concourse of people thronged the judgment hall the day appointed for the trial; and when, after the pleading of Target and the recommendation of Seguier, the restored parliament annulled by a solemn decree the decree of the parliament Maupeou, the wildest excitement prevailed. Beaumarchais immediately addressed the following letter to Vergennes:

"Paris, this Friday, September 6, 1776.

"M. le Comte,

"I have just been judged, *déblâmé*, amidst a universal concourse of applause. Never did so unfortunate a citizen receive greater honor. I hasten to announce to you the news, begging you to place my gratitude at the feet of the king. I am so trembling with joy that my hand can scarcely write all the respectful sentiments with which I am, Monsieur le Comte, your very humble and very obedient servitor, Beaumarchais.

"Do me the kindness, M. le Comte, to announce this very happy news to M. de Maurepas and to M. de Sartine. I have four hundred persons about me who applaud and embrace me and make an infernal noise, which seems to me superb harmony."

The happy man was carried in triumph amid the enthusiastic shouts of the populace from the great chamber of justice to his carriage.

The next day he published a discourse which he had intended to deliver, but from which he had been dissuaded.

It will be remembered that Beaumarchais had been consulted by the ministers in regard to the principles on which the new parliament should be recalled, and that they had not dared to carry out the justice and the liberality of his ideas. Although as we have seen, Beaumarchais utilized the ministers pretty much as he desired, he did so without in the least compromising his own freedom.

In this daring address he combated the existing abuses of the present parliament, as he before had done those of the Parliament Maupeou.

"He contributed," says Loménie, "without being conscious of it, to prepare the ruin of the parliament which applauded him. He combated their abuses and caused to enter into the minds of the masses the necessity for judicial reform."

M. de Loménie says elsewhere: "Beaumarchais at this moment, reinstated in his rights as a citizen, enjoying the brilliant success of his *Barbier de Séville*, already invested with the intimate confidence of the government in the American question; well received at court, popular in the city; directing the dramatic authors in their struggle for literary liberty, might be considered as a man who had at last conquered evil fortune; nevertheless, he was not yet disengaged from the fetters of his past. His first suit with the Comte de la Blache, which had been the origin of his trials and of his celebrity, existed still in the midst of his triumphs, and held in check his fortunes and his honor."

This man, confidant of the ministry in the affairs of the United States, the popular author of the *Barbier de Séville*, was under the blow of an iniquitous sentence which declared him indirectly a forger, and placed his goods at the discretion of an enemy.

In 1775, the first judgment had been revoked and the affair sent before the parliament which met at Aix in the south of France.

The zeal which we have seen Beaumarchais display in carrying rapidly to a successful termination the matter of his rehabilitation was now turned toward the *retarding* of the judgment in the other case.

The Comte de la Blache, on the other hand, vexed at seeing the rapidly rising fortunes of his adversary, endeavored by every means in his power to hasten the decision. Overwhelmed with the multiplicity of his undertakings, Beaumarchais appealed to M. de Vergennes, urging that the case be allowed to stand in *statu quo* for the present. In a letter from the minister, dated June 2, 1776, the following passage occurs:

"I saw yesterday, in relation to your affair at Aix, M. le Guard of the Seals, who immediately gave orders to write to M. de la Tour, the first president of the tribunal, to the effect that all ultimate procedure should be suspended.... You know, Monsieur, the sincerity of my interest for all that concerns you.

"de Vergennes."

Thus with a comparatively tranquil mind, the indefatigable agent of the government was able to turn his attention to the gigantic commercial enterprise which he already had well in hand.

We shall not, therefore, be surprised to see him rise above all adverse circumstances, and notwithstanding the disloyalty of some of his agents, the fury of the English Ambassador, the opposition of the government itself, actually succeed in landing immense cargoes on the American coast in time for the great decisive campaign of 1777.

WILLIAM CARMICHAEL
Member of the Continental Congress.

CHAPTER XIX

> *"I should never have completed what I have but for the generous, the indefatigable and spirited exertions of Monsieur de Beaumarchais, to whom the United States are in every account greatly indebted, more so than to any other person on this side the water."*
>
> Silas Deane to Congress, November 29, 1776.

Suspicions of English Aroused Through Indiscretions of Friends of America—Treachery of du Coudray—Counter Order Issued Against Shipments of Beaumarchais—Franklin's Arrival—England's Attempt to Make Peace Stirs France—Counter Order Recalled—Ten Ships Start Out—Beaumarchais Cleared by Vergennes.

WHILE Beaumarchais, through the intervention of the Ministry, was bringing his own personal interests to a successful termination, he was at the same time carrying vigorously forward his operations in the cause of America. These operations were the most difficult. In the words of Loménie: "It was a question of an officially prohibited commerce, which prohibition was under the vigilant supervision of the English Ambassador,—and could receive the official support of the French government only on condition that it was carefully hidden. The least indiscretion, the slightest diplomatic embarrassment occasioned by the affair would immediately transform this support into persecution. It was under these conditions that the author of the *Barbier de Séville* was obliged to extract without noise and in small quantities, from the different arsenals of the state, 200 pieces of cannon, mortars, bombs, bullets, 25,000 guns, 100 tons of powder; to manufacture the stuffs necessary for the equipment of 25,000 men, collect all these objects in the different ports and send them to the insurgents without arousing the suspicion of the English Ambassador."

It was, however, humanly impossible that suspicions should not be aroused; too many people were interested in the cause of America; too many were eager to aid in the struggle of the colonies for liberty. Especially was the *cher bon ami* of Dr. Franklin constantly bringing things to the brink of exposure through his officious intermeddling. Although he knew nothing of the real basis upon which the commercial house, Roderigue Hortalès et Cie., was founded, yet he was very well aware that Beaumarchais had supplanted him in the confidence of the ministers. Forced to see himself set aside, Dubourg none the less continued collecting supplies on his own account, which he forwarded to the insurgents. His indiscreet zeal led him often into grave difficulties.

"With the best intentions in the world," says Doniol, "he was in danger of interfering with, rather than aiding the cause he hoped to serve."

The letters of Beaumarchais to Vergennes during this period constantly revert to this theme, "Dubourg must be made to keep silence and not to compromise the ministry." "If," he writes in another place, "while we are closing the doors on one side, someone opens the windows on the other, it is impossible that the secret does not escape." At length quite out of patience at some new and serious indiscretion which the good doctor in his simplicity had told to Beaumarchais himself, the latter wrote to Vergennes, "Is there then no way to stop the mouth of that cruel gossiper?... As he told me I could scarcely refrain from dealing him a blow, but I restrained myself, simply turning my back and walking away.... I depend upon you, M. le Comte, to deliver us from this fatal and mischief-making agent."

But Dubourg was by no means the only person interested in the cause of America who was sowing snares in the pathway of Beaumarchais and of Deane. At the worst, the good doctor was only indiscreet, he was never guilty of that personal ambition which in times of great crisis delights to bring ruin upon the schemes of others, and which uses all its power to thwart those enterprises which it cannot lead. Many enemies of this latter type were destined soon to manifest themselves. On the 1st of October, 1776, Silas Deane wrote to Congress of a certain Mr. Hopkins of Maryland, then in Paris, who without official authority was interesting himself in the same cause. "Offended at some supposed personal slight, he formed the dark design," says Deane, "of defeating at one stroke my whole prospect as to supplies.... However thunderstruck I was, as well as my friend Monsieur Beaumarchais at this treachery ... we exerted ourselves and truth prevailed.... It would be too tedious to recount what I have met with in this way.... I do not mention a single difficulty with one complaining thought for myself.... I am happy in being so far successful, and that the machinations of my enemies, or rather the enemies of my country ... have been brought to nought."

But perhaps the most dangerous enemy in the pathway of Deane and Beaumarchais was a man in whom from the first they had reposed the most entire confidence. This was Trouson du Coudray, a French officer of rank and genius, a personal friend of the minister of war, the Comte St. Germain, who had been the military preceptor of le Comte d'Artois. He had afterwards been stationed at the garrison of Metz, where he was associated with the drawing out of old arms and of replacing them by ones of more recent date. As it was precisely these old arms which the French Government was willing to part with to Hortalès et Cie.,—at a reasonable price, du Coudray was admirably placed to further the proceedings of its agent. Had he been truly disinterested in his proffered services, his coöperation would have been invaluable. As a matter of fact, "this officer," says Doniol, "certainly capable, was one of those who whatever employment is made of their services, look first to the personal advantage they can draw from them. Having fascinated Deane and Beaumarchais, he succeeded in having himself named one of the staff officers of artillery and was to go out to the colonies in command of the chief vessel of Hortalès et Cie., the *Amphitrite*. Deane at once wrote to Congress, announcing the great acquisition which he had made. He bestowed the highest praise upon du Coudray, but at the same time evinced a fear lest Congress might consider that he had overstepped the bounds of his commission in appointing him to so high a rank. He excused himself for having been forced to confer upon the officer special marks of favor in order to secure his services, which, he felt sure, would, in the end, justify him for the step he had taken. He humbly expressed a hope that Congress would not consider as too high the salary he had promised, and begged it to confirm the wisdom of his choice."

Du Coudray was not long in showing himself unworthy of the confidence thus reposed in him. It was this unfortunate step of Deane, afterwards imputed to him as a crime by Arthur Lee, which was the chief cause of his subsequent recall and the semi-disgrace inflicted upon him. Beaumarchais, being as deeply inculpated as Deane, fell equally in the opinion of American patriots. But as yet, no foreshadowing of coming events had dampened the zeal of the colonial commissioner, or of his indefatigable friend. On October 15, 1776 (Spark's *Dip. Corres.*, I, p. 51), a contract was signed M. de Monthieu, Roderigue Hortalès et Cie. and Silas Deane, for furnishing armed vessels and merchandise on condition that risks and perils be on account of the U. S. and that "in case the vessels be detained in American ports more than two months, without returning them laden with the cargoes proposed, wages and expenses shall be paid by the United States."

While Deane was thus busily engaged in carrying out the commission with which he was entrusted, he was being left, as far as Congress was concerned, absolutely without support or approval. Communication between the two continents was slow in those days, and it has been shown already that before Deane was able to send any definite information to Congress of his reception by the French Government, Lee had forestalled him by giving that body his own private and unfounded interpretation of the relation entered into between the commissioner and the agent of the French Government. When Lee's letter reached America, Congress was deeply engrossed with the weightier matters which were forcing themselves upon its attention, owing to the decisive step which it was about to take in declaring itself free from British rule. The matter, therefore, was allowed to rest in *statu quo* for the present. Congress preferred to await developments before setting on foot any investigations, and so, though Deane continued to give frequent and full accounts of all his transactions, no reply was ever made to any of his letters. This rendered his situation cruel in the extreme. Wholly unsuspicious by nature, it never occurred to him that an enemy was busily at work, undermining his character and poisoning the minds of his compatriots in regard to the disinterestedness of the motives which actuated him. His irritation began at last to manifest itself. "For heaven's sake," he wrote in a letter to Congress, dated October 1, 1776 (Spark's *Diplomatic Correspondence*, Vol. II), "if you mean to have any connection with this kingdom, be more assiduous in getting your letters here. I know not where the blame lies, but it must lie heavy somewhere, when vessels are suffered to sail from Philadelphia and elsewhere, right down to the middle of August, without a single line. This circumstance was near proving a mortal blow to my whole proceedings."

October 17th of the same year he says:

"Warlike preparations are daily making in this kingdom and in Spain. I need not urge the importance of immediate remittances towards paying for the large quantity of stores I have engaged for, and I depend that this winter will not be suffered to slip away unimproved. I have the honor to be, etc.

"Silas Deane."

By the end of November, notwithstanding the delays and discouragements encountered by the agents of the two governments, several vessels had been loaded with supplies and were about to set sail. Silas Deane wrote to Congress, Nov. 29th, 1776.

"I should never have completed what I have, but for the generous, the indefatigable, and spirited exertions of M. Beaumarchais, to whom the United States are on every account greatly indebted, more so than to any other person on this side the water ... therefore I am confident you will make the earliest and most ample remittances." After giving further details, he proceeds: "A nephew of Beaumarchais, a young gentleman of family, education and spirit, makes a voyage to America with M. Ducoudray (in the various documents, the name of this officer appears, sometimes written as above by Mr. Deane, but more often 'du Coudray,' which is the correct form) and is ambitious of serving his first campaign in your cause. I recommend him therefore to your particular patronage and protection, as well on account of the great merits of his uncle, as on that of his being a youth of genius and spirit.... I have confidently assured his uncle that he will receive protection and paternal advice from you, and am happy in knowing that you will fulfill my engagements on that score.

"I cannot in a letter do full justice to M. de Beaumarchais, for his address and assiduity in our cause. His interest and influence, which are great, have been exerted to the utmost, in the cause of the United States."

On the 3rd of December, 1776, in a letter to John Jay written when the last measures were being taken for the despatching of the vessels equipped by Hortalès et Cie., Deane thus expressed himself:

"If my letters arrive safely they will give you some idea of my situation:—without intelligence, without orders, and without remittances, yet boldly plunging into contracts, engagements, negotiations, hourly hoping that something will arrive from America.

"By M. du Coudray I send 30,000 guns, 200 pieces of brass cannon, 30 mortars, 4,000 tents, and clothing for 30,000 men, with 200 tons of gunpowder, lead balls, etc., etc., by which you may judge we have some friends here. A war in Europe is inevitable. The eyes of all are on you, and the fear of your giving up, or accommodating is the greatest obstacle I have to contend with. Monsieur Beaumarchais has been my minister in effect, as this court is extremely cautious and I now advise you to attend carefully to the articles sent you. I could not examine them here. I was promised they should be good, and at the lowest price, and that from persons in such station that had I hesitated it might have ruined my affairs....

"Large remittances are necessary for your credit, and the enormous price of tobacco, of rice, of flour and many other articles, gives you an opportunity of making your remittances to very good advantage. Twenty thousand hogsheads of tobacco are wanted immediately for this kingdom, and more for other parts of Europe."... (*Correspondence and Public Papers of John Jay*, 1890, p. 97.)

In spite of the remonstrances of Deane, Congress continued deaf and dumb in regard to their Commissioner, neither condemning nor approving his acts, but passing all by with like indifference. In the meantime, Beaumarchais was pushing forward his gigantic operations, being taken with "a sort of drunkenness of activity and of confidence in himself, which," says Doniol, "turned him at times from precautions. He was at this juncture, really a political agent. He had indicated to M. de Maurepas a plan of finance which would enable France to arm itself, without increasing taxation, and the mission had been given him to study the execution of the plan with M. Necker, who had been called to the management of the Treasury. He had discussed with Deane, perhaps somewhat with Vergennes, the creation of a bank, in view of making loans on the lands of America." (*Doniol* II, p. 57.)

Extracts from a Memoir by Beaumarchais, addressed to Vergennes, in regard to a loan to be made to the Congress: "Supposing always," he wrote, "that your intention is neither to let America perish nor to force her to arrange with England through lack of the succor which is indispensable for her defense, if you can procure it; supposing also that my work and my ministry have not ceased to be agreeable to you; I have found a means of supporting the Americans without disbursing considerable sums, which you do not possess, but which the Americans cannot dispense with.

"If you look upon me as the important advocate of that nation before the Ministry of France,—an employment which I have assumed because it was as noble as it was useful to my country; knowing that I have not done this without your secret agreement, you must hear me to-day, even aid me, if you do not wish to leave without results a plan which is without danger." After developing the details of his scheme for rendering more effective aid to the Americans, Beaumarchais continues, "As you see, M. le Comte, this is only an extension adroitly given, to that which I have been doing for the last year. For the past two weeks I have been buried in the meditations and the correspondence which this work requires. To-day I am in condition to treat secretly with you and M. de Maurepas. Any evening which you wish, I will attend upon your orders."

Things were moving, however, far too slowly for the impatient spirit of Beaumarchais. The 14th of October he had written to Vergennes.

"Every time that I think how we hold in our hands the destiny of the world, and that we have the power to change the system of things—and when I see so many advantages, so much glory ready to escape, I regret infinitely not to have more influence over the resolutions of the councils, and not to be able to multiply myself, so as to prevent the evil on one hand, and aid the good on the other. I know too well your patriotism to fear offending you in speaking thus....

"I expect to be at Fontainebleau Thursday at the latest. Until then I shall not sleep until I have finished the work on Finance, promised to M. de Maurepas."

Obstacles of every kind were being thrown in the path of Beaumarchais, though he remained ignorant of their source. He continued to insist that the government permit him to carry forward what it had encouraged him to commence. His letters of this period testify to "a consciousness of being hampered, a desire to act, fear of being too presumptive in his demands, and intentions of rendering effective service." (*Doniol* II, p. 58.) He thought the delays came from Maurepas, whose coldness had distressed him, so he urged Vergennes to plead for him. "If I were not certain," he wrote, November 12, 1776, "that I do not displease you in desiring you to raise as far as possible the obstacles which retard my course, I would not have the indiscretion to make observations when it seems I ought simply to submit. But I know that you are as much annoyed as I by all that tends to spoil my plans. This idea consoles me and enables me not to lose patience...." "Do not," he pleads, "do not, M. le Comte, look upon my impatience as insubordination, it is nothing but zeal." Then he proceeded to urge Vergennes to send him an order through the minister of war, the Comte de St. Germain, that there be delivered to him 2,000 hundredweight of powder, which would enable him to set sail, and he ended by saying how he had "*le cœur bien serré* to see how things are going or in reality, not going."

The fall of New York offered an opportunity for Beaumarchais to press his solicitations, urging that the Americans had been beaten only from lack of supplies. "If I were asking a personal favor," he wrote to Vergennes, "I would have patience, but I shall lose it if you do not come to my assistance." On the second of October he had written: "Everything about me follows me with talk and does all that it can to ruin me. Across all these bitter things I walk with assurance to my ends; unless a pistol shot stops me, I will be found ready to treat with all who present themselves. My zeal and my disinterestedness are the basis of my defense. I have no important paper about me—everything is secure."

In the midst of so many hidden dangers Beaumarchais was soon made to feel a still graver one. The French government suddenly began to thwart all his operations, and this without a word of warning or explanation. The fact was that the suspicions of the Court of St. James had been thoroughly aroused, and, pressed by the English Ambassador, the minister had been forced to take a stand. The fifteenth of November the English Court notified the Spanish Ambassador that everything was known, and the twenty-second of the same month, they expressed themselves still more strongly through other avenues. Vergennes was informed that the aid being rendered by France was no longer a secret. Something had to be done immediately to allay the fears of the English, and from this had arisen the apparent hostility of the ministers.

Even had there been no one directly to blame for these disclosures, entire secrecy still could not have been maintained. The very multiplicity of the operations, "the goings and comings of Deane and Beaumarchais and their intermediaries, the confidence that was inspired by the support of the government leading to indiscretions, all this divulged the acts." (*Doniol* II, 35.) More than this, officers enrolled, or those who wished to be, were spread about in the cafés and public places, in Paris or the seaports, awaiting the moment of embarkation. All these men, "infatuated and needy," were under the control of du Coudray, who was expecting to sail on the largest of Beaumarchais's ships, *l'Amphitrite*, a vessel of 480 tons, which already had received its cargo, and was only awaiting the presence of the officer in order to set sail. For some unaccountable reason, he had returned to Versailles without giving any notice. He remained there for more than a week, causing a delay which threatened to spoil everything. Beaumarchais, supposing that the ministry was at fault, wrote to Vergennes in the following impatient manner: "Everything has gone, everything is waiting. Why cannot I have the whole management of the affair? Then nothing would be delayed and my vessels would already be in America." The truth was that du Coudray, relying upon his powerful support at court, had gone to Versailles in order to succeed in escaping if possible from the hands of Beaumarchais, so as not to go over as his envoy. He had all along been lengthening "by every means in his power the delay in getting off, had sown discontent among the enrolled, sending away such as he could not gain, had encouraged complaint, confided the place of embarkation to indiscreet persons, and then threw upon Beaumarchais the blame of the noise which he himself had made." (*Doniol* II, 61.) In addition to all the rest, Beaumarchais was guilty of a particular indiscretion of his own. Having gone the 6th of December, 1776, to Havre, under the assumed name of Durand, in order to superintend, without arousing suspicion, the despatching of three of his vessels, the *Amphitrite, La Seine, La Romaine*, he could not resist the temptation of busying himself at the same time with his literary productions. Displeased with the way in which his famous comedy, *Le Barbier de Séville*, was being performed, he imprudently collected the actors, making them rehearse the play under his direction. His presence in the seaport thus became known; the English Ambassador was notified and the latter at once addressed to the Government the most vehement remonstrances.

"On the 16th of December a counter order was issued and sent to Havre and Nantes, prohibiting the officers from embarking and the vessels from setting out. But when the counter order reached Havre, *l'Amphitrite*, which bore the greater part of the officers and munitions, already had set sail. The *Seine* and the *Romaine* were alone sequestered, Beaumarchais then returned with all haste to Paris, in order to obtain the revocation of the counter order." (Loménie II, p. 136.)

But in the meantime, an event had happened which, as soon as it became known, roused the French people to the highest pitch of enthusiasm, while it deepened the distrust and anger of the English Ambassador. This event was the arrival of Dr. Franklin upon the shores of France. Beaumarchais already had announced the fact in a letter to Vergennes. "The noise," he said, "caused by the arrival of Mr. Franklin is inconceivable.... The courageous old man allowed the vessel to make two captures, in spite of the personal danger he ran."

Though the French people might welcome with heartfelt enthusiasm, the venerable old democrat and philosopher, yet his presence at this moment was a serious matter to the Court of France. The Government was moving, it is true, directly towards open war with Great Britain, but she was as yet very unwilling that the

CHAPTER XIX

English should have cause of offense in her attitude towards the country which had now declared itself free and independent. All the supplies which she was allowing to be sent by Hortalès et Cie. went out in vessels bound direct to her West Indian possessions, and were ostensibly intended for her own colonists, so that the English Government had no legal right to interfere. England therefore redoubled her watchfulness at the court of her rival, and knowing as she very well did that it was in every way to the interest of France to aid the Americans in their fight for liberty, she was all the more determined to harass and thwart every operation which tended in that direction.

All this time the Americans were far too deeply engrossed with the difficulties of their own situation to spend much thought upon those that surrounded their friends in Europe. On the 26th of September, Congress had appointed three commissioners to the Court of France. Silas Deane already on the spot had been retained; to him were added Benjamin Franklin and Thomas Jefferson. The latter declining to serve, was replaced by Arthur Lee, who was still in London.

Immediately after setting foot in France, Franklin wrote to his *cher, bon ami*, the Doctor Dubourg, a letter full of warm expressions of friendship and of polite messages to Madame. He enclosed under the same cover a letter to Silas Deane, begging his dear friend to see to its speedy delivery. The letter to Deane informed him of his new appointment, and gave orders that Lee be summoned immediately to join them. He bore with him no letter from Congress, nor any message relating to the past services of Deane, news of which, in fact, had hardly reached the colonies at the time of the doctor's embarkation.

Franklin had no personal interest in the work already accomplished, since his *cher, bon ami* had been set aside, as soon as Deane saw "where the confidence of the Government was placed." From the first he had determined not to interfere in the quarrel that existed between Lee and Deane, and he steadily refused to enter into the merits of the zeal displayed by Beaumarchais under cover of Hortalès et Cie. Warned against him by so many of his friends, and having particular reasons for not showing marked favor to Deane (the suspicious jealousy of Lee's character threatened from the start to thwart the entire object of the commission), he chose the course of ignoring all that already had been accomplished. For the moment Deane, himself, seemed alienated from Beaumarchais. Vexed at the delay in despatching the supplies (for he knew nothing of the counter-order issued by the Government), irritated by Lee, annoyed at the indifference of Franklin and dismayed by the silence of Congress, Deane in turn assumed an attitude of cold indifference which perplexed and disquieted his friend. The new duties which were forced upon him, the change in the character of his mission, occupied for the time all his thoughts.

As soon as the three commissioners were united in Paris, Franklin wrote asking for an audience with the minister of foreign affairs, M. de Vergennes. "Sir," he wrote, "we beg leave to acquaint your Excellency that we are appointed and fully empowered by the Congress of the United States of America to propose and negotiate a treaty of amity and commerce between France and the said states.... (Doniol II, 112.)" The minister, however, really anxious to further the plans of Beaumarchais, was slow to give additional umbrage to the English Ambassador by receiving the three commissioners whose presence in Paris it was impossible to hide.

Already Franklin had taken up his quarters in Passy, where he held a little court of his own. Imbert de St. Amand, in his *Les Beaux Jours de Marie Antoinette*, has given a vivid picture of the impression made upon the inhabitants of Paris by the presence in their midst of the aged philosopher. "The idol of the day," he says, "in that Paris, so capricious and so versatile, was Franklin—that peasant, that septuagenarian philosopher, that learned democrat, that man of the future—was acclaimed by the French aristocracy. The philanthropists, the apologists of perpetual peace, demanded war with loud cries. Louis XVI, notwithstanding his scruples of conscience, allowed himself to be won over. The apartments of Versailles filled themselves with solicitors of peril and of glory. All the young nobility wished to start at once. What transport! what madness! what valor in those paladin philosophers, those chivalrous democrats, having the double passion of glory and liberty, full of superb illusions, of generous follies, and so eloquent, so amiable, so brave! With what gaiety these quitted their pleasures, their châteaux, their theatres, to live the life of a soldier, to go to seek the other side of the Atlantic, perils and unknown dangers!"

All this excitement caused by the presence of Franklin did not tend to lessen the vigilance of the English, although from the first they had hope that if France could be prevented from aiding the Colonies, Franklin might in the end be obliged to enter into negotiations with England. It was precisely this fear which haunted the French Government and induced the King to revoke the counter-order issued to prevent the sailing of the ships of Hortalès et Cie. Happy at last in gaining permission to leave port, Beaumarchais thought only of despatching his retarded vessels, when he learned that the *Amphitrite*, the one ship that had set out before the arrival of the counter-order, was at Lorient, a seaport on the west coast of France, whither it had been brought by du Coudray "under the pretext that bad weather encountered in the channel had shown the defective condition of the vessel." (*Doniol* II, p. 314.)

Beaumarchais, still deceived, wrote to Vergennes: "*L'Amphitrite*, after sixteen days of bad weather, has been obliged to return for a moment to take on fresh provisions, those on board having been saturated by the sea. This is what I have from M. du Coudray, who asks that it be kept secret, and who expects to depart in a few days."

The treachery of this officer could not, however, long remain secret. "The English Ambassador, learning the details, complained loudly to Vergennes, who, irritated to find himself again compromised, laid the blame on Beaumarchais withdrawing the permission newly accorded to set sail." (Loménie II, p. 137.) Du Coudray then wrote a long letter full of lame excuses. Beaumarchais, furious on learning the truth, replied as follows:

"Paris, January 22, 1777.

"As your conduct, sir, in this affair is inexplicable, I will not waste time in trying to comprehend it. All that concerns me is to guarantee myself and my friends against occurrences of the same kind in future. As the veritable owner, therefore, of the *Amphitrite*, I send herewith an order to Captain Fautrelle, to take absolute command. You are sagacious enough to see that I have not taken so decisive a step without previously consulting powerful and judicious friends. Have the kindness, sir, to conform to it, or find another vessel to take you wherever you please, with no pretension on my part to hinder you in any respect, except in matters which relate to myself and which tend to injure me."

When Deane learned of the disgraceful conduct of the man in whom he had reposed such entire confidence, he withdrew the commission which he had granted him, and the 8th of February wrote to Beaumarchais. "The strange, ungrateful and perfidious conduct of this man, mortifies and embarrasses me strangely, and as I wish with all my heart that I had never seen him, I wish equally that he may never see America." Beaumarchais at once forwarded this letter to Vergennes, begging him to prevent du Coudray from setting out for the new world. An order from Vergennes arrived commanding him to return to his garrison at Metz. Instead of obeying, he hastened to Versailles, where, as has been shown, he had powerful protection. He succeeded in being privately presented to Franklin and through the intervention of the ministers of war and the navy, du Coudray received from Franklin a recommendation to Congress, which recommendation Deane himself finally consented to sign, although with reluctance, for he informed Beaumarchais at once of the act, assuring him that he had done no more than admit that du Coudray was a good officer. Vergennes, not wishing a quarrel either with the Comte de St. Germain or with M. de Sartine (minister of war and the navy), was obliged to close his eyes to the action of the officer, who at once hastened to set sail for America. (See *Doniol* II, p. 317.)

The 11th of February, Beaumarchais wrote to Vergennes: "Everyone knows the evil which that officer wishes to do me. Having made to myself a law to explain to no one the wise and pressing motives which oppose themselves to the departure of that officer, and owing to the necessity of preventing his indiscretions, I am liable to be taxed with a design to persecute him, whom on the contrary I have from the first endeavored to advance and have aided in sincere good faith.... It is neither in my character nor in my principles to revenge myself on anyone—I should be obliged to pass my life at that odious business...."

"Neither the orders of Vergennes nor the interference of Beaumarchais or Deane having prevented du Coudray from crossing the Atlantic, the evil which followed was inevitable. Arrived in America, he hastened to accuse Beaumarchais of the very acts which he himself had attempted to perform, and he accused not him alone, but in consequence Silas Deane of complicity, as well as the Comte de Vergennes." (*Doniol* II, p. 353.)

"Dreaming of great position in America, he built upon the order to retain him on the continent, and gave it out as an intrigue of Beaumarchais." He at once issued a pamphlet to Congress, in which he explained, "It is to my credit alone, and to my zeal in your service, that you are indebted for the extent of the aid accorded to your commissioner, and in nothing to the Sieur de Beaumarchais; everything was finished when he arrived." He further dilated upon the greed of gain which characterized the French agent, and accused him of fraud in his dealings with the colonies. To minds already prepossessed with similar ideas, this pamphlet was not calculated to increase the confidence of Congress in the good faith either of their commissioner or of his friend. During the two months preceding the open exposure of the perfidy of this officer, the difficulty of the situation of Beaumarchais hardly can be overestimated. "Denounced by the conspiracies of du Coudray as being only incited by desire for lucre; obliged to resort to complicated expediencies in order to spare the Government the recriminations of the English, constrained to defend himself against the mistrust aroused even in the spirit of M. de Vergennes by his at times inevitable indiscretions; forced to fall back on justifications which might seem equivocal, he lent himself to doubt, even to suspicion." (*Doniol* II, p. 308.) On the 30th of January he wrote to M. de Vergennes:

"When one writes to a minister whom one respects and cherishes, one is very much embarrassed to find terms to explain a fact like the one that suffocates me. After Mr. Deane had shown during a month a very bad humor, and saying to myself the whole time that there was something very mysterious in the delay of the vessels at Havre, I was anxious to have an explanation of his offensive tone. He replied that, tired himself of not knowing where the blame lay, he had the honor to send you a memoir by M. Lee, and that the latter reported that Your Excellency had clearly assured him that for a long while there had been no obstacle on the part of the ministry and that if I said there was, it could only be an imposture of mine or of M. Montieu. Pardon, M. le Comte, if after swallowing all the other bitter pills without complaint, this rests in my throat and strangles me in passing. Your Excellency will perhaps be so good as to cast a glance over the four letters that I join to this, written by me to M. de Sartine the 3rd, 18th, 22d and 29th of January. They will inform you of the true state of affairs if it is possible that you are ignorant of it, and you will tell me afterwards up to what point you order me to keep silent and sacrifice myself. This blow crushes me and makes me desire that my whole conduct as a vigilant man and faithful servitor be promptly examined and with the utmost rigor. It is impossible for me to take an instant's repose until you have accorded me this grace. Read, I beg you, my letters to M. de Sartine and judge of my suffering."

Vergennes immediately replied, and the whole situation grew brighter. Beaumarchais wrote the next day, February 1, 1777, "I sincerely thank you for your goodness in tranquilizing me. I have force against everything except your discontent. Never judge me without hearing me, this is the only favor I ask. I know well that you are accused of irresolution, which is very far from your character. Afterwards they cast upon me the reflections of their discontent, making you speak, so that I may feel it more keenly—I will never believe anything again. I have the intimate consciousness that I do my best and even the best that can be done under the circumstances. Across all the obstacles that surround me, a small success pays me for great labor. I feel myself already light-hearted again since yesterday's letters have told me that three of my vessels have started." Beaumarchais was thus after so many delays given full power to act. On the 4th of February, 1777, he wrote to Vergennes:

CHAPTER XIX

"At last I have my delivery.... It is a pity that the Dutch should be destined to have the principal gain from the transport of these materials. No matter, the most important thing is, not to let America come to grief through lack of good munitions...."

By the beginning of March ten vessels of Roderigue Hortalès et Cie. were floating towards America. The seventh of that month he announced the fact to Vergennes: "Never," he wrote, "has commercial affair been pushed with so much vigor, in spite of obstacles of every nature which have been encountered. May God give it good success!"

"Beaumarchais," says M. de Loménie, "naturally expected soon to receive very many expressions of gratitude from Congress, as well as very much Maryland and Virginia tobacco. He did not even receive a reply to his letters." Nevertheless, he continued to send out ships laden with supplies, all through the spring and summer, receiving from his agents alone information of their safe arrival.

The failure of Congress to ratify the conditions offered by its commissioner would have brought to ruin the commercial house of Roderigue Hortalès et Cie. in spite of the subsidy of two millions with which it had been founded, had not the Government again come to its assistance. But though the ministers in general, and Vergennes in particular, never entirely deserted Beaumarchais, other and wholly different measures for aiding the Americans were now seriously occupying their attention. The colonies in declaring themselves free from British rule had forced upon France the necessity of coming to some definite decision. This she was slow in doing, but so inevitable was it that she should take an active part in the great struggle that already the measures necessary for the arming and equipping of her forces were being discussed in her councils, while the nation, gone mad with enthusiasm, was urging her forward in the pathway which could lead to nothing but open war.

LAFAYETTE

CHAPTER XX

> *"Never Greece, never Rome, never any people of the ancient world, exposed the motives of its independence with a more noble simplicity, nor based them upon more evident truths."*
>
> Gudin de la Brenellerie, Histoire de Beaumarchais.

The Declaration of Independence and Its Effect in Europe—Beaumarchais's Activity in Getting Supplies to America—Difficulties Arise About Sailing—Treachery of du Coudray—Lafayette's Contract with Deane—His Escape to America—Beaumarchais's Losses—Baron von Steuben Sails for America in Beaumarchais's Vessel, Taking the Latter's Nephew, des Epinières, and His Agent, Theveneau de Francy—The Surrender of Burgoyne—Beaumarchais Finds Himself Set Aside While Others Take His Place—Faces Bankruptcy—Vergennes Comes to His Assistance.

"THE Act," says *Doniol* (I, p. 561), "which proclaimed to the civilized world the institution of the American Republic and which was destined to open a new phase of civilization, was announced in Europe only as an incident, secondary to the resistance of the rebels.

"The English Government would not admit that the solemn act produced any visible emotion in London. In the beginning Garnier, the French Ambassador, was no more struck than the cabinet of London by the page of political philosophy put into being by the declaration of Congress, and which was to respond so loudly in the country of Voltaire and the Encyclopædia." In France, "when it became known," continues Doniol, "it produced the most vivid sensation which was possible to create a century ago by the means of publicity then existing."

But though the action of the colonies was greeted with wild enthusiasm by the populace, the government remained cold and undemonstrative. Silas Deane had written to Congress, January 17, 1777, "The hearts of the French people are universally for us and the opinion for an immediate war with Great Britain is very strong, but the court has its reasons for postponing a little longer."

The chief cause of the apparent inaction of the government arose from the ruined condition of its finances. Beaumarchais, as was seen in the last chapter, already had been commissioned to draw up a plan of finance which should aid in the present crisis. This he had done, basing his scheme of reform upon the wise and prudent measures adopted by the great Sully. He endeavored to prove that these reforms would, if put into execution, cause such an increase of revenue as would enable France safely to declare war, without increasing the rate of taxation or incurring the risk of bankruptcy. His scheme, however, had been set aside. On the 30th of March, 1777, he addressed a lengthy memoir to the prime minister, M. le Comte de Maurepas, of which the following is an extract: "... I have doubtless explained badly my ideas of help for the Americans, since it seems that you have not adopted them. The fear of giving you too much to read makes me concise to the point of being perhaps obscure.... Read the letter of M. Deane.... Judge if a good Frenchman, a zealous subject of the King, a good servitor of M. de Maurepas, who respects him and wishes to see his administration honored among all the people of the world, judge if he can support your constant refusal to lend him a hand, the earnest solicitations of America at bay, and the insolent triumph of armed England.... M. le Comte, spare your servitors the sorrows of one day hearing you reproached with having been in a position to save America at small cost and you have not done it, to tear her from the yoke of England and to unite her to us by commerce, and that you have neglected it.

"Hear me, I pray you; you distrust too much your own powers and my resources; and above all I fear that you do not sufficiently esteem the empire, which your age and your wisdom gives you over a young prince whose heart is formed, but whose politics are still in the cradle. You forget that that fresh young soul has been turned and brought back from very far. He is tractable, helpless, weak in his whole being. You forget that while dauphin, Louis XVI had an invincible repugnance to the old parliaments, yet that their recall honored the first six months of his reign; you forget also that he swore never to be vaccinated, yet that eight days afterwards he had the vaccine in his arm. No one is ignorant of this, and no one will excuse you for not employing the beautiful power of your place in causing to be adopted the great things which you have in your mind.

"If you find my liberties too daring, go back to their respectful motives, and you will pardon them to my attachment.

"It was not play on my part, M. le Comte, when attaching myself to you, I said with feeling: 'I shall never have a day of true happiness, if your administration passes away without having accomplished the three greatest acts which could illustrate it: the humiliation of England by the union of America and France; the re-establishment of the finances, following the plan of Sully, which I have placed several times at your feet, and the rendering of civil existence to protestants.... These three things are to-day in your hands; I wish only the honor of having often recalled them to you. What work, M. le Comte, what success more beautiful, could crown your career? After such actions, there is no death. The dearest existence of man, his reputation, survives all and becomes eternal. Hear me then, I beg you, in favor of the Americans. Remember that the deputies await my answer to dispatch a courier who will carry encouragement or desolation into Congress.... Do not render my pains unfruitful, through not concurring in them, and may the recompense of my works be the honor of having made them acceptable to you!

"I am, with the most respectful devotion, M. le Comte,

CHAPTER XX

"Your very, etc.,
"de Beaumarchais."

To all this Maurepas made no reply, and the unhappy agent, still harassed and thwarted in his plans, wrote to Vergennes:

"April 13, 1777.

"... If I do my duty, as M. de Maurepas had before the goodness to say to me, in presenting without ceasing and under all its faces, the picture of so important an affair, permit me to represent to you, M. le Comte, what you know better than I, that loss of time, silence and indecision are even worse than refusal. Refusal is a deed, one can act afterwards, but from nothing, nothing ever comes—it remains nothing...."

In the same letter he warmly pleaded his own cause. "In so far as I work alone," he said, "my secret is secure. If the indiscretion of the officers of the *Amphitrite* and their foolish chief make known the destination of the vessel, what can I do more than you? I defy any man in this country, beginning with the ministers themselves, to cite either what name, what charge, from what port and for what destination I have sent the vessels dispatched since.... In a word, M. le Comte, now that all is in operation, when the first pains and labors of so vast an establishment have obtained a certain success, when my profound disdain for the idle gossip of society has turned aside the babblers and now that I can assure the happy consequence of the enterprise, do you refuse to concur any longer? and does my active perseverance inspire the same in no one?... In the name of Heaven, of honor, of the interests of France, retard no longer your decision, M. le Comte! Confer again with M. de Maurepas. No object is more important, and none so pressing.

"In the instant of closing this letter, I receive one from Nantes, by which I am informed of the refusal to provide sailors, and so my richest ship is stopped at the moment it is ready to sail.... I implore you, M. le Comte, promptly to arrange with M. de Sartine what is necessary for the departure of my vessel.... I hope to go myself for your orders upon very many objects Thursday evening, if you do not send them before. I recommend the Americans to your remembrance and their advocate to your good will.... The hour of the post has passed while I was writing. I send this therefore by a man on horseback."

72 BEAUMARCHAIS AND AMERICAN INDEPENDENCE

GENERAL JOHN SCHUYLER

In striking contrast to the outspoken and independent tone assumed by Beaumarchais when addressing the ministers, is the friendly yet authoritative manner which he employs when it is question of a subordinate. To de Francy, his confidential agent, he had written February 28, 1777, in relation to the dispatching of the *Amphitrite*, after it had been brought back by du Coudray: "We shall have to say, like Bartholo (one of the characters in the *Barbier de Séville*) '*le diable est entré dans mon affaire*,' and remedy as best we may the evil that is past, by preventing

CHAPTER XX 73

its happening again. Give the enclosed letter to M. du Coudray. I send it to you open, in order that you may reply in my behalf to his objections, should he make any. Show to Captain Fautrelle, the enclosed order which we give him, in quality of proprietor of the vessel which he commands, and take his word of honor to conform to it entirely. I received yesterday a letter from my nephew along with yours. As unreasonable as the rest of them, my nephew seems to be unwilling to go back to his place on the *Amphitrite*. You can understand the little attention which I pay to such childishness. Simply recommend him again to the special care of M. de Conway and to the Chevalier de Bore. Command the captain to receive on board M. le Marquis de la Rouërie, who comes to us with special recommendations. Give to the Captain the general rule and the secret of the route. If the force of circumstances obliges him to put into Santo Domingo, arrange with him and M. de Conway not to stop there, but to write to the governor of the island in order to notify him that the fear of some unlucky encounter, alone prompted the drawing up of the fictitious order in regard to the destination of the *Amphitrite*, and take from him a new fictitious order for France, in order to shelter yourself by that order in case you encounter an English vessel between Santo Domingo and the true destination of the ship. You know very well that all the precautions of the Ministry are taken in accord with us; it is upon this that we can count.

"As soon as the *Amphitrite* has set sail, go on to Nantes, where, by the way, you will probably find *le Mercure* started, because it is ready now to set sail. Goodbye, my dear Francy. Come quickly back to Paris. You have trotted about enough for this time; other work awaits you here: but I will be there to divide it with you. Bring me back this letter."

The fear of a possible reconciliation of the colonies with Great Britain, which constantly haunted the agent of the French Government, had of late been greatly augmented. The 8th of March, 1777, he had written to Vergennes:

"Sunday morning.

"M. le Comte; Another letter you will say. Will they never stop! Eh! how can I stop, M. le Comte, when new objects unceasingly excite my attention and my vigilance? A private secretary of Lord Germaine arrived yesterday, secretly sent to Messrs. Deane and Franklin. He brings propositions of peace. The most superb recompenses are promised him if he succeeds."...

Monday morning, he wrote ... "America is doing the impossible to hold her own. But be sure that she cannot go much farther without you, or without a reconciliation with Great Britain.... While I am treating with you, I warn you that England is secretly attempting to treat with M. Franklin.... Deane is regarded as a formidable obstacle to any project of adjustment: They will attempt to dislodge him at whatever price. My news is so positive as to the intention of the ministers that my conjectures become facts. They have the project to compel Deane to leave France, and to make of him the expiatory victim." A short time before Beaumarchais had written to the same minister: "The doctor Franklin at this moment, wishes to send away M. Deane from France. My special object is to prevent his leaving. The manly firmness of this Republican alone, can arrest the insinuations of every kind employed against the doctor."

As a matter of fact, Franklin was well aware of the dismay which the noise of his secret communications with agents of Great Britain had caused the ministers, nor did he desire to allay their suspicions. He knew well the value for France of an alliance with the colonies, at least supposing the fact of their independence. He knew, also, how far it was to the interest of England to prevent such an alliance. So long as France remained outwardly inactive, Franklin did nothing to allay the fears of the one government nor to weaken the hopes of the other, although there can be no doubt that in his heart he was bent only upon concluding a treaty with France. In March, 1777, he wrote: "I did not come to make peace, but to procure the aid of European powers to permit us to defend our liberty and our independence, which it is certainly to their interest to guarantee, because our great and growing commerce will be open, and cease to be the monopoly of England.... I think we shall be capable with a little help, of defending our possessions long enough, so that England will be ruined if she persists in destroying us.... I flatter myself to live to see my country established in peace and prosperity, while Great Britain will no longer be so formidable a figure among the powers of Europe." There also seems no doubt but that he had at last secretly concurred with Deane in aiding the escape of Lafayette from the restrictions imposed upon him by the French government, although subsequently, the whole blame was allowed to rest upon Deane alone.

The situation in regard to Lafayette was as follows: Some time during the year 1775, the young Marquis who was then scarcely eighteen, and who was serving under the Comte de Broglie at the garrison of Metz, was present at a dinner given in the fortress where the English Duke of Gloucester was guest. The latter was bitterly opposed to the policy of George III in regard to America, and at table spoke freely of the uprising among the colonists; it was then, so Lafayette tells us in his memoirs, that he formed the resolution of offering his services to the insurgents. Through the intervention of De Broglie, the Baron von Kalb, a Prussian general serving in France, introduced to Silas Deane on November 5, 1776, the young marquis with two of his cousins who had formed the same determination to offer their services to America. Silas Deane received them with enthusiasm, and promised all high positions in the American Army (see *Doniol* Vol. II, p. 63). Eleven other officers were added and the entire group were to sail from Havre on *La Seine*, one of the fleet of Hortalès et Cie. when the order already spoken of, came from the government to prevent further operations of the house. Moreover, a special prohibition was issued regarding the young officers, because it was of great importance for the French Government to seem to oppose the enlistment of such prominent members of the high nobility as Lafayette and his colleagues. Nothing daunted, Lafayette, whose fortune made him independent, bought a vessel of his own, *La Victoire*, and having decided "to go in spite of everything and without regard to consequences" secretly negotiated with Deane, and set sail, April 20, 1777, with some twenty other commissioned officers.

The agreement which had been drawn up between them was signed by Lafayette, the Baron von Kalb, and Silas Deane; it bore the date of December 7, 1776, although it was not really issued until February, 1777. This discrepancy was owing to the fact that since the arrival of Franklin in December, Deane's commission had changed in nature, so that he no longer was empowered to enlist officers for the American service. The date of December 7, 1776 had been chosen because on that day the two noblemen had been presented to the American Commissioner and an informal engagement entered into. This was immediately before the arrival of Franklin in France.

The true patriotism which inspired Deane led him to adopt this subterfuge, feeling as he did that the services of so brilliant an officer as Lafayette, and one belonging to such an illustrious house, would be of sufficient value to his country to warrant the irregularity of the act. The Baron von Kalb had originally, it would seem, stipulated with Deane for a considerable salary, part of which was to be paid in advance. (See *Our French Allies*, Stone, p. 39.) Deane rightly understood the effect which would be produced in the different courts of Europe by the daring deed of the young nobleman and foresaw the consequent fury of the English which could not help but hasten the final decision of the ministry. Therefore he willingly concurred in the designs of Lafayette, aiding them to the utmost of his power (*Doniol*, Vol. II, Chap. VII). Congress afterwards disavowed all the commissions granted by Deane, so that most of the officers were obliged to return to France. Lafayette and the Baron von Kalb, having fortunes of their own, were willing to serve without pay; they were therefore given appointments. The romantic escape of the young nobleman caused all the commotion that was expected of it. The Capital went wild with exultation, openly vindicating his act, while the anger of the English knew no bounds.

England, indeed, had good grounds for discontent with the conduct of her rival. "Public opinion in London," says Doniol, "was more and more for war. France everywhere was accused of aiding the colonies.... It was said that open war was preferable to the insidious peace which we pretended to maintain while according every advantage to the revolted colonies."—(*Doniol* II, p. 455.) Other causes of grievance, especially in regard to the protection granted to American vessels in all French ports, were constantly coming up. "England," says Doniol, "incriminated especially the authorities of Martinique. According to Lord Weymouth, the Americans armed openly in the island, favored by the most notable persons. So much pressure was brought to bear upon the French Government by the English Ambassador, that, not yet ready for war, it was forced to grant the satisfaction which was demanded. As in previous instances, the blow fell heaviest upon Beaumarchais. July 1, 1777, he wrote:

"I have just received news that afflicts me.... M. de Bouille, the new governor of Martinique, has notified the merchants that it is agreed between the courts of France and England, that the English Navy seize the French vessels coming from their islands, taking all the commodities of America which they find.... This is so impossible, that though I have read it, I still cannot believe it!

"Afternoon.... I am indeed, in despair to receive the confirmation of that trying announcement. It seems certain that France has ceded to the English the right to seize all French vessels coming from the islands, which are charged with American commodities. What distress, M. le Comte, could have brought about such an arrangement?... I learn by letters from Cape Francis of the 18th of May, that the cargo of the *Amétie*, happily arrived in that port, has started for America, divided on several American and Bermudan vessels, bought at my cost at Santo Domingo for....

"P. S. You are not to blame, M. le Comte, for the consequences of that sorrowful convention with the English. Your hands were tied to sign it. But I am in despair. I made my payment of the 30th yesterday, selling all the paper money which I had, at a disadvantage. A quarter of an hour is so important, that a million arriving the next day could not repair the lack of but thirty thousand *louis d'or*. I was compelled to pay yesterday £184,328 2s., and £21,864 8s. 4d. remain unpaid from the 15th on which I have only received £200,000 instead of £221,864 8s. 4d. From now until the 15th, I must pay £268,304 8s. 3d. I am lacking therefore £490,168 16s. 7d. with the loss of my paper money, and the three last payments which I must replace so as to be abreast of my affairs. I therefore beg you to send me an order for 5,000,000 fr., after that I can go forward, but as my destination is not a matter of indifference, I shall have the honor of conferring with you about it."

The documents deposited in the bureau of foreign affairs, show that M. de Vergennes "taking into consideration the desperate situation into which Beaumarchais found himself thrown, owing to the obstinate refusal of Congress to send him returns, had advanced successively, the 13th May, 1777, 400,000 livres, the 16th of June, 200,000 livres, and the 3rd of July 474,496 livres." (*Loménie* II, p. 145.) By this means alone, Beaumarchais was able to continue his active services in the cause of America.

Although the court of Louis XVI were making pretense of not favoring the Americans, they already had decided on war and were endeavoring to bring the court of Spain to a similar decision.

"The 26th of June," says Doniol, "a memoir was addressed to the Spanish cabinet explaining the seasonableness of associating themselves positively with the colonies, and in consequence, of making war upon England."

"By the means so far employed," wrote Vergennes, "the reconciliation of the colonies with Great Britain cannot be prevented; those means have been all that have been prudent, but they will not suffice any longer; it is necessary that the assistance become sufficiently effective to assure a total separation and so compel the Americans to gratitude."

Madrid was finally forced to follow the course laid out for it at Versailles; but before openly declaring their alliance, both courts awaited some decisive act of the Americans. The capture of Burgoyne determined the King, although several months more elapsed before the treaty was actually signed.

But if the court was thus apparently inactive, Beaumarchais continued as assiduous as ever in aiding the Americans, and this notwithstanding the coldness of the commissioners, the total absence of returns and the unbroken silence of the Continental Congress. The Hon. John Bigelow, in his admirable paper *Beaumarchais, the Merchant*, speaking of Beaumarchais at this period, said: "He received no tobacco, nor money, nor thanks, nor even a letter from Congress.... His funds were

CHAPTER XX

exhausted, and all his expectations of returns were disappointed.... At last, reduced to extremities, he resolved to send a confidential agent to the United States, to obtain, if possible some explanation of results so chilling to his enthusiasm, and for which he was so poorly prepared. For this mission he selected a young man named Theveneau de Francy, a person of considerable talent, generous and enthusiastic, but poorly trained for the delicate duty assigned him. De Francy embarked for the United States at Marseilles on the 26th of September, 1777, on board of one of Beaumarchais's ships, carrying twenty-four guns, called *Le Flammand*."

"De Francy," says Loménie, "went out with the double mission of obtaining justice from Congress for the past, and to prevent cargoes from being delivered gratis in the future."

But before entering into a consideration of his mission, let us pause to note among the passengers of the *Flammand* a now justly celebrated personage, who was destined to render such effective aid in training the American troops; this was Baron von Steuben. In his life of that famous Prussian officer, Frederick Kapp has given a detailed account of the incidents which led up to his entering the American service. The French minister of war, the Comte de St. Germain, had long been a pronounced admirer of the military tactics employed by the king of Prussia. He had endeavored to have those tactics introduced into the French army but without success. Being on intimate terms with the Baron, the latter made a halt in Paris with the intention of visiting his friend at Versailles on the occasion of a voyage to England in the spring of 1777. Having notified the count of his desire to wait upon him, the Baron was surprised to be requested not to come to Versailles, but to meet him at the arsenal in Paris. "You have arrived very apropos," the count said; opening a map and pointing to America, he continued, "Here is your field of action, here is the Republic you must serve. You are the very man she needs at this moment. If you succeed, your fortune is made and you will acquire more glory than you can hope for in Europe for many years to come." He then pictured the bravery, the resources of the Americans, and intimated the possibility of an open alliance. After this he sketched the other side of the situation; spoke of the disadvantages under which the Americans labored: bad training, lack of order and discipline among the troops, and ended by saying "You see now why you must not be seen at Versailles." The Baron, however, seemed but little touched by the eloquent appeal of his friend. He told the count that he was no longer young, that he had no ambition; though he was without fortune, yet his position was all that he desired.

After a second interview, his interest seemed somewhat aroused. The Count gave him a letter to Beaumarchais, who introduced him to Deane; and Deane took him to Passy to see Franklin. Both commissioners seemed anxious that Steuben should enter the service. "But," says his biographer, "when Steuben mentioned a disbursement for the expenses of his journey, they expressed some doubts of their power to grant it. Mr. Deane made no difficulties; Franklin, however, made several. He spoke a great deal of presenting him with a couple of thousand acres of land,... but Steuben did not care for them.... As to any advances, Franklin positively declared that it was out of the question; he told him this with an air and manner to which Steuben, as he remarked in a letter written at that time, 'was then little accustomed,' whereupon he immediately took leave, without any further explanation.

"He went thence to M. de Beaumarchais, telling him that he intended to set out immediately for Germany, and that he did not wish to hear any more of America. As soon as Beaumarchais was informed of the cause of Steuben's resolution, he said to him, that if he wanted nothing but money, a thousand *louis d'or* and more were at his disposal. Steuben thanked him for his generous offer, but said his determination was fixed. The Count of St. Germain endeavored to dissuade him, but to no effect.

"Arrived at Rastadt, he found a very persuasive letter from M. de Beaumarchais, who wrote that the Comte de St. Germain expected his prompt return to Versailles; that a vessel was ready at Marseilles for his embarkation, and that Beaumarchais's funds were entirely at the Baron's disposal.

"Prince William of Baden, with whom Steuben conferred, urged him to accept; accordingly he returned to Paris, August 17, 1777."

On the 26th of September he set sail. Beaumarchais wrote to Congress:

"The art of making war successfully being the fruit of courage combined with prudence, knowledge and experience, a companion in arms of the great Frederic, who stood by his side for twenty-two years, seems one of the men best fitted to second M. Washington."

Baron von Steuben was well received in America. As he asked for no pay, and wished to enter the army as a simple volunteer, no objection was made to his enlistment. He soon was raised to a position suitable to his rank and talents. A little more than a year after his arrival, Beaumarchais, overjoyed at the success which had attended the Baron, wrote to his agent, Theveneau de Francy: "Recall me often to the memory of M. the Baron von Steuben.

"I congratulate myself from that which I learn of him, to have given so great an officer to my friends, the free men of America, and to have forced him in a way to follow that noble career. I am in no way disquieted about the money that I lent him for his voyage. Never have I made an investment which gave me greater pleasure, because I have been able to put a man of honor in his true place. I learn that he is Inspector General of all the American troops. Bravo! Tell him that his glory is the interest of my money, and that I do not doubt but at that title, he will pay me with usury."

On the same vessel went also the nephew of Beaumarchais, the son of his elder sister married to the watchmaker, De Lépine, who on entering the American service took the name of des Epinières. It was the same of whom Beaumarchais had spoken impatiently on the occasion of his refusing to continue his voyage upon the *Amphitrite*, when du Coudray had brought that vessel back to port. That he had his way, is proved by the fact that his name is mentioned amongst the six aids who accompanied the Baron von Steuben to America. An idea of the young man's character may be gained from the following brief extract of a letter written by him the evening of an engagement: "Your nephew," he wrote, "my very dear

CHAPTER XX

Uncle, may perhaps lose his life, but he will never do a deed unworthy of one who has the honor of belonging to you. This is as certain as the tenderness which he always will have for the best of uncles." According to Loménie, he never returned to France, but died on the field of battle, after having attained the rank of Major.

At the time when the Baron von Steuben set sail for America, Beaumarchais was no longer the confidential agent of the government. As has been seen, Franklin had from the first, refused to treat with him, while Lee's influence at home and abroad was at all times used to bring about his ruin. More than this "everything," says Doniol, "seemed to cost too much; they (Franklin and Lee) had allowed themselves to be persuaded that Beaumarchais ought to serve them for nothing. The *Barbier de Séville*, as he was called familiarly, passed with too many people for gaining great profit, for there not to be many interested in ruining him. It was also of the utmost importance to England to interfere with his operations, and the English Ambassador fed the flames.... Dubourg had his part to play ... but whatever the reasons, it remains true that Franklin never missed an opportunity openly to contest the operations of Roderigue Hortalès et Cie., and to attempt to bring them to naught." (Doniol II, 611.) Other intermediaries, therefore, began to be employed.

Although less recognition was given to Beaumarchais by the government, the ministers continued to make use of his advice. "At the moment," says Doniol, "when he was treated with the greatest coldness, his counsels were appropriated.... They used his political estimates almost in the terms in which he expressed himself, sometimes textually. At the end of October he was admitted to discuss with Vergennes and Maurepas the definite stand to take in offering propositions of alliance with the American colonies. Three months later when the King was about to sign the treaty, it was evident that the Secretary of State had demanded of Beaumarchais a résumé of their discussion. This résumé entitled, *Mémoire particulière pour l'Etat*," was drawn up by Beaumarchais under circumstances peculiarly distressing. It was at the moment when he first realized with absolute certainty that his coöperation in the aid soon to be freely and openly accorded the Americans was no longer desired. Nevertheless, he continued to express himself with the same manly vigor as previously. After setting forth the actual situation of France and Spain with regard to England, he said: "What remains for us to do?

"Three courses are open to us. The first is worth nothing, the second is the most sure, the third, the most noble; but a wise combination of the third and second could instantly raise the King of France to be the first power of the civilized world.

"The first course, which is worth nothing, absolutely nothing, is to continue to do what we are doing, or rather what we are not doing; to remain longer passive by the side of the turbulent activity of our neighbors, and obstinately to refuse to take sides while still awaiting events." After setting forth at length the actual condition of affairs in England, the perils which menaced France, the desire which actuated all parties in Great Britain to make peace with America while wreaking their vengeance upon France, he continues warningly, "But the first step towards peace being once taken, be sure that it will be too late for France to declare in favor of America." Then follows a narration of preparations then making in England to take France unawares. "After having become the laughing stock of all Europe," cries the daring advocate of the alliance, "a fatal war and the bankruptcy of America will be the worthy reward of our inaction.

"The worst course therefore, of all the courses, is now, to take no course and to attempt none in conjunction with America, waiting until England shall have closed up every way; something which will certainly happen very shortly.

"The second course which I regard as the most sure, would be to accept publicly the treaty of alliance proposed to us for more than a year by America,... As soon," he says, "as the English learn that there is no longer any hope to treat with a country which has treated with us, they will instantly make war upon us, declaring us to be aggressors."... One objection after another that might present itself to the minds of the ministers is then taken up and weighed, especially in relation to the ignorance which existed among them with regard to the "extent of the powers entrusted to the legation at Passy, the uncertainty of the consent of Congress, the possible mobility of an assembly of which the majority was the only law, and which made them fearful that France might have to regret too late, a step which naturally would exasperate the English.

"These fears, Beaumarchais knew how to turn aside by reasons and considerations (*Doniol* II, p. 742) which would not have been out of place in the mouth of a minister."

The third course open to France, "the noblest of all," was to declare to the English in a manifesto which should be announced at the same time to the other potentates of Europe, that the King of France, after having, through delicacy and regard to England, long remained a passive spectator of the war existing between England and America, to the great disadvantage and injury of French Commerce; "that conditions being so and so," which he proceeded to clearly define, "His Majesty obliged by circumstances to decide upon some definite course ... and not wishing to declare war against England, nor to insult her ... His Majesty contents himself with declaring that he will hold the Americans for independent, and desires to regard them as such from henceforward, relatively to their commerce with France, and the commerce of France with them."...

"After drawing up his manifesto, Beaumarchais entered into the exposition of the measures to take, and discussed the shades of opinion of each minister exactly as though he had been part of the council.... It is not one of the least singularities of the times to see the author of the *Barbier de Séville* deliberating as it were with the ministers, saying 'I would do' and putting himself naïvely in the place of the King of France." (*Loménie*, II, p. 160.)

It was early in December that news of the surrender of Burgoyne reached Europe. "The joy of the news of Saratoga brought Beaumarchais to Passy, in spite of the bitter griefs which he had against the Commissioners." (*Doniol* II, 646.) The same day he wrote to Vergennes:

"December 5, 1777.

CHAPTER XX

"Monsieur le Comte:

"... Yesterday I was at Passy with the courier who arrived from Congress, and I passed the morning in comforting my heart with the excellent news of which we had that moment received the announcements.

"I came back to Paris, bringing M. Grand in a light carriage with a postillion and two horses. The carelessness of my postillion ... caused us to be overturned.... Mr. Grand had his shoulder broken; the violence of the fall made me bleed profusely at the nose and mouth;—a piece of broken glass entered my right arm—the negro who followed was badly hurt. See me then prostrated, but more ill in mind than body ... it is not the postillion who kills me, but M. de Maurepas. Nevertheless the charming news from America is a balance to my soul.... I am the voice which cries from the depths of my bed, '*De profundis clamavi ad te Domine; Domine exaudi orationem meam.*' Although you received the *Gazette* of Boston yesterday, I will send you the extract which I myself made to insert in *le Courrier d'Europe*. It is just that I give them in England by my phrases all the poniard thrusts which their Ambassador gives me here with his. I salute you, respect and cherish you, and will sign, if I can with my wounded arm, the assurance of the unalterable devotion with which I am, etc.

"Beaumarchais."

Two days later, he wrote:

"M. le Comte:

"Your honorable and sweet interest consoles me for everything. In thanking you for the counsels which you have been so good as to give me I can assure you that I did not allow myself to be too vivacious in the letter of which I sent you a copy; I cannot explain myself in writing, but you will be much more surprised than I, because you are less acquainted with the persons of whom it is a question, when I give you an account of all that has happened. I always have put a great difference between the honest deputy Deane, and the insidious Lee, and the silent Dr. Franklin.

"The movement which the news of America has given to all idle heads is inconceivable; the English of the cafés do not know where to hide themselves;—but all that is nothing like so curious as what will take place in London from the shock of the different reports. I await the details with a pleasure equal to all the trouble which they have tried to make me. I thank you for the interest which you take in my health. I am getting up to-day for the first time, and to-morrow I hope to go out.... Receive with your ordinary goodness the assurances of the very respectful devotion with which I am, etc.

"Beaumarchais."

Wounded in body and sick at heart, the zealous patriot and vigilant friend of America continued to give notice to the government of the news which, through his agents and friends in London, he received before anyone else.

Thursday, the 11th of December, he wrote:

"To M. le Comte de Vergennes, to be communicated, if he pleases, to M. le Comte de Maurepas.

"M. le Comte:

"Although I find it difficult to use my right arm, still I must force it to aid me in announcing to you that I received last night very particular news from London. Everything is in such a state of fermentation since the news of Burgoyne that the crisis has arrived, when the deceived King, the audacious ministry, and the most corrupt parliament must cede to the cries of a furious nation....

"What is the true moral sense of this crisis? It is, that whichever one of the two nations, France or England, recognizes first the independence of America, she alone will reap all the fruits, while that independence will certainly be ruinous to the one which allows her rival to get the advance. This word sums up everything; this moment accomplishes everything. As to the details, in spite of my grievances and my sufferings, if my poor body can endure the *broutage*, and if you have the time and the desire to receive me to-day, or better, to-morrow, my postillion has orders to await yours.

"I renew, with the same devotion, M. le Comte, the assurances of the very profound respect of the poor turned and overturned

"Beaumarchais."

A few days later he had still more startling news to announce; a mysterious stranger had arrived in Paris, had visited M. Deane, had dined with him, remaining more than two hours. At the end of that time, a lackey of Mr. Deane came into the street, looked anxiously about; seeing a cab (which was none other than the one in the employ of Beaumarchais) he asked if it was engaged; being told that it awaited two ladies, the lackey entered the house and soon the mysterious stranger came into the street and went away on foot, followed, of course, by the cab.

Two more days passed, and at the end of that time, Beaumarchais was able to give more definite information. The mysterious stranger proved to be a secretary of the Lord Germaine. "Beaumarchais," says Doniol, "informed as usual before all others, dispatched at once a notice to the ministers. He had followed the English Emissary from the moment of his arrival, informed himself of what he already had accomplished, found out his lodgings and notified the ministers, who sent at once an agent to confer with Deane." (*Doniol* II, 64.) Vergennes hastened to inform the Court of Spain of the secret actions of England, with a design to rouse it to action. The moment was indeed a critical one, for the English government was leaving nothing undone to come to terms with the Americans.

January 1, 1777, Beaumarchais wrote to Vergennes:

"I hasten to inform you that an emissary from Lord North arrived in Paris yesterday. He has been watched ever since he left London. He has orders to gain the deputation at Passy at any price whatever. This is the moment or never, to cry *tu dors Brutus*. But I know that you are not asleep. From your side you see very well that I do not keep bad guard either.... Be sure that the English ministers are working seriously to make peace with America, and that it is of as much value to the nation that they make it, as it is for Lord Chatham and others.... And so peace with America is absolutely resolved; this is what has been very expressly communicated to me. As for myself, I am informed by the same avenue that the minister of France has given the Americans here help of money by means of Messrs. Grand, that the English ministers know it on good authority and that I am shifted off, which annoys no one in England. I easily believe it. Then I have lost the fruits of the most noble and unbelievable labors, by the very means that lead others to glory; I have several times guessed as much by the strange things which have struck me in the conduct of the Americans towards me.... Miserable human prudence, thou canst save no one when intrigue is bent upon ruining us.

"M. le Comte, you are the man upon whose equity I have the most counted; you have not even refused at times esteem and well-wishing to my active zeal. Before I perish as merchant, I demand to be fully justified as agent and trader. I demand to lay before you my accounts, in order that it be proved well that no one else could have done so much with so little means across so many difficulties. It is certain that this summer M. le Comte de Maurepas permitted me to send guns to America, and he promised me that when they were gone I should be reimbursed, because he feared at that time the indiscretion of those about M. le Comte de St. Germain. I bought them, sent them and gave my notes which fall due soon, and yet M. de Maurepas seems to have forgotten his promise. This article and the charging of my vessel at Rochefort, arrives at more than 800,000 francs.

"By the unbelievable retention of my vessel in port, everyone considers me lost and demands his money; nevertheless, though ready to perish through this delay and money not reimbursed, I do not lose my head. You can judge of that by the cold and reasoned work which I put into your hands Saturday. But I avow that I am at the end of my courage and my strength by the assurance that Messrs. Grand have secured the confidence which I believed I so well merited.[1] This breaks my heart. I have fulfilled the most thorny of tasks; I must be allowed to prove that I have fulfilled it well; it is in giving my accounts that this truth will appear....

"Be happy, M. le Comte, this year and all years. No one merits to be so, more than you, and no one desires it more truly than

"Beaumarchais."

Although no longer made use of as intermediary, the former agent of the government was not wholly abandoned by Vergennes.

A few days previously Beaumarchais had written:

"M. le Comte: I felt yesterday the sweet influences of your goodness. If I did not obtain what I asked for, at least I could judge by the gentle tone of the prohibitions that they were less directed against me than forced by events and promises already made. To lose much money is a great evil, when one has very little; but to carry in one's heart the mortal sorrow of displeasing when one has done one's best, and even the best that could be done, under the circumstances, is a state which kills me. Receive, M. le Comte the warmest testimony of my gratitude."

[1] Beaumarchais had aided in placing Grand on firm footing with the American Commission (Doniol II, 613).

On the 22nd of January, 1778, the discarded agent handed in the résumé required of him by the ministers. In writing to Vergennes he said: "This sorrowful Memorial (*Mémoire Particulière, pour les ministres du Roi, et une manifeste pour l'Etat*) which at another time, and on another subject, I could have finished in two hours, has taken me eight days to write, my head being so confused by the frightful medley of objects which it contains, and in regard to which I claim your justice while invoking your mercy.

"I even thought for four days that it had become useless through delay, and abandoned everything to work upon my consular balance-sheet. By a *tour de force*, I put myself on my feet for twelve or fifteen days;—But *grand Dieu*, is this to live? The more I assume a tranquil air, the more my secret torment increases. I have examined myself well, I have not done the least wrong, and in going over my papers to assure myself of my state, I have been frightened at all it has been necessary to overcome in the last two years, to arrive where I am. If I am to be aided, you cannot do it too quickly or too secretly for the letters of change are like death, they wait for no one.... If I am not to be, Amen—I have done what I ought, and more than what I could. I learn by sure news that my two vessels of Marseilles are certainly at Charlestown. This, in spite of France and England. Sixty-six cannons, twenty-two mortars, bombs and bullets in proportion; eighty thousand weight of sulphur and my poor guns which have not yet been paid for. All this is in America, by my indefatigable labor, and I have had to deceive all the world, with unbelievable pains, in order to make this shipment secretly. Ah, M. le Comte, it is my balance sheet which will show what an active man you have allowed to be lost and dishonored if you permit this fearful misfortune to accomplish itself. I have no courage to talk of England, because in truth I am dying of sorrow."

That the Comte de Vergennes did not lend an altogether deaf ear to this cry of despair, may be judged from the following letter, dated February 15, 1778,

"M. le Comte:

"You have seemed to take a too obliging interest in my fearful situation, for me to allow you to remain ignorant a moment of the excessive joy which I have felt since yesterday. Yesterday, my teeth clenched with fury to be without news, I waited the moment to close my case, refusing to make any payment the 15th, which falling due to-day Sunday, was exigible yesterday, the 14th. Read, M. le Comte, read I implore you what I received at 2 o'clock, and what I replied this morning, see, my joy is excessive. I am no longer exposed to the dishonor of a bankruptcy, which, notwithstanding all my efforts, I could never have justified, without an involuntary and fatal indiscretion. M. le Comte de Maurepas received me Monday, like a corsaire who had failed in respect to our flag. I did not say a word, I would have had too much to say. I withdrew, death in my heart. Not that I thought the interests of America abandoned. I know very well that they are not....

"The profound silence which I have imposed upon myself for the past two months, since the departure of the brother of M. Deane, secretly embarked at Bordeaux and bearing ... but this shall be matter for another letter. It is just that M. de Maurepas learns through me of this affair, for if the fear of the most frightful misfortune has rendered me pressing solicitor, I am not a man without virtue; it will be the strongest proof which I can offer of the resignation with which I know how to support the coldness and disdain of those who have protected me. Ah! but I am again saved. It is to you that I render a million thanks for all the efforts which you have made in my favor. Never will I forget the generous efforts which you have made to save me from ruin...."

The moment of the open alliance between France and America was now hastening forward. With it, ends the first phase of the war of the United States against England, "phase heroic by its enterprise, its constancy, its privations, by the serenity of its chief and by the results obtained, if one considers the nature and quality of the soldiers." (*Doniol* III, 260.)

It was to this period that the activities of Beaumarchais in the cause of America essentially belong. The operations, however, now so well under way, he continued to carry on through his agent de Francy, though from henceforward they are wholly private in character.

GENERAL BARON VON STEUBEN

CHAPTER XXI

> *"Any crisis which puts in peril all that society undertakes to secure to us by its laws, uncovers our hearts to the world, strips our native selfishness of all its disguises, and makes us appear to each other pretty nearly as bad as we must always appear to the angels."*
>
> Hon. John Bigelow in *"Beaumarchais the Merchant."*

De Francy Sails for America—His Disappointment in the New World—Beaumarchais Recounts His Grievances against the Deputies at Passy—Rejoices Over American Victories—Manœuvers to Insure Safety to his Ships—The Depreciation of Paper Money in America—De Francy Comes to the Aid of Lafayette—Contract between Congress and De Francy Acting for Roderigue et Cie.—Letters of Lee to Congress—Bad Faith of that Body—Deane's Signature to Documents Drawn up by Franklin and Lee—Beaumarchais's Triumph at Aix—Gudin Seeks Refuge at the Temple—Letters of Mlle. Ninon.

THEVENEAU DE FRANCY arrived in the States the 1st of December, 1777. He was the bearer of letters to Congress from Roderigue Hortalès et Cie., filled with polite reminders of the fact that great advances had been made for arms, ammunition, etc., and that it was very important that much tobacco should be returned as soon as possible. (Spark's *Diplomatic Correspondence*, Vol. 1, p. 112.)

De Francy, young and enthusiastic, had set out full of admiration for the brave people with whom he had to deal. A little experience, however, convinced him that it was no easy or brilliant task which lay before him. On the 14th of December, two weeks after his arrival, he addressed a lengthy letter to his superior, in which, after giving details of the voyage, he proceeded to describe the condition of the country to which he had come. He begged Beaumarchais to obtain for him a captain's certificate from the Ministry, "for," he said disconsolately, "it is all I am likely to get out of this enterprise. Government currency is in such poor credit that the 28 per cent. you promised me, to-day is worth only 1/2 per cent. The paper money is so discredited that merchants prefer keeping their merchandise to selling it at any price for paper. The farmers bring nothing to market, so that everything is selling at the most extravagant prices; chickens sold for $25.00 after the capture of Burgoyne. There is no doubt that what you have done has been presented here in a false light. I expect to have many prejudices to destroy, and many heads to set right, for the sending of several vessels without invoices (a thing which, to tell the truth, is unprecedented) and the errors found in the bills of lading of the *Amphitrite* especially, have caused it to be suspected that the shipments were not made for a merchant. I have explained to General Whipple the reason for this apparent disorder, and have made him admit that it was inevitable. Nevertheless, there were articles furnished at Havre, which differ so widely from what was delivered, that the General told me that our correspondent in this country is either a poor merchant or a swindler. For example: on my invoice there are 62 boxes or barrels of tinned iron. Captain Fautrelle has delivered but 41.... They have given him notice of missing boxes, but will they ever arrive?"

In his second letter, written two days later, he announced that Silas Deane had been recalled and John Adams appointed to replace him. He recommended Beaumarchais to put his affairs in order and get his accounts regulated at once, "for," said he, "Mr. Adams has the reputation of being the first statesman on the continent and he has in fact an air, *extrêmement fin*. I fear that, aided by his colleagues, he may be disposed to play sharp with you. Be on your guard.

"The Colonel Langdon thinks that the affair of the officers has had something to do with the recall of Deane. I am almost sure that it is the work of that famous politician of Spain and Berlin, Arthur Lee. It is he in part who has alienated Doctor Franklin from you, and no doubt he will do what he can to have his opinion adopted by Deane's successor."

"I have not yet been able to obtain direct news of your nephew but I am assured that he is in the Army and well placed, and that he has received honorable mention. As to his contract with Deane, I warn you not to reckon upon that. I do not doubt that he will obtain by his own merits, the grades which Mr. Deane promised him, but Congress will give no heed to a contract made with him. Mr. Deane has far exceeded his powers in granting commissions to officers who were recommended to him in the beginning of his sojourn in France. He had not even the right to make a lieutenant, consequently nearly all who came out with commissions signed by him, and who have not wished to serve until they were placed, have been obliged to return. If M. du Coudray had not died, they would have been greatly embarrassed to place him.... Almost all our officers who brought letters of recommendation, and have conducted themselves well, have advantageous places. La Rouërie is colonel and much esteemed. The Marquis de Lafayette has been wounded in the leg. This did not prevent his keeping the saddle, however, all day. He cried, 'There, I am wounded, now I am content.'"

In the meantime, Beaumarchais had written to de Francy from Paris, "I profit, my dear Francy, of every occasion to send you news; let it be the same with you, I beg of you. Although it is to-day the 20th of December, 1777, my largest ship has not yet set sail; but this is the common lot of all merchantmen destined for America. The ministry fears that our commerce will take away too many sailors at a time when the state may have need of them from one day to another. The most rigorous orders have been given in all the ports, and especially in the ports where I arm. It seems that the force and capacity of my ships have made Lord Stormont attack the ministry in a way to make them fear that he suspects them of favoring an operation, which in truth, is carried on without them and in spite of them. Ready to set sail, my artillery has been taken from me, and the delay in getting it back or in forming another is what detains me in port. I struggle against obstacles of every kind, but as I struggle with all my force, I hope to conquer with patience, and courage and very much money. The enormous loss which all this occasions me seems to touch no one. The minister is inflexible; there is no one, even to Messrs. the deputies at Passy, who do not pretend to the honor of thwarting me,—me—the best friend of their country. At the arrival of my vessel, the *Amphitrite*, which at last unloaded at Lorient a small cargo of rice and indigo, they had the injustice to seize upon it, saying that it was sent to them and not to me; but, as M. de Voltaire has very well said, 'Injustice in the end produces independence.' They have very probably taken my patience for weakness, and my generosity for stupidity. In proportion as I have been attached to the interests of America, in so far I have been offended by the dishonest liberties which the deputies of Passy have wished to take with me. I have written them a letter of which I send you a copy, and which they have left without reply up to the present. While waiting, I have left the cargo in the hands of MM. Berard brothers, of Lorient, and in so doing I have not believed myself to have deviated in any way from the frank and generous attitude I always have maintained towards Congress, but simply to use my legitimate right in regard to the first and very small return which they make upon an enormous advance; that cargo is worth about 150,000 livres. You can see the great difference between that drop, and the ocean of the debt owing me." (Note of Loménie, "Franklin and Lee, who in this instance acted in spite of Deane, did not dare insist, and the cargo remained for Beaumarchais.")

"As for you, my dear, I suppose you have arrived and that you have obtained from Congress a reasonable adjustment, such as the situation of America permits them to give. I hope that following my instructions, you have obtained and will continue to obtain much tobacco, and I expect that my vessels will find their return cargoes ready to be embarked as soon as they arrive where you are. I still hope that if events should retard my vessels still longer, that you will send me at least by *le Flammand* a ... cargo that will deliver me from the horrible pressure in which I find myself.

"I do not know whether I flatter myself, but I count upon the honesty and equity of Congress as I count upon mine or yours. The deputies here are not in comfortable circumstances, and pressing need often make men indelicate; this is the way I explain the injustice which they tried to do me. I do not despair even of winning them back to me by the gentleness of my remonstrances and the firmness of my conduct."

Loménie says, "This explanation may seem strange ... but the fact is that the deputies from America received no more remittances from Congress than Beaumarchais. Silas Deane had been obliged to borrow from the latter the funds absolutely necessary for his personal expenses. Arthur Lee tried later to make use of this fact to inculpate Deane ... but it has been well proved that necessity alone forced Deane to contract the debt. As for Franklin, he was a little richer when he

CHAPTER XXI

landed in France, because he wrote to his colleague, Silas Deane, from Quiberon, December, 1776; 'Our vessel has brought indigo to the value of about 3000 pounds sterling which will be at our orders to pay our expenses.'...

"During the year 1777, the French Government itself gave money at different times to the deputies at Passy, up to the moment when it passed to them, through the Banker Grand, the two millions, which were used partly to support the agents and under-agents of America in France, and partly to buy munitions for Congress."

To return to Beaumarchais's letter:

"It is very unfortunate my friend, for the cause of the colonies that their interests in France have been confided to several persons at once; a single one would have succeeded better. As for what regards myself I must do M. Deane the justice to say that he is ashamed and sorry both together, at the conduct of his colleagues with me, of which the blame belongs entirely to M. Lee.

"I am having trouble also with the provincial Congress of South Carolina, and I wrote by L'Estargette to M. the President Rutledge demanding justice from himself to himself. L'Estargette, who will correspond with you, will inform you of the success which follows my just demands.

"Across all these annoyances, the news from America overwhelms me with joy. Brave, brave people! whose military conduct justifies my esteem, and the beautiful enthusiasm felt for them in France. In a word, my friend, I only want returns in order to be in a condition to serve them anew, to meet all my engagements, so as to be able to make others in their favor.

"It seems to me, from what I hear, that our French soldiers have done wonders in all the battles in Pennsylvania. It would have been a disgrace for me, for my country, for the name of a Frenchman, if their conduct had not been equal to the nobility of the cause they had espoused....

"The City of London is in a terrible commotion; the ministry at bay—the opposition triumphant, and the King of France, like a powerful eagle, hovering above all these events, reserves to himself another moment of pleasure to see the two parties, divided between the hope and fear of his decision, which will have such a great weight in the quarrel of the two hemispheres.

"To prescribe to you your conduct when you are three thousand miles from me would be foolishness ... serve me to the best of your ability is the only way to render yourself useful to me, to yourself, and to become interesting to the Americans themselves.

"Do as I do; despise small considerations, small measures, small resentments. I have associated you in a magnificent cause; you are the agent of a just and generous man. Remember that success is always uncertain, that the money due me is at the risk of a great concourse of events, but that my reputation is my own, as you are to-day the artisan of yours. Let it be good my friend, then all will not be lost, even if everything else should be. I salute you, esteem you, and love you."

In the postscriptum which follows, "we see Beaumarchais," says Loménie, "applying the resources of comedy to politics, and ingeniously combining the means to elude the ministerial orders, as he would have arranged a theatrical play."

"Here," wrote Beaumarchais in the postscriptum, "is what I have thought out relative to my large vessel—*le Fier Roderigue*. I must keep my word given to M. de Maurepas, that my ship is to carry only seven or eight hundred soldiers to Santo Domingo, and that I will return without touching the continent. Nevertheless, its cargo is very valuable to Congress and to me; it consists in ready made clothing for the soldiers, cloth, blankets, etc. It carries an artillery of sixty-six bronze cannons, ... and much other merchandise.

"After much thinking, it seems to me that you might arrange secretly with the committee of Congress, to send two or three American corsaires immediately to Santo Domingo. One of them will send its gun-boat to Cape Francis ... then M. Carabasse (Beaumarchais's agent at the Cape) will go aboard her with M. de Montaut, the captain of my vessel *le Fier Roderigue*. They will arrange together that when my vessel sets out, the American Corsaire will capture it under any pretext he chooses, and carry it off. My captain will protest violently, and threaten to complain to Congress. The vessel will be taken to where you are. The Congress will disavow the brutal act, liberate my vessel, with obliging excuses for the French flag; during the time this takes, you will have unloaded the cargo quickly, and filled the ship with tobacco, and you will send her back to me with just what you have been able to gather together. As the bearer of this, M. Carmichaël, returns directly, you will have time to arrange this manœuver either with the Secret Committee of Congress, or directly with a friendly and discreet corsair. By this means, M. de Maurepas will be disengaged from his promise made to others, I from mine to him, because no one can oppose himself to violence, and my operation will have been successful in spite of all the obstacles which cross my path.... My vessel starts before the 15th of January. It bears orders to wait news from you at Cape Francis. After all that I am doing, the Congress cannot longer doubt, I hope, that the most zealous partisan of the republic in France is your friend

"Roderigue Hortalès et Cie."

Commenting upon the above letter, James Parton has written:

"Such was Caron de Beaumarchais; unique among merchants and men. Whether it was by those or by other manœuvers that the ship was enabled to reach America, no one has informed us. Certain it is that she arrived safely at Yorktown, Virginia, and was loaded with tobacco for her return. I trust M. de Maurepas was satisfied." (*Life of Franklin*, Vol. II, p. 271.)

The next letter in this series which has been preserved to us is from De Francy and is dated May 14, 1778. In it he announced that it was the twelfth since his arrival, all of which he feared had failed in reaching their destination. Continuing his account of the disorderly consequences of the depreciation of paper money, he said, "I have just extricated the Marquis de Lafayette from a serious mistake into which he had fallen unsuspectingly.

"You have, of course, heard of the excessive depreciation of paper money. At one moment in Pennsylvania it reached the point of absolute worthlessness.

CHAPTER XXI 91

The expenses of the Marquis at this time, as he received no pay, were absolutely enormous. He at first borrowed money on bills of exchange at 2 for 1, afterwards at 3 for 1. He supposed that was borrowing at the rate of $2 for $1 and $3 for $1; instead, the rate was 2 and 3 pounds Pennsylvania currency for 1 pound sterling. The pound sterling was worth 34 shillings Pennsylvania currency. He had signed the bills presented to him without reading them and his expenses far exceeded the amount he supposed them to reach. I informed him of his error and ... have advanced him very considerable sums on account of the House ... my arrangement with him is that he shall reimburse the principal in one year in Paris, paying 6 per cent., the same as Congress allows you."

The allowance of 6 per cent. made by Congress to Beaumarchais, to which De Francy here alludes, had been settled in a contract drawn up the 6th of April, 1778 duly signed, sealed and delivered to the indefatigable agent, of which the following is the substance: (The contract in full is given by Durand, p. 119-126 in his *New Material for the History of the American Revolution*.)

"To whom it May Concern:

"Whereas, Roderigue Hortalès et Cie. have shipped or caused to be shipped ... considerable quantities of cannon, arms, ammunition, clothing, and other stores, most of which have been safely landed in America ... and Whereas as Roderigue Hortalès et Cie., willing and desirous to continue supplying those stores ... provided satisfactory assumption be made and assurance given for the payment in France of the just cost, charges, freight of the cargoes already shipped as well as those to be hereafter shipped....

"Now know ye that John Baptist Lazarus Theveneau de Francy, agent of Peter Augustin Caron de Beaumarchais, as representative of the house of said Roderigue Hortalès et Cie., by him especially appointed and empowered to act ... in virtue of the powers in him trusted, to contract, agree and engage to and with M. Ellery, Jas. Forbes, Wm. Henry Dayton, Wm. Hurer, Esq., a Committee of commerce, properly appointed and authorized by the delegates of the United States of America in Congress assembled to enter into, execute, ratify and confirm this contract for and in behalf of the said United States as follows:

"1st. That the cost and charges of the cargoes already shipped shall be fairly stated in current prices ... at the date of shipment.

"2nd. The freight to be charged agreeably to contract entered into by Caron de Beaumarchais, Silas Deane, and M. Monthieu.

"3rd. All orders to be transmitted to Messrs. Roderigue Hortalès et Cie. or their agents, subject to the inspection and control of an agent appointed under the authority of Congress, who shall have liberty to inspect the quality of such merchandise.

"4th. All articles hereafter shipped to be provided as nearly as possible to order ... and not higher than the current price ... attended with most moderate charges.

"5th. Good ships shall be chartered or bought at moderate price for transportation of the stores.

"6th. That agents appointed under the authority of Congress, shall have free liberty to inspect the quality, and require the prices of all articles to be shipped for the account of the United States, with power to reject such as they judge unfit or too high priced; they shall also be party in the charters and purchasing of ships to be employed in the service.

"7th. Bills on the House of Roderigue Hortalès et Cie., for 24,000,000 *livres tournois*, annually, shall be honored and paid....

"In consideration whereof, the said William Ellery, James Forbes, William Henry Dayton, William Durer, Esq., Committee of Commerce for Congress ... agree and engage with Roderigue Hortalès et Cie., by their said agent as follows:

"1st. That remittances shall be made by exports of American produce ... for the express purpose of discharging the debt already justly due, or thereafter to become justly due in consequence of this agreement....

"2nd. That all cargoes ... for the discharge of said debt, be addressed to Roderigue Hortalès et Cie. ... subject to the inspection and control of an agent appointed under the authority of congress, who shall have liberty to inspect the quality of such merchandise, assent to or reject the prices offered, postpone the sales and do everything for the interests of his constituents.

"3rd. That the customary interest of France not exceeding 6 per cent. per annum shall be allowed on the debt already due, or that from time to time, shall be due to the said Roderigue Hortalès et Cie.

"4th. That any payments of Continental Currency in America ... shall be computed at the current, and equitable course of exchange at the date of payment ... and interest to be discounted on the amount from that date.

"5th. That remittances to be made for the purpose of discharging the debt now due, or to become due to the said Roderigue Hortalès et Cie., shall be made at such times and seasons, as shall be most convenient for the American interest, but are to continue until the entire debt, principal and interest, shall be fully and fairly discharged.

"6th. That a commission of 2-1/2 per cent. shall be allowed to the said Roderigue Hortalès et Cie. ... on all charges and monies paid and disbursed by them for the account of the United States.

"In witness whereof the contracting parties have hereunto set their hands and seals, this 16th day of April in the year of our Lord, 1778.

Signed: "William Ellery,
James Forbes,
William Henry Dayton,
William Durer,
Jean Baptiste Lazarus Theveneau de Francy.

Signed, sealed and delivered in the presence of

Charles Thomson,

CHAPTER XXI

Secretary of Congress."

ROBERT MORRIS

Naturally enough, having obtained a contract of such precise stipulations, signed, not as formerly, by an agent three thousand miles from the seat of Congress, but by a committee chosen from the bosom of that body, de Francy thought the greatest difficulty of his mission already accomplished, and Beaumarchais, when he received the glad tidings, set about with renewed vigor, the gathering together and dispatching of supplies. The Americans, however, still found reasons for delaying the fulfillment of their part of the contract; and it was only after two more months of ceaseless activity that de Francy succeeded in getting enough tobacco to freight the *Fier Roderigue* for its return voyage. Which cargo, the second that had reached Beaumarchais, was destined when it arrived in France to be seized upon by Lee, as that of the *Amphitrite* had been, with the same results. In a letter to Beaumarchais, June, 1778, de Francy announced the order which he had received for the delivery of the tobacco, "The rest of the letter," says Bigelow, "is filled with complaints of the bad faith of these republicans, who refuse him the vessels they had promised to carry off his tobacco, and urges Beaumarchais to send out at least six himself."

A letter dated July 11th is filled with still more bitter complaints. "In spite of the most formal engagements," he wrote, "these people find the means of obstructing all business, the pretext for breaking promises the most solemn." In a word, he thinks it better to suspend business until "laws better established put a bridle upon the bad faith which reigns in the country." A little later he wrote: "If this business were to be continued, which I do not advise unless you have special reasons, it would be one of the greatest commercial operations ever engaged in, if one could only rely upon the good faith of these republicans. But they have no principle and I desire sincerely to see all your accounts closed with them.

"I believe Carmichaël is the only one who appreciates all you have done for this country. He arrived at York two days ago, before I went to Virginia. The moment of our meeting was one of the most agreeable that I have passed in this country. We did not quit each other for two days. During these two days, I rendered him a service by letting him into the private character of all the members of Congress. I told him those who were his friends, and those who were opposed to his nomination as Secretary of Legation. In gratitude I hope he will serve you well.... I made the President feel that your letter to M. Sartine clearly demonstrated that the assertions of du Coudray and Lee were vile and infamous lies. The force and energy of this letter astonished him. He could not help saying to me that he would not have believed that anyone could have written with such freedom to a minister in France....

"I believe Carmichaël is your friend; if I am mistaken, I never wish to speak to an American again, as long as I live." Then follows a most doleful picture of the discord, selfishness, and greed, which seemed to reign everywhere. Upon this part of the letter, Hon. J. Bigelow has commented admirably. He says:

"A little more experience with the world would probably have taught the young man that any crisis which puts in peril all that society undertakes to secure to us by its laws, uncovers our hearts to the world, strips bare our native selfishness of all its disguises, and makes us appear to each other, pretty nearly as bad as we must always appear to the angels. There is no doubt but the revolted colonists, struggling for their very existence, appeared disadvantageously to a sentimental enthusiast like de Francy, but we have yet to hear of any people while having so much at risk, appearing better.

"Of course after having been kept so long without tobacco, and treated with undisguised distrust as a swindler or as the agent of one, de Francy takes very dyspeptic views of the men who compose the Continental Congress."

CHAPTER XXI 95

As a matter of fact, he hits off one after another of our great heroes with anything but the reverential tone which we are wont to use in referring to them. "President Laurens," he says, "is a very upright merchant, but no more; in important affairs he is an old woman." "Samuel Adams is an old fox who has genius." "The famous Hancock is precisely the *Corbeau revêtu*." "Robert Morris works for himself while working for the Republic." "General Washington," here his tone changes, "has honor, courage, and a truly disinterested patriotism.... I have seen much of him and I really believe he is the first man on the continent, although to tell you the truth, he is very difficult to know well...."

The unaccountably bad faith of Congress began to arouse the suspicions of the agent of Beaumarchais, which he hastened to communicate to his superior. On the 31st of July, 1778, de Francy wrote: "I have not been able to obtain a perusal of the letters of Lee. Two of his brothers, members of Congress, had possession of the foreign correspondence during the past year, and they have abstracted all his letters for fear they would be prejudicial to him; but I cannot doubt but you are there painted in the blackest colors. I know at least that anonymous letters were written against you, filled with lies, insults, and atrocities; and what is of a marked fatality, your excessive zeal for the Americans has been the basis of the lies of Lee, and of all the misgivings with regard to you. Doubtless you recollect that at the commencement of 1776, while you were in London, you promised this little doctor, then humble and suppliant, that if the Americans fully decided never to reunite with England, you would send out under the name of Roderigue Hortalès et Cie., all the succor of which they would have need; and the enthusiasm which then animated you, gave great latitude to your promise. At least, the doctor so communicated it; and to give importance to what he said, he made an ambassador of you, and instead of naming you, he remarked that the promise came from the ambassador of France. Behold here the origin of his elevation! His brothers have strongly supported his high pretensions and he was named agent. He was obliged to maintain what he had written, but fearing lest the reserve of the ministers towards the agents in France should make Congress suspect that the French Ambassador never had spoken to him in England, he abandoned his first assertion and then wrote that it was you who called upon him in London to make him such beautiful promises on the part of the French Minister. The Memoir of du Coudray attests, on the other hand, that the minister put you forward that he might disavow you if he desired. Congress readily allowed itself to be persuaded that everything that arrived on your vessels was a present, or at least a loan from your government which it might acquit at its pleasure.

"When after my arrival at York, I announced my purpose and the reclamations I came to make, I did not find a single member of Congress disposed to believe that it was an individual who had rendered them such signal services, and that he was to be paid for them, as it was impossible to find on this continent a man who would ever have attempted for the freedom of his country the one-hundredth part of what you have done.... True Americans are infinitely rarer here than in Paris, and I am satisfied there is not one whose zeal approaches yours."

As a sample of what Lee had been writing to Congress, the few following passages quoted at random, will suffice: "Upon this subject of returns I think it my duty to say ... that the ministry have repeatedly assured me that no returns are expected for these subsidies." At another time he wrote, speaking of a shipment just being made, "this is gratis as formerly, and what has been sent I have paid for; so that those merchants Hortalès et Cie. have no demand upon you; nor are you under any necessity of sending effects to them, unless you think it a proper market for some things, as it certainly is for fish." (See *Vindication of Arthur Lee.*)

"These assertions," says Loménie (Vol. II, p. 178), "offering the advantage of dispensing America from all gratitude and all payment to Beaumarchais, Congress was naturally disposed to adopt." It must be remembered, however, that at this moment the party which upheld Arthur Lee, headed by his two brothers and Samuel Adams, were at the height of their power, so that the opposite side, in whose ranks stood the upright and clear-sighted John Jay, was temporarily overruled.

Before inserting the last letter which we give of de Francy, a short explanation is necessary. Already the reader has been apprised through these letters, of the difficult position in which Silas Deane had been placed, through the secret disavowal of his acts by Congress, even while he still remained their credited commissioner in France. Unconscious of the perfidy of Lee, yet thoroughly distrusting him, dismayed at the attitude of Franklin, who explained nothing, but who took from the first the part of ignoring all Deane's previous transactions, the latter was forced to submit for the present to this embarrassing state of affairs, and to place his whole hope of adjustment in the equity of Congress in which he still firmly believed. Slowly it began to dawn on him, that the ground of his colleagues' resentment to him was largely a matter of money. In the beginning Deane, realizing to the full the lack of trained military men among the insurgents, had freely promised commissions of high rank, with proportionately high pay, to the French officers who came to him well recommended and who had a desire to serve. As most of these men were either unable or unwilling to provide their own equipment and traveling expenses, Deane had advanced them money in the name of Congress, but taking it, not from his own resources, for he had none, but from those of his friend Beaumarchais, with the understanding, of course, that it should all be repaid.

When Franklin arrived, Deane soon realized that repayment would be very difficult, and dreading to face the effect which the whole truth would have produced, he had begged Beaumarchais to delay sending in his accounts until Congress should have ratified his agreements. This Beaumarchais, with characteristic generosity, readily conceded. De Francy wrote: "You appear still to have the blindest confidence in Deane and you neglect your own interests.... Well, now, on February 16th, when Deane passed the morning with you, they had written to Congress—(I have seen the letter signed by the three agents)—that you got possession of the cargo of the *Amphitrite* contrary to their expectations, and that they did not oppose it because their political situation did not permit them to come to any explanation with you. They add that they had been informed that you had sent an agent to Congress to solicit the payment of a very considerable debt, but that it was not necessary to settle anything with this agent; that the commercial venture to which it related was a mixed business which it was necessary to sift before closing

CHAPTER XXI

the account; that they would occupy themselves with the business, and that it was better to leave it with them to arrange with you.

"I will make no reflections upon this transaction; I will only say that it appears to me very extraordinary, an incredible weakness even, that Mr. Deane should have consented to sign what it pleased his colleagues to write, up to the very moment when you had the generosity to sacrifice everything for him and he knew it. You can well imagine, that with such news, doubts are reinforced, objections multiplied, etc., etc."

Of the recall of Deane, already announced in a previous letter of De Francy, we shall speak at length, in another chapter. For the present let us return to France to follow Beaumarchais in his private career as citizen.

It will be remembered that when, in 1776, the restored parliament had annulled the decree of the parliament Maupeou, Beaumarchais had petitioned the Ministers to obtain for him the adjournment of the final decision in the matter of the suit instituted against him by the Comte de la Blache so many years before. "This suit," says Loménie (Vol. II, p. 54), "which had been the origin of his tribulation, and of his celebrity, still subsisted, and in the midst of his triumphs held his fortune and his honor in check.... The Count de la Blache, seeing the credit of his adversary so rapidly growing, urged on with all his force the final decision. Beaumarchais was in less haste; occupied in organizing his operations with America, and in reconquering his civil existence, he did not wish to terminate the other case until he had assured himself very well of his position.

"The decisive combat came off at Aix in July, 1778. The author of the *Barbier de Séville*, accompanied by the faithful Gudin, started for Provence. He was going at the same time to despatch two vessels from Marseilles for the United States and to finish with the most desperate of his enemies."

"At Marseilles," says Gudin in his memoir, "Beaumarchais covered the part he played in public affairs, by the veil of amusements or his private business."

Of the memoirs which he published at Aix, in relation to this important suit, Loménie has said: "They contain passages which are not below the best to be found in the memoirs against Goëzman ... one feels a man who is conscious of his power, who conducts vast operations, who enjoys a great celebrity and who considers his social importance as equal at least to that of a field-marshal.

"The city of Aix seemed predestined to famous lawsuits. In the same place where Mirabeau was soon to come to give forth the first bellowings of his eloquence, was seen to glitter the sparkling fancy of the *Barbier de Séville*. Vainly, the Count de la Blache surrounded himself with six lawyers, and prepared from very far back his triumph.... At the end of a few days, Beaumarchais had conquered the public."

"You have completely turned the city," his attorney said to him. His triumph was complete; a definite decree of Parliament disembarrassed him forever of the Comte de la Blache. The latter was condemned to execute the agreement drawn up and signed, du Verney, 1770.

"The affair," says Gudin, "was examined with the most scrupulous attention and judged after fifty-nine seances. The legatee, all of whose demands were rejected, was condemned, and his memoirs were suppressed."

Beaumarchais, in turn, was condemned to pay 1,000 *écus* to the poor of Aix as a punishment for the severe witticisms against his antagonist, in which he had indulged in his memoirs. They were also publicly condemned. Beaumarchais, however, was triumphant. Overwhelmed with joy to find his honor and his fortune restored to him, he desired only that the good people of Aix should rejoice with him. Instead, therefore, of the 1,000 *écus* demanded of him, he instantly doubled the sum, requesting that it might be distributed in dowries to twelve or fifteen poor, but worthy young women; the benediction of so many families happily established seeming to him the most beautiful which he could draw upon himself.

"The intoxication of this triumph, after so many years of uncertainty and combat, the enthusiasm with which he was received by the people of Aix," are graphically described by Gudin in a letter written at the moment of his triumph.

"All the city," wrote Gudin, "which subsists on suits, was in a state of the greatest impatience. While the judges deliberated, the doors of the court house were besieged; women, idlers, and those interested, were under the trees of a beautiful avenue not far off. The cafés, which bordered this promenade, were also filled. The Comte de la Blache was in his well lighted salon, which looked out on this avenue. Our friend was in a quarter at some distance away. Night came; at last the doors of the court house opened and these words were heard: 'Beaumarchais has gained;' a thousand voices repeated them, the clapping of hands spread down the avenue. Suddenly the windows and doors of the Comte were closed, the crowd arrived with cries, and acclamations, at the house of my friend; men, women, people who knew him and those who knew him not, embraced him, and congratulated him; this universal joy, the cries and transports overcame him, he burst into tears, and see him, like a great baby, let himself fall fainting into my arms. It was then who could succor him, who with vinegar, who with smelling salts, who with air; but, as he himself has said, the sweet impressions of joy do no harm. He soon returned to himself, and we went together to see and thank the first president.... On returning ... we found the same crowd at the house; tamborines, flutes, violins succeeded before and after supper; all the fagots of the neighborhood were piled up and made a fire of joy.... The mechanics of the place composed a song, and came in a body to sing it under his windows. Every heart took part in his joy, and everyone treated him like a celebrated man, to whose probity, due justice had at length been rendered."

Gudin's enthusiasm for his friend was destined, however, to a singular recompense. Arrived in Paris, he had composed a lengthy epistle to Beaumarchais (Loménie II, p. 66), which began as follows:

"The severe justice of Parliament has confounded the malice of thy enemies, though they had hoped that the dark art, which a *vile senator* in unhappy times had made to incline the balance, would surprise the prudence of our true magistrates."

This chef-d'œuvre, composed of a hundred or more verses, had been inserted in a copy of *Courrier de l'Europe*, which was published in London, and which had altered the text by putting at the place of the words, "of a *vile senator*"—"*a profane senate*," so that the personal allusion to the judge Goëzman was transformed into an allusion to the whole parliament Maupeou. But most of the members of this judicial body had gone back to their places in the grand council, from whence Maupeou had drawn them. Irritated at the triumph of Beaumarchais, and not daring to attack a man so strong in the favor of the public and the confidence of the ministers, "they seized this opportunity of scourging Beaumarchais over the back of his friend."

The latter was absent from Paris, busy with the despatching of vessels from one of the seaports, when, suddenly, a warrant, "issued," says Loménie, "without the slightest warning, came to surprise the pacific Gudin." As he sat at table one evening with his mother and niece, a letter was handed him, which proved to be from a friend, Mme. Denis, niece of Voltaire. He glanced it through and there read the startling announcement: "You are about to be arrested, and that for verses printed in the *Courrier de l'Europe*. You have not an instant to lose."

"I lost none," wrote Gudin. "Having read the letter, I quitted the table without a word and passed into my room, where I hastily dressed myself, and then took refuge at the house of Beaumarchais. I read the letter to Mme. Beaumarchais....

"My first care was to send a messenger to prepare my mother for the strange visit she was about to receive, and bidding her not to alarm herself, and to reply that she did not know where I was, and that it was possible I was with Beaumarchais at a hundred leagues from Paris."

After calling about him several of his friends, men of experience, they deliberated what was to be done. "Do not allow yourself to be taken, these men of the grand council hate Beaumarchais, and are quite capable of revenging themselves upon his friend...."

"I decided therefore to withdraw into the enclosure of the Temple. This castle, ... so scandalously taken by Philipp the Bel from the Templars, and since ceded to the Chevaliers of Malta, was at this time, owing to the privileges of that order, an asylum, not for criminals, but for any person, who, without having given serious offense, found himself in difficulty, as for instance, a debt, a challenge, in a word, an affair like the present. (The Temple, famous for being the stronghold in which a few years later the royal family was imprisoned, and from which Louis XVI was led to execution, was subsequently destroyed by Napoleon. It stood near the present Place de la République. Much of its site is now occupied by the *Magasins du Temple*, the great second-hand shops of Paris.)

"The custom was to inscribe one's name upon the bailiff's register on entering the Temple; he asked me why I had come to claim the privileges of the place.

"'Is it debts?'

"'I have none.'

"'An attack?'

"'My enemies, if I have any, have never used any weapon against me except their pen.'

"'A quarrel at cards, or an affair with a woman?'

"'I never play cards, and I have never caused either disorder in a family, nor scandal in a house of joy.'

"'But why then?'

"'For verses, which grave personages do not find to be good, verses printed I don't know how in London, denounced, I don't know why in Paris, and which the grand council, who has not the control of books and is in no way judge of what takes place in England, pretends to be injurious to a tribunal which no longer exists.'"

"Beaumarchais, on his return to Paris, learned of my adventure, and was justly angry. He came and took me from my retreat. 'Be sure,' he said, 'they will not dare to arrest you in my carriage or in my house.'"

"At the end of several days," says Loménie, "Beaumarchais had succeeded in liberating his friend; nothing could paint better his situation at this period than the tone of his letters to the ministers, especially to the keeper of the seals:

"'Monseigneur,' he wrote, 'I have the honor to address to you the petition to the council of the King, of my friend Gudin de la Brenellerie, who unites to the most attractive genius the simplicity of a child, and who, in your quality of protector of the letters of France, you would judge worthy of your protection if he had in addition the honor of being known to you.'"

Beaumarchais thus was able to ignore the smoldering resentment of his enemies and to press forward his vast enterprises. The war had now broken out between France and England. French merchantmen went to sea completely at the mercy of events. The French flag, instead of a protection, was now a signal for attack. It was therefore clear that if Beaumarchais was to continue his mercantile operations, it must be upon a new basis. But before we follow him into the equipping of armed vessels to protect his merchant fleet, let us linger a moment, that we may gain a still nearer view of Beaumarchais, the man.

The popular enthusiasm which everywhere had welcomed the uprising amongst the colonists continued to voice itself in every quarter of France and on all occasions where it was a question of the rights of man. The wild joy which had greeted the triumph of Beaumarchais at Aix was due largely, Gudin tells us, to the fact that for the first time in the annals of that city a nobleman had been so signally humiliated as had been his antagonist. In this general desire for a recognition of human rights, the aristocracy of France themselves took the lead. Rousseau, calling so loudly for human beings, men and women, to leave the lines marked out for them by authority and tradition and to return to nature as their guide, was heard, not only in the remotest hamlet of the realm, but his voice found echo in its lordly castles and its palace halls. In *Emile*, he traced the revolution which was to take place in the instruction and training of the child; in *La Nouvelle Heloïse*, he laid down a scheme of morals, the teaching of which was directly opposed to the Christian code. The effect of these teachings upon contemporary France could not be more strikingly exemplified than in the following letter addressed to Beaumarchais by a girl of seventeen. It gives at the same time an idea of the confidence which the name of the latter inspired among the masses of the people. The letter is written from Aix and is dated not long after the successful termination of his suit:

"Monsieur:

"A young person crushed under the weight of her anguish, comes to you and seeks consolation. Your soul, which is known, reassures her for a step which she dares take, and which, were it anyone else, would remain without consequences. But are you not Monsieur de Beaumarchais, and do I not dare hope that you will deign to take my cause and direct the conduct of a young and inexperienced girl? I am myself that unfortunate who comes to lay her sorrows in your bosom; deign to open it to me. Allow yourself to be touched with the recital of my woes.... Ah! if there are hard hearts, yours is not of that number.... Shall I say to you, Monsieur, that I feel in you a more than ordinary confidence? You will not be offended; my heart tells me to follow that which it inspires. It tells me that you will not refuse me your succor. Yes, you will aid me, you will support despised innocence; I have been abandoned by a man to whom I have sacrificed myself. I avow, with tears that I yielded to love, to sentiment and not to vice.... I enjoyed a certain consideration; it has been taken from me. I am only seventeen, and my reputation is lost already. With a pure heart and honest inclinations I am despised by everyone. I cannot endure this idea; it overwhelms me and I am in despair.... Ah, Monsieur, lend me your aid, reach out to me your generous hand, cause to spring up in my oppressed soul, hope and consolation. I do not wish to injure the perfidious one who has betrayed me; no, I love him too much. It is at the foot of the throne that I wish to carry my plaint. If you will deign to aid me, I promise myself everything. You have powerful protectors, Monsieur; you know the Ministers, they respect you. Say to them that a young person implores their protection, that she sighs and groans night and day; that she desires only justice.... (The ungrateful one must in the end do me justice.) I can say without presumption that I am not unworthy of his tenderness. He opposes nothing to my happiness but my fortune, which is not sufficient to arrange his affairs, which are not in too good order. He has no aversion to me. There is nothing about me to inspire it. The only crime of which I am culpable is to have loved him too well. Do not abandon me, Monsieur; I put my destiny in your hands.... If you are kind enough to reply to this, be so good as to address your letter to M. Vitalis, rue de Grand-Horloge, at Aix, and above the address simply to Mlle. Ninon. You will be so good as to pardon me, Monsieur, if I still hide my name.... I know that with you I have nothing to fear, but still a certain fear that I cannot conquer, that I would not know how to define, holds me back. You have connections in Aix; I am very well known here. In small towns one knows everything; you know how they talk. I implore you, do not divulge the confidence which I have taken the liberty of making to you.... Monsieur, I have the honor to be, with sentiments of the most perfect consideration, your very humble and very obedient servant,

"Ninon."

"Let one imagine a similar letter," says Loménie, "suddenly falling from six hundred miles away, upon a man forty-six years of age, the busiest man of France and Navarre, who had need to confer every morning with the Ministers, who had forty ships on the seas, who pleaded against the comedians, who was preparing a pamphlet against the English Government, who was busy founding a bank, who dreamed of editing Voltaire; surely this man would throw into the waste basket the sorrows of a young and unknown girl. Not in the least. Beaumarchais had time for everything. Here is his reply to Mlle. Ninon:

"'If you are really, young stranger, the author of the letter which I have received from you, I must conclude that you have as much intelligence as sensibility, but your condition and your sorrows are as well painted in this letter as the service which you expect of me is little. Your heart deceives you when it counsels you an act like the one which you dare conceive; for although your misfortune might secretly interest all sensible persons, its kind is not one whose remedy can be solicited at the foot of the throne. Thus, sweet and interesting Ninon, you should renounce a plan whose futility, your inexperience alone hides from you. But let me see how I can serve you. A half confidence leads to nothing and the true circumstances of an open avowal might perhaps furnish me the means of seeing how the obstacles may be removed which separate a lover from so charming a girl. But do not forget that in desiring me to keep the matter secret you have told me nothing. If you sincerely believe me the gallant man whom you invoke, you should not hesitate to confide to me your name, that of your lover, his position and yours, his character and the nature of his ambition; also, the difference in your fortunes, which seems to separate you from him.' He next attempts to persuade the young girl to forget a man who has shown himself so unworthy of her regrets. 'Forget him, and may this unhappy experience of yours hold you in guard against similar seductions. But if your heart cannot accept so austere a counsel, open it to me then entirely, that I may see, in studying all the connections, whether I can find some consolation to give you, some view which will be useful and agreeable.

"'I promise you my entire discretion, and I finish without compliment, because the most simple manner is the one that should inspire the most confidence. But hide nothing from me.

'Beaumarchais.'

"Mademoiselle Ninon," continues Loménie, "asked for nothing better than to unburden her poor heart; she addressed to Beaumarchais an avalanche of letters of which several contain no less than twelve pages; she gave her name, the name of her seducer, and recounts her little romance with a curious mixture of naïveté, of precocity, sensitiveness, intelligence and garrulity. This *Provençale* of seventeen is literally saturated with the *Nouvelle Heloïse*.

"'Fatal house,' she cried, in speaking of the place where she first met her lover, "tis thou which causes my pains.' She has all its contradictions, ... protesting that if she has left the path of virtue, she has only all the more felt the worth of a pure and virtuous soul. 'Lovely innocence,' she cried, 'have I lost thee? Ah! no, no; I have sounded to the remotest depths of my heart; it is too sensitive, but it is still honest. I implore you, Monsieur, do not believe it corrupt.'

CHAPTER XXI

THE TEMPLE

"Whether," continues Loménie, "these rather wordy dissertations of the little philosopher in skirts gave to Beaumarchais the idea that it would be too difficult to correct such an exalted brain, or whether it was that the work which was crushing him on every side prevented his following this strange correspondence, true it is that he replied no more to the long letters of Mlle. Ninon, although she addressed to him the most melancholy reproaches. But what could he do? The war had just broken out between France and England. Beaumarchais, who had had his own part in bringing about that result, was engaged himself in the conflict; he drew up political memoirs, he armed vessels; where could he find the time to reply to the confidences of Mademoiselle Ninon? Nevertheless it would seem that these letters interested him because he has classed them in a package by themselves, upon which he has written with his own hand: 'Letters of Ninon, or affair of my young client, unknown to me.'"

CHAPTER XXII

"After the perplexing and embarrassing scenes you have just had to pass through, it must give you the most solid joy to see an armament going out to America.... I congratulate you on this great and glorious event, to which you have contributed more than any other person."

"Silas Deane to Beaumarchais."

March 29, 1778.

"It seems to me that we cannot consistently with our own honor or self-respect pay off an undisputed debt with a doubtful or disputed gift."

Speech of Mr. Tucker of Virginia, Relative to the Claims of Beaumarchais, 1824.

Deane's Recall—Beaumarchais's Activity in Obtaining for Him Honorable Escort—Letters to Congress—Reception of Deane—Preoccupation of Congress at the Moment of His Return—Arnold and Deane in Philadelphia the Summer of 1778—Deane's Subsequent Conduct—Letters of Carmichaël and Beaumarchais—Le Fier Roderigue—Silas Deane Returns to Settle Accounts—Debate Over the "Lost Million"—True Story of the "Lost Million"—Mr. Tucker's Speech—Final Settlement of the Claim of the Heirs of Beaumarchais.

IN accounting for the recall of Deane, Wharton, in the beginning of his Diplomatic Correspondence, Vol. I, p. 560, says:

"Deane had, or was supposed to have had, a considerable amount of business patronage which to Arthur Lee's eye gave too much opportunity for speculation, and not only did he suppose that Deane made use of this opportunity for his own benefit, but he himself desired to have the entire control of the business side of the mission placed in the hands of his brother William Lee, then, through the influence of Wilkes, alderman of London. The close connection which existed between Lee in Paris and the center of the opposition in London was not unknown to the French Ministry."

From the first, Vergennes had distrusted Lee, and held him at a distance. "Having had occasion," says Loménie (Vol. I, p. 115), "to study closely the work of the deputation at Passy, I am able to affirm that Lee never had any credit with the French Government, who, rightly or wrongly, suspected him of having secret relations with the English Cabinet.... It is this which perfectly explains his permanent irritation against his two colleagues."

Doniol (Vol. I, p. 368) affirms positively, "spies of the foreign office were in communication with him and he aided them to arrive even to M. de Vergennes."

"In his heart," continues Doniol, "he had an antipathy for France, which was shared by the majority of his countrymen. He was willing to accept everything from us, but on condition that no obligation be incurred."

"It is certainly not too much to say," says Jared Sparks in his *Life of Franklin* (Vol. I, p. 450), "that the divisions and feuds which reigned for a long time in Congress with respect to the foreign affairs of the United States are to be ascribed more to Lee's malign influence than to all others."

It was the same that at the most perilous moment of the war, which was precisely this same winter of 1778, was exerting itself to the utmost of its power to place a creature of its own at the head of the American forces. So bitter had party spirit become, that a member from New England, whose patriotism was undisputed, had allowed himself to write in a letter which has been preserved: "I would rather that the whole cause should come to ruin, than that Mr. Washington should triumph."

Lee succeeded so well in poisoning the minds of Congress with regard to their commissioner that after much discussion a resolution was passed on December 8, 1777, recalling Deane. The reason given being the importance of obtaining information as to the true state of affairs in Europe.

"It was originally proposed," says Parton (*Life of Franklin*, Vol. I, p. 250), "to accompany the resolution of recall by a preamble of censure. But John Jay took the defence of his absent friend and succeeded in getting the offensive preamble condemning a servant of the public unheard, stricken out." "In this case," continues Parton, "Jay was warmly his friend and defender, and not on this occasion only, but whenever he was attacked by Congress."

Franklin also warmly pleaded his cause by letter. Knowing that Congress had received unfavorably the foreign officers sent over by Deane, he wrote as follows:

"I, who am on the spot, and who know the infinite difficulty of resisting the powerful solicitations of great men, ... I hope that favorable allowances will be made to my worthy colleague on account of his situation at that time, as he long since has corrected the mistake and daily proves himself to my certain knowledge an able, faithful, active and extremely useful servant of the public." (Parton, *Life of Franklin*, Vol. II, p. 350.)

Franklin indeed might well plead for his friend in regard to the commissioning of officers, since, as has been seen, it was he who was responsible for the departure of du Coudray for America.

When the news of his recall reached Deane, he was filled with consternation. It was easy for him to pierce the thin veil of the reason given. The treatment which he already had received from Congress seemed the guarantee of further trouble.

He at once communicated his fears to Beaumarchais and his resolution not to return to America until a satisfactory explanation of the charges held against him were given. Beaumarchais, however, warmly urged his complying with the command of Congress, assuring him that his presence and the positive proof of his integrity which he would bear with him quickly would dispel the gathering storm.

Deane seems to have been convinced that the wisest course would be to yield to authority; accordingly, he at once set about his preparations for the journey. Beaumarchais, equally active, addressed a lengthy memoir to the ministers.

The memoir is given in full in the Deane papers (Vol. II, p. 399). In it, with characteristic boldness, he prescribes the rôle necessary for each minister to play, in order that Deane's enemies may be outwitted. Though Beaumarchais was no longer entrusted with the millions which were being handed over to the Americans, yet from the tone of his memoir there can be no doubt that he was still an indulged favorite.

"March 13, 1778.

"Secret Memoir to the King's Ministers, Sent to the Comte de Vergennes:"

(After explaining clearly the character and ambitions of Lee, his English connections, his influence in Congress, Beaumarchais continued:) "To succeed in his design, it was necessary to dispose of a colleague so formidable as Mr. Deane. This he has done by rendering him in many respects an object of suspicion to Congress.

"Having learned that foreign officers demanding commissions were not received favorably by the American Army, he put the worst construction upon the conduct of his colleague who sent them, maintaining that Mr. Deane arbitrarily and in spite of good advice, was responsible for the sending…. Another reason is the officious zeal displayed by M. Lee in constantly writing to Congress that all merchandise, etc., was a present…. Nothing then is easier than for the adroit Lee to blacken the conduct of Mr. Deane by representing it as the result of underhand measures contrived to support demands for money in which he expected to share; and this explains the silence, more than astonishing, that Congress has observed in regard to over ten letters of mine full of details."

Then he draws a faithful picture of Deane's situation and speaks of his having at first formed the determination not to return until charges should be communicated to him.

"I have, however, urged him to go back to face the storm. 'Lee,' I have said, 'accuses you of having arbitrarily sent officers to America; your complete defense is in my portfolio. I have in my possession a cipher letter from this time-serving Lee, urging me to send engineers and officers to the assistance of America, and the letter is written before your arrival in France.'"

Then he urged the importance for French interests to have so true and tried a friend as Mr. Deane back in America.

"I would desire," he wrote, "a particular mark of distinction, even the King's portrait or some such noticeable present to convince his countrymen that not only was he a creditable and faithful agent, but that his personality, prudence and action always have pleased the French Ministry.... I strongly recommend his being escorted by a fleet.... Once justified before Congress, his opinion becomes of immense weight and influence.... His enemies will remain dazed and humiliated at their own failure.... Should the ministry be unable to grant a fleet as he wishes, he ought at least to have a royal frigate to be furnished by M. de Sartine. His friend Beaumarchais will with pleasure undertake the composition of an explanatory and defensive memoir. He should have a testimonial, laudatory of his conduct, and this important writing is the province of the Comte de Vergennes. Finally I believe that there should be accorded to him some special favor, showing the esteem entertained for him personally and this would properly come from M. le Comte de Maurepas in the name of the king. (This seems to have been the only suggestion not carried out by the ministers.)

"There is not a moment to lose...."

Beaumarchais then recommended that everyone assume a dejected air at the news of Deane's recall, so that the enemies of the latter might be thrown off their guard. "If it is thought advisable, I will even quit Paris as one driven to despair. My lawsuit at Aix will furnish an excellent excuse. I suggest in addition that a reliable person accompany Mr. Deane, to return in the same frigate under order to await his convenience, bringing back the result of M. Deane's labors with Congress....

"Upon the assurance that these considerations be regarded as just, I will neglect everything else until I have completely vindicated Mr. Deane."

If anything could be more curious than the tone of the above memoir, it is the docility with which each minister filled the rôle mapped out for him. Not only was the portrait of the King with the personal testimonials given to Deane, but a fleet was sent out under the popular Comte d'Estaing to bear him safely to America, and with him the first minister sent by France to the new world went as his companion, charged with orders to follow closely his interests in the ensuing combat.

To the president of Congress he bore the following letter from the Comte de Vergennes:

"Versailles, March 25, 1778.

"Monsieur Deane being about to return to America, I seize this occasion with pleasure to give my testimony to the zeal, activity and intelligence with which he has conducted the interests of the United States and for which it has pleased his Majesty to give marks of his satisfaction."

To Deane himself Vergennes wrote the same day:

"March 26, 1778.

"As I am not, Sir, to have the honor of seeing you again before your departure I pray you to receive here my wishes that your voyage may be speedy, short, and happy, and that you may find in your own country the same sentiments which you inspired in France. You could not, sir, desire anything to be added to that which I feel for you and which I shall keep as long as I live. The King, in order to give a personal proof of the satisfaction which he has had in your conduct, charged me to communicate it to the Congress of the United States. This is the object of the letter which Mr. Gérard will give you for Mr. Hancock. He will also give you a box ornamented with a portrait of the king. You will not refuse to carry into your country the image of its best friend."

On the 23rd of March, Beaumarchais had written to Congress in a letter in which he set forth the proofs in his possession of the innocence of Deane.

"These, gentlemen," he wrote, "were the real motives that determined us both in sending you the officers. As I have never treated with any other, as my firm never has transacted business with any other in France, and as the other commissioners have been lacking even in common civility towards me, I testify that if my zeal, my advances of money, and my shipments of supplies and merchandise have been acceptable to the august Congress, their gratitude is due to the indefatigable exertions of Mr. Deane throughout this commercial affair.

"I hope that the honorable Congress, rejecting the insinuations of others, who are desirous of appropriating for themselves the credit of the operations, will accept in perfect faith the present declaration of the man most capable of enlightening them and who respectfully signs himself and his firm, gentlemen, yours, etc.

"Caron de Beaumarchais,

"Secretary to the King and Lieutenant-General of the King's Hunt, known in America under the title of his firm, Roderigue Hortalès et Cie."

Before quitting France, Silas Deane addressed a letter to Beaumarchais, dated March 29, 1778. Obliged to quit France during the absence of his friend, he wrote thanking him for his letter to Congress, which he hoped would throw light upon the vexed question. "It is unhappy," he said, "that the short time allowed me to prepare for my voyage will not admit of our making at least a general settlement of our accounts.... I hope to return to France early in the fall; immediately after my return it shall be my first business to adjust and settle with you the account for your several expeditions and disbursements.... After the perplexing and embarrassing scenes you have had to pass through, it must give you the most solid joy to see an armament going out which will convince America and the world of the sincere friendship of France, and their resolution to protect its liberties and its independence.

"I again congratulate you on this great and glorious event, to which you have contributed more than any other person....

"I shall improve my first opportunity of writing to you, and rely on being honored with a continuance of your correspondence and friendship. Wishing that you ever may be happy and fortunate, I am, etc.,

"Silas Deane."

The misgivings which had haunted the American commissioner seemed entirely to disappear during his voyage, so confident was he of being able to justify himself before Congress, and if ever commissioner had the right to look forward with joy to setting foot again on his native land, that commissioner was Deane. When he had gone out two years previously he had left his country poor, unrecognized and not yet decided to declare its independence. By his unhesitating and

CHAPTER XXII

indefatigable zeal, aided by that of Beaumarchais, supplies and officers of priceless value had been sent to its aid, arriving at the moment when they were most needed.

Mistakes had been made, it is true, but those mistakes were all of a nature that no man of honor need blush to acknowledge. Far from having enriched himself during those two years of service, he had spent not only all his own private savings, but had been obliged to draw very heavily upon the generosity of his friend, since all the stores brought with him from America had fallen into the hands of the English. In the words of Parton, "He was returning now the acknowledged minister of a victorious nation, the honored guest of a French Admiral, bringing back a powerful fleet (twelve line of battleships and four frigates) to aid his country, and accompanied by an ambassador of the King of France! Well might he write exultingly to the president of Congress, well might he expect a warm welcome and a hasty adjustment of his claims; as the proud French vessel was dropping anchor in Delaware Bay, July 10, 1778, he wrote: 'I shall embark this afternoon ... and I hope soon to have the honor of presenting my respects to your Excellency and the Honorable Congress in person. . . .'

No reply came to him from Congress. No one paid him the smallest attention. His testimonials were ignored and even the presence of the French fleet had no power to rouse Congress from a stony indifference. He was in despair.

"He had brought with him," said Parton, "only a hundred pounds, not expecting to be detained in America many weeks. When at last given audience, he told his story to distrustful and estranged employers. All the friends of Arthur Lee, all the ancient foes of France, and a large proportion of the faction who desired to put Horatio Gates into the place of Washington, were disposed to believe the foul calumnies sent over by every ship from Paris."

As a matter of fact the time of his arrival in Philadelphia was not well suited to a fair consideration of Deane's claims. The city recently had been evacuated by the British Army. During the occupation, Toryism had been rampant and the state was retaliating with indictments for treason. Disputes over questions of jurisdiction engaged the civil authorities in quarrels with Arnold, the commander of the garrison, who numbered among his sympathizers Silas Deane and the mercantile class.

Arnold, after his brilliant exploits at Saratoga, had seen himself thrust aside at the moment of victory to make way for Gates. Wounded at Saratoga, and burning for revenge, Arnold was already so much disgusted with the Continental Congress that he began seriously to wish to see Great Britain triumph.

Washington had put him in command of the garrison at Philadelphia in June, 1778. The reigning belle of the Quaker City was at that moment Miss Margaret Shippen, "the most beautiful and fascinating woman in America." She was the daughter of a wealthy merchant, who along with his whole class, was eager for the war to come to an end through a speedy adjustment with Great Britain, whose liberal offers, since the surrender of Burgoyne, seemed more than satisfactory to their moderate patriotism.

No sooner had Arnold entered into his new post than he fell a captive to the charms of the young woman in question, then under twenty years of age.

"As no one kept a finer stable of horses, nor gave more costly dinners than Arnold," it was natural that he should invite the Tory friends of the young lady whose hand he hoped to win. Although he was "thirty-five years of age and a widower with two sons" ... his handsome face, his gallant bearing and his splendid career, made him acceptable. In the fall their engagement was publicly announced, while the Tory sentiments of the commander of the fort of Philadelphia became definitely fixed.

The bitterness of his own grievances against Congress led him to give ear willingly to the complaints poured out by the exasperated French commissioner, whose patriotism was also rapidly vanishing in the gulf of his private wrongs.

It was during this summer of association between Arnold and Deane that the sentiments of the latter underwent the profound change which induced a subsequent conduct so disappointing to his dearest friends. Silas Deane never has been accused of treason to his country, for he was incapable of such an act as that which rendered Arnold an object of contempt to our enemies even—but that he was untrue to his own past cannot be denied. No one in the beginning had been a warmer advocate of independence or had worked so indefatigably for an alliance with France. In the end, this was completely reversed. The unfortunate course which he took to avenge himself for the atrocious wrongs heaped upon him by the party in Congress then in power led him to exile, where he died destitute and dishonored. However, "the most bitter reproach," says Wharton, "ever heaped upon this loyal patriot was that he had joined hands in friendship with the traitor Arnold."

While the condemnation of Lee at the bar of history seems unanimous, it is unfair to allow the blame of his conduct to rest wholly upon him, for it must be shared by that party in Congress which was dominant during most of the existence of the body, and which supported the pretensions of Lee and shared his antagonisms.

A consideration of the complex causes which led to the ruin of Deane is in place here, only as these causes relate to his connection with Beaumarchais. Up to a certain point the credit of the two men is inseparable, and it must not be forgotten that the same party which planned Deane's downfall was also the one that tried to prevent the alliance with France, and was unwilling to admit any debt of gratitude to Roderigue Hortalès et Cie.

Gérard de Rayneval, first ambassador of France to America, who accompanied Deane on the occasion of his recall, attributes the action of Congress at this time to an *"esprit d'ostracisme,* which," he says, "already has begun to make itself felt against those men who, having rendered important services, are no longer deemed necessary...."

The private secretary of Deane while in France, W. Carmichaël, had returned to America some time before. Having aided Beaumarchais and Deane in the shipment of supplies to the new world, there was no one who understood better the exact nature of the difficulties against which they had labored, or the real debt of gratitude owed them by America. Under date of September 3, 1778, he wrote to Beaumarchais from Philadelphia:

"I have written you twice lately about your affairs, so that I have the pleasure of repeating that Congress begins to feel its lack of attention to you and to realize that it was too ready to believe the base insinuations of others, which I truly believe would have had no weight if du Coudray had not circulated such prejudicial reports concerning you.... I have applied myself with my whole power to convince my compatriots of the injustice and ingratitude with which you have been treated and this before the arrival of Deane, and I flatter myself to have had some success. His efforts have been the same, so that justice, although tardy, should now prevail. I wish for the honor of my compatriots that it had never been necessary for us to plead for you.

"M. de Francy is in Virginia and works sincerely and indefatigably for your interests. I expect him here soon.

"Your nephew spent several weeks with me, but is now commanded with his general to join the army under the orders of General Sullivan. He is a brave young man who makes himself loved very much when he is known; he has all the vivacity of his age and desires to distinguish himself. General Conway assures me that he conducted himself like a young hero at the battle of the Brandywine. I take the liberty of entering into these details because I know they will delight his mother, since bravery always has been a powerful recommendation to the fair sex, and she will be charmed to find so much in her own son.... I do not know whether I shall be continued in my place as Secretary of the Embassy at your court, or be employed in some other department.

"Dr. Franklin certainly will be continued at the Court of Versailles, and an attempt will be made to force the Lees to fall back into the obscurity from which they have lifted themselves, but whether this will succeed is doubtful. We have as many intrigues and cabals here as you and your friends suffer from on the other continent. And why not? Are we not sovereign states and are we not friends and allies of Louis XVI?

"I beg you to believe me always, Yours,

"W. Carmichaël."

The spirit of the letter, as well as the news it brought, must have been consoling to the heart of Beaumarchais. But in the meantime, he had been pushing forward his vast commercial enterprises and with his usual vigor prepared himself for new dangers to which the open alliance with France exposed his undertaking. He wrote to De Francy:

"I am dispatching the *Zephyr*, so that you may know that I am ready to put to sea a fleet of more than twelve vessels at whose head is *le Fier Roderigue*, which you sent back to me and which arrived safely the first of October. This fleet will carry six thousand tons, and it is armed absolutely for war. So arrange yourself in consequence. If my ship, the *Ferragus*, leaves Rochefort in September, keep it there to join my fleet in returning. This is an armament which I hold in common with

M. de Montieu.... Allow the ships to remain in port no longer than is absolutely necessary, for although strong and well armed, our enemies must not be allowed to interfere with their return.

"They will not arrive until some time in February, as they are to make a detour to provision our colonies with flour and salt provisions, of which they are in great need, and the payment of which, sent to us in bills of exchange upon our treasurers before the return of the fleet, will enable us to meet the terrible outlay which this armament costs us.... You will receive by the *Fier Roderigue* all my accounts with Congress.... The result is that Congress will pay for nothing which it does not receive, or that was destroyed en route. I join the exact account of what I have received from Congress, in spite of the unjust deputation at Passy who have disputed every return cargo and who would have seized upon that of *La Thérèse* if M. Pelletier, instructed by me, had not sold it by authority. This perpetual injustice makes me indignant and has made me take the resolution to have no more to do with the deputation as long as that rogue Lee is there....

"I have been promised, my dear Francy, your commission of captain. I hope to be happy enough to send it by *le Fier Roderigue*, but do not count upon it until you see it in your hands. You know our country; it is so vast that it is a long way from the place where things are promised to the place where they are given. In a word, I have not received it yet, although it has been promised....

"I have received no other money from the comte de Pulaski than that which he himself gave me. I send you his exact account. He should write me but I have heard nothing. I approve of what you have done for M. de Lafayette. Brave young man that he is. It is to serve me as I desire, to oblige a man of his character. I have not yet been paid for the money I advanced to him but I have no uneasiness about that.

"As for you my dear de Francy, I will write you later what I will do for you. If you know me, you will expect to be well treated. Your fate is hence forth attached to mine. I esteem you and love you and you will not have long to wait for the proof of it. Remember me often to Baron von Steuben. I congratulate myself after all I hear of him, for having given so great an officer to my friends the *free men*, and for having in a way forced him to follow that noble career. I am not in the least disturbed by the money I lent him. Never have I made a use of funds the investment of which gratified me as much as this does, since I have succeeded in putting a man of honor in his true place. I learn that he is inspector-general of all the troops; bravo! Tell him that his glory is the interest on my money and at that title I have no doubt he will repay me with usury.

"I have received a letter from M. Deane and also one from Mr. Carmichaël; assure them of my warm esteem. Those two are brave republicans. They have given me the hope that I may soon embrace them both in Paris, which will not, however, prevent me from writing them by the *Fier Roderigue*, who is very proud to find himself at the head of a small squadron, and who I hope will *ne se laissera pas couper les moustaches*, on the contrary he promises to do some cutting for me,

"Adieu, my Francy, I am yours for life,

CHAPTER XXII

"Caron de Beaumarchais."

Silas Deane returned to France in 1781, to settle all his accounts. On the 6th of April of that year the indebtedness to Beaumarchais by Congress was fixed by him at 3,600,000 *livres* after the deduction of all receipts and comprising the interest promised. This sum, then, Beaumarchais demanded of Congress.

CÆSAR AUGUSTUS RODNEY — ATTORNEY GENERAL OF THE U. S.

Two years passed. Congress paid no attention to the demand. In 1783, another emissary, Mr. Barclay, arrived from America in the capacity of consul-general, and with the mission to revise all the accounts rendered by Silas Deane. Beaumarchais refused to submit to this treatment, but Mr. Barclay told him Congress would pay nothing until there had been a new inspection of the accounts. After a year Beaumarchais was forced to submit.

In revising the statement made by Deane, Mr. Barclay admitted all the claims, but gratified Congress by lessening commissions, expenses, etc. Still Congress refused to pay the new and reduced accounts. Soon after this, an incident arose which determined Congress to postpone payment indefinitely.

In the fall of 1783, after signing the treaty which ended the war, the United States wished to borrow six millions from the French Government. It was decided to grant the request and at the same time to make an exact recapitulation of all the sums already furnished, whether loaned or presented.

In the first class were announced eighteen millions; then another loan of ten millions from Holland, guaranteed by the king of France and of which he paid the interest; finally the six millions about to be loaned. This constituted a sum of thirty-four millions which the United States promised to refund at future times. Finally the King announced as a gift, the three millions conveyed to the colonists before her treaty of Alliance in 1778, and six millions given in 1781. It was therefore nine millions which the king of France relinquished without expecting any return, and this in addition to the enormous expenditure made in sending the fleets and armies of France to America. (See *Loménie* Vol II, p. 186.)

The statement was signed by Franklin and received without comment by the United States, but three years later, in 1786, Franklin made the discovery that the king of France stated that three millions had been given to the cause of independence in America before 1778, whereas he, Franklin, had received but two millions.

What had become of the other million?

Inquiry was at once made of the United States banker in France, and an explanation demanded. After much difficulty it was learned that this million was one delivered by the royal treasurer on the 10th of June, 1776.

"It was," says M. de Loménie, "precisely the million given to Beaumarchais, but the reticence of Vergennes showed that an embarrassing mistake had been made, though unconsciously, by the royal treasurer."

It was impossible in 1786 for the French government to avow the secret aid she had given to the colonies before her open recognition of American Independence. The two millions given to Franklin in 1777 through the banker, Grand, after France had decided upon the policy of open recognition, but before the act, had never been a secret—but the million given to Beaumarchais, while really intended to help the American cause, had been conveyed to him under stress of secrecy at a time when it was unsafe to submit to writing even the most informal engagement in regard to it.

Whatever the stipulations made concerning the use of the money, they were verbal and have never been revealed. Nothing could attest the profound confidence inspired in the magistracy by Beaumarchais more than this absence of documents relative to the loan. There can be no doubt that whatever the arrangement made by Vergennes, he was satisfied with the account rendered him by Beaumarchais, for we find him coming repeatedly to the latter's aid when the failure of Congress to return cargoes, placed the house of Hortalès and Company in danger of bankrupt-

CHAPTER XXII

cy. The confidence of the minister is also further attested by his refusal to deliver the receipt for the million, signed by Beaumarchais, on the 10th of June, 1776, and so become a handle to the calumny which Congress was directing against him.

To summarize the exposition of that conscientious historian, Loménie: "Why," he asks, "did the government insert this million in the list of those given directly to America? Was it simply a recapitulation of the accounts of the treasury made without thought of the inconvenience that might result for Beaumarchais; or did the government really intend Beaumarchais to render an account of it to the United States?... We have the right to affirm that the government never intended that he should be accountable for it to anyone but to the minister.

"By refusing constantly to name the person to whom the million had been given, the minister said implicitly; 'I class this million with those given gratuitously because in effect it was given; but since it was not given to you, and as the man to whom it was given, engaged himself by his receipt to render an account of it to me, and not to you, that man cannot be accountable except to me. If I asked to have the million returned, you would then have the right to demand it of him who received it; but since I ask nothing, I am the one to decide whether that million, gratuitously given by me, shall profit you or the man to whom I gave it. It was given to aid in a secret operation very useful to you, but which, by your refusal to acquit and by losses which he has experienced in his commerce with you, seems to have been more harmful than fruitful to him.'" (See *Loménie*, Vol. II, p. 190.)

Of all this that was transpiring Beaumarchais knew nothing, nor could he obtain from Congress any explanation of their reason for totally ignoring their debt to him. At last his patience at an end, on the 12th of June, 1787, he wrote to the President of Congress as follows:

"A people become sovereign and powerful may be permitted, perhaps, to consider gratitude as a virtue of individuals which is beneath politics; but nothing can dispense a state from being just, and especially from paying its debts. I dare hope, Monsieur, that touched by the importance of the affair and by the force of my reasons, you will be good enough to honor me with an official report as to the decision of the honorable Congress either to arrange promptly to liquify my accounts, or else to choose arbiters in Europe to decide the points debated, those of insurance and commission as M. Barclay had the honor of proposing to you in 1785; or else write me candidly that the sovereign states of America, forgetting my past services, refuse me all justice: thus I shall adopt the method best suited to my interests which you have despised, to my honor which you have wounded, although without losing the profound respect with which I am of the General Congress and of you, Monsieur le President, the very humble, etc.

"Caron de Beaumarchais."

It was at this juncture that Beaumarchais, stung by the reproaches of his own countrymen, made a ringing vindication of his acts in the cause of American independence, which will be given in the next chapter.

The reply which Congress made to the letter above quoted, was to appoint Arthur Lee to examine the accounts.

"The work was soon done," says Loménie, *"d'un tour de main*. Arthur Lee pretended to discover that instead of 3,600,000 livres owing Beaumarchais, he not only had nothing to reclaim but on the other hand owed 1,800,000 francs to the United States!" The absurdity of this account could not fail to appear to Congress, and after four years more of protestations, in 1793 it confided a new examination of the debt to "that most distinguished American Statesman, Alexander Hamilton," who established the sum owing Beaumarchais as 2,280,000 francs, but at the same time he proposed to suspend payment until the question of the lost million was settled.

In the meantime the Revolution was advancing upon France with awful strides. Already the royalistic government had fallen, that government whose greatest glory was its noble service to the cause of American independence.

When in 1794 Gouverneur Morris applied to Buchot, then minister of Foreign affairs for the new French government, there was no one left who knew or cared for the details that had prevented Vergennes from producing that famous receipt. At the demand of Congress, therefore, it was given to Morris.

Armed now with what it chose to consider as proof that Beaumarchais wilfully had appropriated to himself a million livres intended by the French Government for it, Congress refused all settlement.

They not only repudiated the payment of the 2,600,000 livres surplus of the debt honorably acknowledged by Deane, who alone knew the immense advances that had been made by Beaumarchais to cover the expenses of the commissioner as well as of the officers whom he had commissioned, but that august body considered that it might even dispense with paying the 1,800,000 livres surplus over and above the million, out of the sum accorded by Alexander Hamilton in which he ignored those advances, together with a part of the commission and interest freely granted by Congress in the contract already quoted in this volume, and arranged by the agent of Beaumarchais, Theveneau de Francy, in 1778.

Congress refused all this, arguing that, as M. de Loménie says: "Since the interest of the million given in 1776 will absorb the difference, therefore we owe nothing, and will pay nothing."

The interest on the surplus, as it would have much more than absorbed the million in question, they, of course, conveniently ignored.

This turn in his affairs with Congress was a crushing blow to Beaumarchais, but it did not prevent him, during the entire remainder of his life, pleading with the representatives of the American people to pay their debt to him.

But at the moment when Congress held triumphantly aloft the receipt for the 1,000,000 livres, and flaunted it in his face, Beaumarchais was in no position to defend himself, for the Revolution which had overwhelmed France had so shattered and ruined his fortune that he was obliged to take refuge in a garret in Hamburg. Here, devoured by anguish,—unable to obtain news from home, knowing only that his goods had been confiscated, that his wife, his daughter, and his sisters had been thrown into prison, his thoughts turned to the people for whom he had performed such herculean labors and to them he addressed one last appeal. This was in April, 1795.

"Congress," says Loménie, "remained deaf to all his reclamations; not only it allowed him to die without liquidating the debt, but during the thirty-six years following his death, all the governments which succeeded one another in France, and all the ambassadors of those governments, vainly supported the demand of the heirs of Beaumarchais."

During the years which follow his death, from 1799 to 1835, "The claims of the heirs of Beaumarchais" occupy congress after congress of the United States. In the progress of the suit all the French governments, from the Empire under Napoleon down to the reign of the "bourgeois King," Louis Phillippe, always take the stand of Vergennes. The following letter from the Duc de Richelieu, dated the 20th of May, 1816, may be said to express the attitude of the French Government in the whole matter. He wrote:

"The notes successively presented by the ministers of France are so particular and positive, that they seem to remove all doubt on the facts of the subject in dispute, and consequently all hesitation as to the decision to be given. It was in fact stated that the French Government had no concern in the commercial transactions of M. de Beaumarchais with the United States.

"By this declaration it was not only intended to convey the idea that the government was in no ways interested in the operations or in his chances of loss or gain, but a positive assurance was also given that it was wholly unconnected with them; whence it results that in relation to them France is to be considered neither as a lender, a surety nor as an intermediate agent. The whole of these transactions were spontaneous on the part of M. de Beaumarchais and the right and agency derived from them appertain exclusively to him....

"The million delivered on the 10th of June immediately reached its intended destination and a simple authorization of the King, but a few months subsequent to the payment of the sum, was the only document which finally placed the expenditure in the regular train of fiscal settlement.

"I am therefore warranted, Sir, after a fresh examination of the facts, in presenting the declaration of the above as stated, and in considering it a matter of certainty that the million paid on the 10th of June was not applied to the purchase of shipments made to the United States at that period by M. de Beaumarchais....

"There is no member of the Government who can be ignorant of the services rendered by the head of that family to your cause and the influence produced on its early successes by his ardent zeal, extensive connections and liberal employment of his whole fortune.

"Be pleased, Sir, to receive, etc., etc.

Signed "Richelieu."

This claim, so repeatedly stated before Congress, was taken up and examined by a succession of committees which seem each to have adopted the views of the

French Government. To the honor of the United States let it be stated that such men as John Jay and Thomas Jefferson, had from the first recognized the debt due to Beaumarchais and had urged the payment of the debt. Later it was James Madison, Cæsar Rodney, William Pinkney and others, who similarly urged Congress to appropriate the money to liquidate the claim.

To close this long debate we have selected a few paragraphs taken here and there from reports of committees, terminating with an extract from a speech delivered by Mr. Tucker of Virginia, in order to demonstrate clearly that the enlightened opinion of the most representative Americans always has stood for the recognition of this claim.... "Only two points," the report says, "are to be decided: Did Mr. Beaumarchais receive from the French Government 1,000,000 livres in behalf of or on account of the United States? If so, has he, or his representative at any time accounted with the United States for their expenditure? ... On the face of the instrument itself it appears that Beaumarchais was to account to Vergennes and not to the United States, for the expenditure of the money.... This contradicts the idea that he was accountable to us for its application.... The engagement of Beaumarchais was positive, express and unqualified to account to Vergennes and to him only for the money received. The United States are no parties to the instrument; there is no stipulation to render them any account of the expenditure.... It is not easy to conceive on what principle he ought twice to account for the same money.... The French government have uniformly declared that they furnished no supply of arms or military stores. Vergennes is full and explicit; he states that all the articles furnished by Beaumarchais are on his private account, who had settled with the artillery department for them by giving orders or bills for their value. This expressly excludes the idea that the million livres in question were intended to be applied to the payment in advance of the account of Beaumarchais.... This construction was acquiesced in by our government in the contract of 1783, when we knew neither the date nor the person to whom the money was paid....

"... The United States allege that the French Government paid this debt for them. The Government through their ministers declare officially that they did not. There seems therefore no room for dispute. Considering that the sum of which the million livres in question made a part, was a gratuitous grant from the French Government to the United States, and considering that the declaration of that Government clearly states that that part of the grant was put into the hands of M. de Beaumarchais as its agent, not as the agent of the United States, and that it was duly accounted for by him, to the French Government; considering also the concurring opinion of two attorneys-general of the United States that the said debt was not legally sustainable in behalf of the United States; I recommend the case to the favorable attention of the legislature whose authority alone can finally decide on it. Signed

"James Madison,
"C. A. Rodney,
"Wm. Pinkney.
"January 31, 1817."

From the speech of Mr. Tucker of Virginia, 1824:

"Mr. Chairman: It is well known to most of the assembly that in the first years of the Revolution, M. de Beaumarchais furnished military supplies and clothing to the amount of several million livres....

"The merits of this claim have hitherto hinged upon the fact whether the million in question was received by Beaumarchais for the purpose of supplies or not;...

"In regard to this there is the solemn declaration of M. de Vergennes that the king had furnished nothing. Again there can be no doubt that M. de Beaumarchais must have been held accountable to his government for the million, for whatever purpose it was put into his hands.... If it was intended for such services as those for which secret service money is employed, it is said, and it seems not improbable, that the vouchers in such cases are destroyed.... But there could be no reason to destroy them if they related merely to the purchase of supplies....

"On weighing all the considerations there is some preponderance of testimony that M. de Beaumarchais received the million in dispute for the purpose of supplies, and if France had been passive on this occasion or if we had paid any valuable consideration to her for this million I should think that we were justified in charging M. de Beaumarchais with that amount. But when it is recollected that we received these supplies directly from him, having arranged the settlement of the account on our own terms; that the million that we claim as a credit was paid not by us, but by France, and that, as an act of bounty; and when France insists that it was for another purpose;... it seems to me that we cannot, consistently with our honor or self respect, pay off an undisputed debt with a doubtful or disputed gift....

"As an individual, I could never seek to give the bounty of a benefactor a direction which he objected to, for the purpose of making a discount from the acknowledged debt of a third person.

"Sirs:—in this matter France is right or she is wrong.... Then the error consists in claiming our gratitude for 9,000,000 livres instead of 8,000,000 ... which can in no way affect the claim of M. de Beaumarchais.... The whole present difficulty comes from the mistake of Dr. Franklin in the treaty of 1783....

"Assuredly if our agent had signed a treaty under a mistake as he himself states, that mistake should be rectified with the French Government which should give us a satisfactory explanation or hold us bound in gratitude for only 8,000,000 livres, neither of which can affect the claims of M. de Beaumarchais....

"Mr. Chairman: We ought to be consistent with ourselves with regard to the declaration of the French Government. When M. de Vergennes declared to our commissioners in September 1778, that the military supplies were furnished by M. de Beaumarchais, we acquiesced in that assurance and required no further proof....

"On every ground then, Mr. Chairman, I am free to say, I would vote at once for the appropriation to the whole amount of this claim ... and I hope the committee will adopt the resolution for that purpose offered by the Committee."

But the government of the United States still refused to listen to reason. However, in 1835, under pressure of necessity, the United States having a claim against

France which it wished to bring forward, offered the heirs of Beaumarchais the choice of taking 800,000 francs and considering the affair closed, or nothing. The heirs chose the former and so at last ended the long drawn out debate regarding "the lost million."

CHAPTER XXIII

"It was to take from the Ministers all idea of my ambition, to conjure the storm, that I began again to amuse myself with frivolous theatrical plays, while guarding a profound silence upon my political actions."

Petition to MM. the Representatives of the Commune of Paris by
P. A. Caron de Beaumarchais.

The *Mariage de Figaro*—Its Composition—Difficulties Encountered in Getting it Produced—It is Played at Grennevilliers—The First Representation—Its Success—*Institut des mères nourrices*—Beaumarchais at Saint Lazare.

SEVERAL years before Beaumarchais had written in answer to the question,—"What gives you so gay a philosophy?"

"The habit of misfortune, I hasten to laugh at everything so as not to be obliged to weep."

So now in 1778 after seeing Deane recalled, his own service ignored, and jealousies aroused even among the ministers themselves he turned from all this bitterness, to develop in his own inimitable way, the gay scenes of his *Mariage de Figaro*.

"In this piece," says Gudin, "the combinations were so new, the situations so varied that one would be tempted to believe that such a work would have absorbed all the faculties of the mind of its author during many years, but for him it was only a relaxation from the many and diverse affairs in which he was engaged."

M. de Maurepas said to him one day, "And how, occupied as you are, have you been able to write it?"

"I, M. le Comte! I composed it the day when the ministers of the King had sufficient leisure to go together to the Redoute."

"Are there many repartees equal to that in your comedy? If so, I answer for its success," retorted Maurepas; for just the day before all the ministers had gone in a body to spend several hours at one of the new and fashionable pleasure gardens of Paris known as the Redoute.

But having written his play was very far from having it produced, for the daring boldness of the author since the marvelous success of his first comedy was known not to have diminished. The authorities rightly suspected that the new play would contain even more pointed criticisms upon the existing social order than had the *Barbier*. To be produced in public it must first pass the censors and have the approbation of the king.

La Harpe has said of this play, "It took much wit to write it—but not so much as to get it played."

Letters given by Loménie show that already in October, 1781, the actors of the Théâtre-Français had seen the piece and were discussing with Beaumarchais the distribution of the parts. The author had appealed to the lieutenant of police to name a censor and asked as a special favor that the play should not leave his office. Six weeks later Beaumarchais learned that the king had read his play and that it had been condemned.

Madame Campan in her Memoires speaks of the incident.

Marie Antoinette who had always liked and protected Beaumarchais said to the King,

"Will the piece not be played?"

"Certainly not," answered the King, "it is detestable. Why, the Bastille would have to be pulled down if that were allowed!"

The situation against which the versatile author had to contend was the positive prohibition by the supreme head of authority—the King himself, but who was seconded, however, by very few of those personages who were nearest to him. In fact this very prohibition excited the curiosity of the court to such an extent that everyone from the loftiest personages down, and notably the Duke d'Artois, brother of Louis XVI, was demanding the favor of hearing Beaumarchais read his play.

"Every day," explained Madame de Campan, "one hears on every side, 'I have heard,' or 'I shall hear the piece of Beaumarchais.'"

Flattered as the author must have been by the enthusiasm of the courtiers, he was far too clever to lose his head or grant lightly the privilege of a reading.

"Even the most considerable personages of the realm," says Loménie, "obtained the privilege on condition that they asked at least twice. The Princess Lamballe, for instance, personal friend of the queen, had a violent desire to have Beaumarchais read the *Mariage de Figaro* in her salon. She sent an ambassador to him, one of the greatest nobles of the court, the oldest son of the Maréchal de Richelieu, the Duc de Fronsac—an ardent patron of the *Mariage.*—Beaumarchais refused to see him. The duc wrote next day:

"You closed your door against me yesterday which was not well. However, I do not hold against you enough malice to prevent me from speaking of the negotiation with which I am charged by Mme. the Princess of Lamballe—and I propose you come next Wednesday to Versailles to dine with me, after which we will go to her. Your very humble servant, etc.

"Le duc de Fronsac."

CHAPTER XXIII   123

Beaumarchais evidently refused a second time for again the Duke wrote another letter, more urgent, to which the author finally yielded.

The grand Duke (afterward Paul I) and Duchess of Russia, while visiting Versailles in the spring of 1782, also became ardent supporters of the piece, after Beaumarchais had accorded them the privilege of a reading.

Strong now with the support of so many notables, he took occasion to write a vigorous letter to M. the *Garde des Sceaux*, to which august personage he began by apologizing for bothering him with such a "frivolous subject" but ended by a very ardent plea that his play be permitted to appear before the public.

"In June of 1783," says Loménie, "Beaumarchais, who, it must not be forgotten, conducted twenty other operations at the same time, seemed on the point of succeeding.... By the influence of some one unknown, the comedians received an order to learn the piece so that it might be played before the court of Versailles. Later it was decided that it should be performed in Paris itself at the *hôtel des Menus-Plaisirs*."

Everything was ready, even the tickets were out, when suddenly an express order of the king arrived, forbidding the performance. "This prohibition of the king," says Madame de Campan, "seemed like an attack upon the liberty of the public. The disappointed hopes of the people excited discontent to such an extent that the words, '*oppression,*' '*tyranny*' were never pronounced in the days before the fall of the throne, with so much passion and vehemence."

Beaumarchais could well afford, as he writes, "to put his piece back in its portfolio, waiting until some event should draw it out again," for the prohibition of the king had acted only as the most serviceable advertisement. Therefore he had not long to wait.

Being in England on business the latter part of the summer, he received a letter from the Duc de Fronsac, from which the following is an extract:

"Paris, the 4th of September, 1783.

"I hope, Monsieur, that you will not object that I shall write to obtain your consent to have the *Mariage de Figaro* played at Grennevilliers.... You know that I have for several years turned over my estate of Grennevilliers to M. de Vaudreuil. M. le Comte d'Artois comes there to hunt the 18th and Madame the Duchess de Polignac with her society comes to supper. Vaudreuil has asked me to arrange a spectacle, for there is a good enough hall. I told him that there was nothing more charming than the *Mariage de Figaro*, but that we must have the consent of the king. *We have secured that and* I went running to find you and was astonished and distressed to find that you were far away in the north.

"Will you not give your consent that the piece be played? I promise you that I will do my utmost to have it well given. M. le Comte d'Artois and his whole society are waiting with the greatest eagerness to see it, and certainly it will be a great step in advance towards having it given at Fontainebleau and Paris.... I, in particular, have the greatest desire and I beg you to reply quickly, quickly. Let it be favorable, I beg you, and never doubt my gratitude and the esteem and friendship with which I shall always be, Monsieur, yours, etc.

"Le duc de Fronsac."

"While the duc de Fronsac," says Loménie, "sent after Beaumarchais, the comte de Vaudreuil who was arranging the festival in honor of the comte d'Artois and Madame de Polignac, waited with impatience for the consent of Beaumarchais. We have under our eyes a letter of the comte written to the duc de Fronsac which was found among the papers of Beaumarchais, apparently because the latter fearing some sudden change of feeling in the King, had requested that the duc give him the entire correspondence, in order that he might be in a position to prove that he had acted only at the urgent solicitations of the courtiers.

"This circumstance enables us to observe closely what was passing in those frivolous heads that were soon to be stricken off, and to realize with what blind impatience those thoughtless patricians aspired to be pointed out by Figaro for the contempt of the masses."

In this letter of the count, after running over a half dozen plays that do not satisfy him, he says: "Fearing the permission of M. de Beaumarchais would not reach us in time we will postpone the spectacle for three or four days so it will not be given until the 21st or the 22nd. Will you please see that the comedians hold themselves ready for that date? But *hors du 'Mariage de Figaro,' point de salut* (our only salvation is in the *Mariage de Figaro*). Thank you a thousand times, my dear Fronsac, for all your trouble. I know that it is for these ladies and M. the comte d'Artois, who join in my gratitude. Receive the renewed expression of my deep regard which is yours for life;

"Le comte de Vaudreuil."

Again to quote Loménie:

"Beaumarchais, then in England, learned that nothing was now lacking but his own consent to play the piece prohibited by the king several months before. He returned immediately to Paris and it was he now who was the one to make the conditions. He was not satisfied simply to amuse the court, but wished rather to reach the public and to make them laugh at the expense of the court, which was a very different matter. If, however, the one would lead to the other, Beaumarchais would be charmed to gratify MM. de Vaudreuil and de Fronsac, but before consenting to the representation taking place at Grennevilliers, he required that the favor be accorded him of a new censure. Singular request!

"'But,' they said to him, 'your play has already been censored, approved, and we have the permission of the king.'

"'No matter, it must be censored again.'

"To M. de Breteuil he wrote, 'they found me a little difficult in my turn and they said it was only because I was so sought after; but since I desired *absolutely* to *fix public opinion* by a new examination of the piece, I insisted, and so they have accorded me the severe historian, Gaillard of the French Academy.'

"This," continues Loménie, "was well thought out. Just before a court festival, where all were eagerly awaiting the representation, what censor, no matter how arbitrary, would dare interfere by spoiling their joy and provoking the anger of the powerful lords who ordered the festival? And so, as was to be expected, the report of the censure was 'completely favorable.'"

But Beaumarchais was not yet satisfied. "The play approved once more," he wrote in his memoirs to M. de Breteuil, "I carried my precaution so far that I required before I would consent to its being played at the festival, the express promise of the magistracy that the Comédie-Française might consider it as belonging to their theater and I dare certify that that assurance was given by M. Lenoir, who certainly believed everything complete as did I myself."

"To appreciate the diplomatic value," continues Loménie, "of this passage, and the art with which Beaumarchais in the suppleness of his tenacity knew how to bind over the people who inconvenienced him, and that he could not openly attack, it is well to recall that at this moment he was struggling against an express prohibition of the representation of his play by the king, a prohibition that his majesty consented to lift only for one day, in a particular house and that only to gratify his brother the Comte d'Artois and M. de Vaudreuil."

Beaumarchais, on his side, was sincere in not wishing to let it be played at Grennevilliers except on condition that he be formally promised that sooner or later it would be given to the public; but since he did not dare to push the matter so far, he saw the way to take one step in advance, by inventing the beautiful paraphrase that had just been read, which became a sort of vague engagement contracted with him and upon which he would depend very soon to push matters still further.

On these conditions he finally accorded the permission asked, and M. de Vaudreuil thanked him in a letter which proves as far as he was concerned, that he accepted the engagement in the sense understood by Beaumarchais. He wrote:

"The comte de Vaudreuil has the honor to thank M. de Beaumarchais for the kindness which he has shown in allowing his piece to be played at Grennevilliers. The comte de Vaudreuil has seized with alacrity this opportunity of giving to the public a chef d'œuvre which it awaits with impatience. The presence of Monseigneur the comte d'Artois and the real merit of this charming piece will in the end destroy all the obstacles which have retarded its representation. The comte de Vaudreuil hopes very soon to be able to thank M. de Beaumarchais personally.

"This Monday, Sept. 15th, 1783."

"The success of this representation at Grennevilliers was such," to continue the account of Loménie, "that a complete change operated in Beaumarchais's attitude toward the piece. Resigned hitherto under the royal prohibition, working slowly and carefully to gain ground, he now became impatient, pressing and almost imperious. It is clear to anyone who will reflect, that on the day when Louis XVI permitted at the insistence of the Queen, the Comte d'Artois and M. de Vaudreuil to the representation at Grennevillier, he placed himself where he would be unable long to resist public curiosity, carried now to the heights by that very representation, of which everyone spoke, and by the address of Beaumarchais." It was not, however, until March, 1784, that the desired permission was given.

JOHN JAY

"The picture of that representation of *Le Mariage de Figaro*," says Loménie, "is in all the chronicles of the times, it is the best remembered scene of the eighteenth century. All Paris from earliest morning, pressed the doors of the Théâtre-Français; the greatest ladies dining in the boxes of the actresses so as to be sure of their places — the guards dispersed, the doors broken down, the iron railings giving way before the crowd of assailants. When the curtain rose upon the scene, the finest reunion of talent which the Théâtre-Français had ever possessed was there with but one thought, to bring out to the best advantage a comedy, flashing with *esprit*, carrying one away in its movement and audacity, which if it shocks some of the boxes, enchants, stirs, enflames and electrifies the parterre."

And what is this play that roused such wild enthusiasm a century and more ago, and which to-day, although its political significance has long vanished, would still give its author, had he done nothing but create its characters, a right to a place among the immortals?

"The *Mariage de Figaro*," to quote his own words, "was the most trivial of intrigues:

"A great Spanish nobleman, in love with a young girl whom he wishes to seduce, and the efforts of that same girl and of him to whom she is engaged, and of the wife of the nobleman united to outwit his designs—and he an absolute master whose rank, fortune and prodigality render all powerful its accomplishment—that and nothing more."

The characters are those in the main of the *Barbier*: the Comte Almaviva, the Comtesse Rosine, and the valet Figaro, are old friends. But there are new ones, the page Cherubim, and Suzanne, lady's maid to the Comtesse—"Always laughing, tender, full of gaiety, of *esprit*, of love and delicious!—but good."

"Like the *Barbier*," says Lintilhac, "it is here a question of marriage, but it is the valet this time who is to marry and the obstacles which retard this desired *dénouement* arise, not from the jealousy of a guardian, or the resistance of a father but from the covetousness of a young libertine master.... It is the master who is outwitted, the valet and his fiancée who triumph, and in this *dénouement* lies the whole secret of the wild enthusiasm with which the piece was greeted. Right here lies the Revolution."

But the master is as truly painted in the play as the other characters. "The Comte Almaviva," says Imbert de Saint Amand, "is the old régime, Figaro is the new society. Almaviva is corrupt, but he is always *comme il faut*. Even in his anger he remains the man of good society; no doubt his faults are great; he is a libertine from ennui, jealous from vanity, but he is not odious, not ridiculous."

But to return to Lintilhac: "We may see that Figaro, by the aid of two clever women and his own *esprit* has the opportunity to interest the public and to bring all to a happy ending.

"'Be on your guard that day, M. Figaro! First put the clocks in advance so as to be a little surer of marrying. Get rid of Marceline who wants to marry you herself—take all the money and the presents, let the count have his way, in little things; drub Basil roundly,... (Act I, Scene II). And let us finish the programme which the fat doctor interrupts,—giving yourself full rein, invective politics, graft and those who live by it; ridicule censorship, and the law, as well as those who abuse both—banter privileges and the privileged and all that attaches itself to either, in a word—open the way for the men of genius who are preparing there below in the obscure crowd, and who wish to emerge.

"But the time to laugh, *la folle journée* commences. *Quel imbroglio!* Twenty times everything seems finished, and suddenly, an unexpected incident, but always arising out of the situation, throws forward in rapid movement that brilliant group of personages. They seek, they evade one another, group themselves in tableaux turn by turn, animated and gracious, laughing or grotesque....

"And the new song to the old music! And the scene which a moment ago framed these charming groups, suddenly fills with the noise of the crowd and the whole village which sings. *Quel crescendo* of gaiety!...

"Take the most ingenious comedy of Lope de Vega, or Calderon, add the gaiety of Regnard, the comique of George Dandin, the amusing of Vadé, and one will scarcely have in imagination the equivalent of the scene on the night which terminates the *Mariage de Figaro*."

And his faithful friend Gudin says of it: "In this piece the parterre applauded not only scenes founded upon true *comique*—that of situations, new characters, like Cherubim and Bridoison—but also the courageous man who dared undertake to combat by ridicule the libertinage of the great lords, the ignorance of magistrates, the venality of officers and the unbecoming way of pleading of lawyers.

"Beaumarchais might perhaps consider himself more authorized in this than anyone else since he had been calumniated so outrageously by great lords, and injured by the insolent pleadings of lawyers, and *blâmé* by bad judges.... Let us dare to say what is true, that since Molière no author had better understood the human heart, or better painted the manners of his time."

And his latest critic, Lintilhac, a hundred years after Gudin, corroborates his judgment. "By the creation of Figaro, Beaumarchais is the first comic French author after Molière, the incomparable painter of character."

Of the famous monologue of the piece, Gudin says, "I remember that when the author composed it in a moment of enthusiasm, he was alarmed himself at its extent. We examined it together; I regarded it with severe attention. Everything seemed to me in its place; not a word could be omitted without regretting it. Every phrase had a moral or a useful object proper to cause the spectator to reflect either on human nature or on the abuses of society."

Of its moral significance Beaumarchais has commented in his preface to the play: "An author has but one duty; to correct men in making them see themselves as they are, whether he moralizes in laughing or weeps in moralizing."

And let us now close this brief summary of the famous play by the description given by Imbert de Saint-Amand in *"La fin de l'ancien Régime."*

"Beaumarchais, that marvelous wit, was scarcely aware perhaps of the weight of his attacks and of the gravity of the piece. He did not desire the fall of the throne any more than the overturning of the altar, at heart he was monarchic.... The first representation was given April 27, 1784, by the Comédie Française.... The success went to the stars. Beaumarchais himself could not help crying out, 'There is something more astounding than my piece, it is its success.' ... Actors and actresses surpassed themselves. Every word told. Each bit of satire was welcomed by acclamations and bravos without end. The public recognized itself in the portrait of

CHAPTER XXIII 129

Figaro. 'Never angry, always gay, giving over the present to joy and not worrying about the future any more than the past,—lively, generous, *generous!*'

"'Like a robber,' says Bartolo.

"'Like a lord,' replies Marceline.

"What joy for all that assembly, his definition of a courtier:

"Figaro—'I was born to be a courtier.'

"Suzanne—'hey say it is a very difficult business.'

"Figaro—'Receive, take, ask, that is the secret in three words.'

"What joyous laughter at the reflection, very true, by the way:

"Le Comte—'The domestics here take longer to dress than their masters.'

"Figaro—'That is because they have no valets to help them.'

"What an excellent remark upon the chances for functionaries:

"Le Comte—'With character and intelligence you may one day be promoted in office.'

"Figaro—'Intelligence will advance me? Monsieur is making sport of mine—to be mediocre and cringing, one can arrive at anything.'

"And after this very subtle observation, what a picture of diplomacy:

"'Pretend to be ignorant of what everyone knows, and to know what others do not know, seem to understand what nobody comprehends, not to hear what all hear, and most of all appear able to do the impossible. Seem profound when one is only empty; spread spies, pension traitors, loosen seals, and intercept letters; magnify the poverty of the methods by the importance of the object,—that's politics, or I'm a dead man.'

"The diplomats who were in the audience were transported with pleasure in hearing their business so exactly judged.

"The great ladies went into ecstacies at the remark of Suzanne to the countess: 'I have noticed how a knowledge of the world gives an ease to ladies well brought up, so they can lie without showing it.'

"They applauded with enthusiasm that democratic observation, but profoundly true of this same Suzanne: 'Do you think women of my position have hysterics? That is a malady which is only to be found in the boudoir.'

"The great lords, always surrounded with flatterers and parasites, applauded with transport that phrase of Figaro to Basil: 'Are you a prince that you must be servilely flattered? Suffer the truth, wretch, since you cannot pay a liar.'

"But the moment when the enthusiasm became delirium, frenzy—the moment when the dukes and peers, the ministers, the *cordons rouges*, the *cordons bleus*—were transported to the seventh heaven of acclaim, was when the daring *Barbier* transformed himself into a tribune and said to all of them in the monologue under the chestnut tree:

"'Because you are a great lord you believe yourself a great genius. Rank, fortune, position, all that make you so proud! What have you done to deserve so many gifts? You have taken the trouble to be born, nothing else!'

"The functionaries charged with the censure were particularly enchanted with this phrase of the same monologue: 'On condition that I do not speak in my writings, either of authority, or religion, or politics, or morals, or of people in position, or bodies in favor, or anyone who holds to anything, I am allowed to write, to print everything freely under the inspection of two or three censors.'

"The ministers charged to fill public functions found the following phrase very just: 'They thought of me for a position, but by ill luck I was suited to it; they needed a calculator, it was a dancer who received it.'"

"The *Mariage de Figaro*" says Loménie, "was presented sixty-eight times consecutively, something unheard of in that day. The receipts for the first presentation amounted to 6,511 livres, that of the sixty-eighth was 5,483. During eight months, from the 27th of April, 1784, to the 10th of January, 1785, the piece had brought to the Comédie Française (not counting the fiftieth presentation which at Beaumarchais's request had been given for the benefit of the poor) a gross sum of 347,197 livres, which left when all expenses were deducted, a net profit to the Comedians of 293,755 livres, except the part of the author which was valued at 41,499 livres....

"This sum the author of the *Mariage de Figaro*, as if to sanctify the piece, consecrated to works of charity.

"'I propose,' he wrote in the *Journal de Paris*, the 12th of August, 1784, '*un institut de bienfaisance*, to which any woman recognized as needy and inscribed in her parish, can come, her infant in her arms and with her certificate from the parish priest, say to us, "I am a mother and a wet nurse, I gain twenty sous a day, my infant makes me lose twelve." Let us give her nine livres a month in charity.... So if the comedians have gained two hundred thousand francs from my Figaro, my nursing mothers will have twenty-eight thousand which with the thirty thousand of my friends, will produce a whole regiment of *marmots* stuffed with maternal milk.'"

"This institute," continues Loménie, "of *les pauvres mères nourrices*, encountered obstacles at Paris which prevented its establishment in that city; but since the idea was good it did not remain fruitless. The Archbishop of Lyon, M. de Montazet, adopted it. He accepted the help and money of Beaumarchais, and the *Institut de bienfaisance maternelle*, if I am not mistaken still in existence in Lyon, was the outcome of the *Mariage de Figaro*. Beaumarchais was one of its most constant protectors and in 1790 he sent six thousand francs to it and received in return the following letter signed by three of the most respectable and important inhabitants of Lyon:

"'Lyon, the 11th of April, 1790.

"'Monsieur:

"'To speak to you of the success of *l'Institut de bienfaisance maternelle*, is to entertain you in regard to your own work. The idea of it is yours, therefore the plan

CHAPTER XXIII 131

of the work belongs to you. You have aided it with your generous gifts and more than two hundred children saved to the country, already owe their lives to you. We consider ourselves happy to have contributed to it and our gratitude will always equal the respectful sentiments with which we are Monsieur, etc., *Les administrateurs de l'Institut de bienfaisance maternelle.*

"'Palerne de Sacy, Chapp et Tabareau.'"

It was jealousy, Gudin tells us, that prevented the establishment of the institute at Paris. A storm of protest arose from his enemies on every hand.

"It is not enough," they wrote, "to have gained at the bar the crown of Cicero and Parru; to have received at the theater, from the hands of Thalie, the laurels of Molière, he must needs add to the just applause with which he is greeted, the cries of joy and benediction of the unfortunate!... From this feeble stream of money will flow rivers of milk and crowds of vigorous infants." An engraving was circulated showing Figaro helping mothers and opening the prison doors of poor debtors....

Gudin says: "The design made known, redoubled the solicitation of the unfortunates addressed to him as well as the insults which the envious poured upon him. He scarcely could open a letter which did not contain either a demand for charity if it was signed, or a series of invectives if it were anonymous."

One of these letters contained a curious request, not for money, as was usually the case, but asking that the author of the *Mariage de Figaro*, send the applicant a ticket to his play. "Misfortune," he wrote, "has driven me to despair, but before ending my life I desire once more to indulge in unrestrained laughter."

With characteristic generosity, Beaumarchais sent at once a message, to inquire into the cause of the young man's misfortune and not only gave him the desired ticket but restored hope to his distressed mind, found a position for him and warmed him back to a desire for life.

"But thus," Gudin tells us, "while with his wife, his daughter, his sisters, and a few friends, he was receiving the applause of the people and the benedictions of the fathers of families—a frightful outrage and one without motive was inflicted upon him by authority.

"I was supping with him; we were at the table when the commissioner Chenu was announced and asked to speak privately with Beaumarchais. They passed into an adjoining room.

"We knew that the commissioner was his friend, still the conference made us uneasy. At length they came out together. Beaumarchais embraced us, as he said he would be obliged to go out and perhaps to pass the night away from home. He begged us not to be uneasy and that the next day we should be informed as to the cause of his going.

"These words, far from calming, troubled us. We could not doubt that he had been arrested, but why? Where would they take him? Perhaps to the Bastille?...

"Not to the Bastille, nor to Vincennes, but to St. Lazare, a prison house of correction for delinquent youths, he, a man of mature age, of the constancy, of the fortune of M. de Beaumarchais, treated as a depraved adolescent! It was a cowardly outrage.

"His enemies were charmed to see him thus humiliated. The consternation was general. Lafayette, the Prince de Nassau-Siegen, and other noblemen appealed instantly in his favor. At the end of five days he was liberated....

"I went with his wife and daughter and the Commissioner Chenu to bring him the news of his release. His first reaction was to refuse liberty.

"'I have done nothing to merit having lost it,' he said, 'I shall not go from here until judged and justified....'

"If he had not been husband and father, his obstinacy would no doubt have carried him to the point of demanding justice of the king against the king himself ... but he could not permit himself to pierce the hearts of his wife and daughter by condemning them to eternal tears in the vain hope of tearing from power the avowal of an injustice....

"Princes, Marshals of France, persons of every rank had inscribed their names at his door during his detention and came to felicitate him on his return...."

And what was the cause that had operated to bring about this sudden outburst of power directed against the author of the *Mariage de Figaro*?

It was this. In a dispute carried on with vigor in the pages of *le Journal de Paris*, between Beaumarchais and certain anonymous attacks directed against him, the former had made use of the expression, "After having been forced to conquer *lions* and *tigers* to have my comedy played...."

"*Lions* and *tigers*!" Evidently the daring man meant the King and Queen of France! The news was brought at once to the royal presence. Louis XVI, already annoyed beyond measure at the success of the play, to the performance of which he had been forced to consent in spite of himself, only needed some pretext to vent his displeasure, "so without rising from the card table at which he was seated," says Loménie, "he wrote, if we may credit the authority of the author of *Souvenirs d'un Sexagénaire*, M. Arnault, ... upon the back of a seven of spades, in pencil, the order for the immediate arrest of Beaumarchais and joining insult to rigor, something which no sovereign is permitted to use, he ordered him conducted, not to an ordinary prison, but one ridiculous and shameful for a man of his years, to Saint-Lazare, where depraved adolescents were detained.

"To treat as a young good-for-nothing, a man of his age and celebrity, a man to whom confidential missions were entrusted, who carried the secrets of state, who was charged with the most important operations, and whose talents were a powerful attraction to the public and to the aristocracy, was not only a gross injustice, it was a most serious fault, because it became manifest to everyone how pernicious the influence of uncontrolled power might become even in the hands of the best prince. This arbitrary act is the only one of its kind that can be held as a reproach to Louis XVI....

"The next day, when the motive was demanded for that incarceration, the government said nothing, as it had nothing to say, for it would have been difficult to make anyone believe that Beaumarchais intended to compare Louis XVI to a *tiger*. The public became uneasy and began to murmur, and the day after to murmur loudly."

"Every one," says Arnault, "felt himself menaced, not only in his liberty but in his reputation." The fourth day there was a general movement of indignation.... The fifth day Beaumarchais was turned out of prison almost in spite of himself ... and Loménie continues:

"A few days' reflection had made the king realize that he could not decently admit the intention given to the author, and coming back to the sentiments of justice and goodness so natural to him, he almost begged Beaumarchais to come out of prison, and set about in every way to make up to him for the wrong done him. Grimm affirms that nearly all the ministers were present at the first performance of the play after his release, which was made the most brilliant possible, when they had the slight unpleasantness of hearing this passage of the famous monologue applauded with fervent energy: 'Not being able to debase the spirit, they take revenge in abuse.'"

Louis XVI, very soon after this, hastened to make amends in the noblest manner and the one most worthy of a sovereign who felt that he had done wrong. "*Le Barbier de Séville*," says Grimm, "was given at the little theater of the Trianon, and the very distinguished favor was accorded the author to be present at the performance."

In the chapter on the *Barbier* we have spoken already of this striking scene, where the queen herself, the Comte d'Artois, M. de Vaudreuil, etc., were the actors. There is one more line to this touching picture which we have from the pen of Gudin.

"A zealous partisan of royalty, after making himself trusted by those in power and in the guise of a Sans-culotte, had penetrated to the presence of the unhappy queen, then prisoner in the Temple. He was able to speak to her and asked if there were anyone of whom she could think who might help her, and he suggested Beaumarchais. The queen's countenance instantly fell.

"'Alas,' she said, 'he now has it in his power to avenge himself for the insult once offered him.'" And Gudin adds, "She did not know the heart of Beaumarchais or that if it had been possible, now that she was in trouble, he would have come to her relief with far more alacrity than in the hey day of her power."

But the storm now gathering, that was to sweep the mighty from their seats, was destined also to vent its fury upon the man of the people whose riches and honors long had been the objects of their jealous rage. Twice he owed his safety to the poor whom he had assisted, but in the general *débâcle* which followed there was no opportunity for his wit or his ingenuity to save him; the author of the *Mariage de Figaro* and the *Barbier* was forced himself to bend before the storm.

D'ESTAING

CHAPTER XXIV

> *"In my feeble childhood I was always astonished to see that the cheval de bronze had its foot in the air, but never advanced.... Sad emblem of my affairs, which like this image seem always to march, but which have no movement."*
>
> Beaumarchais to Ramel, Minister of Finance.

The Marine of Beaumarchais—Success of His Business Undertakings—His Wealth—Ringing Plea of Self-Justification in the Cause of America, Addressed to the Commune of Paris, 1789—The Beautiful House Which He Built in Paris—His Liberality—His Friends—His Home Life—Madame de Beaumarchais—His Daughter, Eugénie.

SINCE the official declaration made by the French Government to the Court of London, recognizing the independence of the United States, England had considered that war had been declared, and on June 18, 1778, she struck the first blow.

"Beaumarchais," says Loménie, "disposed himself to make war as well as to carry on commerce. See him now demanding sailors from the Minister of the Navy, M. de Sartine, for the service of his great vessel, *le fier Roderigue*!

"'Paris, the 12th of December, 1778.

"'Monsieur:

"'If I presented myself to-day before you, and if I had the honor to propose to you to construct and arm a vessel of this importance, as one able to take the place of a vessel of the King, wherever I should send it, do you think, Monsieur, that you would refuse cannon and the title of Captain of a battleship to its Commander? How then can it be less precious when all is ready than if it were still to be built?

"'I beg your pardon; but the multiplicity of objects which occupy you may very easily hide from you the importance of my armament, consecrated to the triple employment of encouraging the commerce of France by my example and my success, of promising to provision the islands most in need, and of conducting to the continent of America, in the most stormy times, a French merchant fleet important enough to convince the new states by this effort of the great desire of France to support the new commercial bond that already joins us....

"'It is to your wisdom that I present these serious matters, and I dare say that there are none more worthy of the attention and protection of an enlightened minister such as you.

"'Caron de Beaumarchais.'

"*Le Fier Roderigue,*" continues Loménie, "set sail, with her sixty cannon, convoying ten merchantmen. At the Isle of Granada it encountered the fleet of the Admiral d'Estaing, which prepared to give battle to that of the English Admiral Biron. Sighting the beautiful vessel of Beaumarchais passing in the distance, the admiral made a sign for it to come. Seeing that it belonged to His Majesty, Caron de Beaumarchais, he assigned it to its post of battle without the authorization of its proprietor, allowing the unfortunate merchantmen which this vessel was protecting to go on at the mercy of the seas and of the English. *Le Fier Roderigue* resigned itself bravely to its fate, and took a glorious part in the Battle of Granada and contributed its part to making the English Admiral retire, but its captain was killed and it was riddled with bullets. The evening of the combat the Comte d'Estaing, feeling the need of consoling Beaumarchais, wrote to him a letter, which he sent through the Minister of the Navy, the like of which is not often found in the archives of a dramatic poet:

"'On board the Languedoc, the 12th of July, 1779.

"'I have only the time to write you that *le Fier Roderigue* has held her post in line, and contributed to the success of the arms of the king. You will pardon me all the more readily for having used her, since your interests will not suffer from it, be sure of that. The brave M. de Montaut unfortunately was killed. I will urge the minister without ceasing for the favor of the state, and I hope you will aid me in soliciting that which your navy has very justly merited.

"'I have the honor to be, with all the sentiments which you have so well known how to inspire, Monsieur, your very humble and obedient servant,

"'Estaing.'

"The minister hastened to send the letter to Beaumarchais, who replied as follows:

"'Paris, September 7, 1779.

"'Monsieur:

"'I thank you for having sent me the letter of the Comte d'Estaing. It is noble of him, in the moment of his triumph, to have thought that a word from his hand would be very agreeable to me.... Whatever may happen for my affairs, my poor friend Montaut died on the bed of honor, and I feel the joy of a child to know that my vessel has contributed to take from the English the most fertile of their possessions....

"'You know my tender and respectful devotion,

"'Beaumarchais.'

"However, the joy of the patriot," continued Loménie, "was somewhat mitigated by the distress of the merchant. The report of the captain, second in command of the *Fier Roderigue*, arrived at the same time, and though it contributed equally to the glory of Beaumarchais, it was very disastrous from the point of view of his coffer. He, therefore, addressed a vigorous appeal to the King, asking for an indemnity which would save him from ruin." That the request was subsequently granted, we may judge from the following extract from a letter to Necker, written a little more than a year after the date of the battle, and given by Gudin:

"Paris, July 18th, 1780.

"You have rendered, Monsieur, an act of justice in my regard, and you have done it with grace, which has touched me more than the thing itself. I thank you for it; but I owe you more important thanks upon the indemnity, which the King has been so good as to offer me for the enormous losses which the campaign with d'Estaing has caused me."

Loménie asserts that the indemnity had been fixed at 2,000,000 francs, and was to be paid in installments, the last coming to him in 1785.

But to return to the American Congress. After long debates a reversal of parties had placed at the head of that body the honorable John Jay, who hastened to address Beaumarchais with the first letter which came to him from Congress, although his earliest shipment of supplies had been made almost two years previously:

"By express order of Congress, sitting in Philadelphia, to M. de Beaumarchais.

"January 15, 1779.

"Sir:

"The Congress of the United States of America, recognizing the great efforts which you have made in their favor, presents to you its thanks, and the assurance of its esteem. It laments the disappointments which you have suffered in the support of these States. Disastrous circumstances have prevented the execution of its desires; but it will take the promptest measures to acquit itself of the debt which it has contracted towards you. The generous sentiments and the breadth of view, which alone could dictate a conduct such as yours, are the eulogy of your actions, and the ornament of your character. While, by your rare talents, you have rendered yourself useful to your prince, you have gained the esteem of this young Republic and merited the applause of the New World.

"John Jay, President."

This beautiful expression of the best feeling in the States must have been soothing to the heart of Beaumarchais. That he understood the attitude of America and knew very well the complexity of the situation in which the young republic found itself involved, may be judged from the following extract from his *Mémoire justicative à la cour de Londres,* printed in the first collection of his works and written in 1779. He says:

"In truth, my ardent zeal for my new friends might well have been a little wounded at the cold reception which was made to brave men whom I had myself brought to expatriate themselves for the service. My pains, my work, and my advances were immense in this respect. But I am afflicted only for our unhappy officers, because even in the very refusal of the Americans, I don't know what exultation, what republican pride attracted my heart, and showed me a people so ardent to conquer their liberty, that they feared to diminish the glory of success in allowing strangers to divide with them the perils. My soul thus is composed; in the greatest evils it searches with care, and consoles itself with the little good which it encounters. And so, while my efforts had so little fruit in America ... sustained by my pride, I disdained to defend myself, leaving the evil-minded to their proper channel.

"The idle of Paris envied my happiness, and were jealous of me as a favorite of fortune and of power; and I, sad plaything of events, alone, deprived of rest, lost for society, exhausted by insomnia and troubles, *tour à tour* exposed to the suspicions, the ingratitude, anxieties, to the reproaches of France, England and America; working day and night and running to my goal by constant effort across a thorny land—I exhausted myself with fatigue and advanced little. I felt my courage revived when I thought that a great people would soon offer a sweet and free retreat to all the persecuted of Europe; that my fatherland would be revenged for the humiliation to which it had been subjected by the treaty of 1763; in a word, that the sea would become open to all commercial nations; I was supported by the hope that a new system of politics would open in Europe."

But notwithstanding all his difficulties and losses, the affairs of Beaumarchais were advancing steadily. His merchant fleet, after the Treaty of Paris, signed in September, 1783, was no longer subject to the risks of war, and soon began to bring him in vast returns. But as late as March of this same year, we find him writing to Vergennes, in a letter quoted by Gaillardet:

"The taking of my two vessels cost me more than 800,000 livres, and since the publicity of my losses I have been drawn upon, through fear, for a similar sum. Remittances have come to me from America, and now unfortunately their payment is suspended. I have two new vessels at Nantes, one of 12,000 tons, which I destined for China, and which I am now unable to sell.

"I have 80,000 livres worth of bales of merchandise on the *Aigle*, destined for Congress, and the *Aigle* has been taken. A sudden inundation, which happened at Morlaige, has submerged two warehouses where I had 1,000,000 pounds of tea. The whole is damaged to-day.

"Day before yesterday, at the instant of payment, the exchange agent of Girard by his fraudulent bankruptcy carried off near 30,000 livres.

"Two vessels must be sent to the Chesapeake before the middle of May if I am not to lose all the miserable remains of the tobacco of my stores in Virginia, the main part of which was burned by the English, because for four years *le Fier Roderigue* has been detained at Rochefort, where it has at last decayed. This is the most trying time of my life; and you know M. le Comte that for three years I have had over 200,000 livres in disuse, because of the enormous mass of parchments which M. de Maurepas ordered me secretly to buy, wherever I found them. I shall perish if M. de Fleury does not promptly arrange with you to throw me the 'on account' which I demand, as one throws a cable to him whom the current carries away. I always have served my country well, and I will serve it still without recompense; I wish none. But in the name of Heaven, of the King, of compassion and of justice, prevent me from perishing or from hiding shamefully in a foreign country the little courage and talent which I always have sought to render useful to my country and to my King. What I ask is of the most rigorous equity and I will receive it as a favor.

"I present to you the homages of him who has not slept for two months, but who is none the less, with the most respectful devotion, M. le Comte, your very humble and very obedient servitor,

"Caron de Beaumarchais."

But let us now turn from this gloomy picture and cast a glance at the home life of this man so buffeted before the world.

Bonneville de Marsangy, in his life of Madame de Beaumarchais has drawn the picture for us. He says:

"Beaumarchais, in consequence of the noise which continued to be made about his name, was none the less one of the personages the most sought after of the capital. Whatever he says about it, the fact is that he lived in great style. His stables contained as many as ten horses. He kept open table; strangers of distinction, desirous of knowing the popular author of so many celebrated works, solicited the honor of being presented to him. He received men of distinction in politics, in letters and arts, and women the most sought after, in the midst of whom the mistress of the house shone in the first rank by her *esprit*, her education, and her charms.... Nearly every evening in the Hotel Boulevard St. Antonie, there was talking, music, playing, although the master never took part in play. His *esprit* was equally free, equally alert, his fancy inexhaustible. It is there he loved to read his new productions, and he excelled at that. Arnault recounts one of these literary reunions at which he assisted, 'in a great circular salon, partly ornamented with mirrors, partly with landscapes of vast dimensions, and half of which was occupied by seats for placing the auditors. Upon an estrade, furnished with a desk, stood the armchair of the reader. There, as in a theatre, Beaumarchais read, or rather played his dramas; because it is to play, if one delivers a piece in as many different inflexions of the voice as there are different personages in the action; because it is to play if one gives to each one of the personages the pantomime which should characterize him.'" (Arnault, *Souvenirs d'un sexagénaire*, Vol. IV.)

And Gudin adds another touch to the portrait of this many-sided man; after speaking of the loss of his mother, dying in her eighty-third year, he said:

"Beaumarchais came at once to see me, offered me all the consolations of friendship, and reclaimed the promise which we had given one another long ago, to unite the rest of the days which nature reserved to us.

"It is thus that I found in the family of my friend all those attentions which could sweeten the irreparable loss of the tenderest mother and one whom I had quitted almost never."

THE BASTILLE

In 1787 Beaumarchais had accumulated a sufficient fortune to contemplate the building of a superb residence, for which he already had bought the land in that section of the City of Paris now occupied by the Boulevard which bears his name. It was directly opposite the Bastille, and was not yet completed on the memorable 14th of July, 1789, when the ancient fortress was destroyed. This residence cost the owner one million six hundred and sixty-three thousand francs. *"Une folie,"* Napoleon called it. When in 1818, the government bought the property so as to make way for the new boulevard, they paid the heirs of Beaumarchais only five hundred thousand francs. As an investment, therefore, it was far from successful; but as a residence, it was, while it lasted, one of the sights of the city, and was regarded as such. It was the very last word in elegance and comfort, and rivaled the most sumptuous palaces of the capital. In the beginning, it was always open to the public, but so vast became the horde of visitors, that very soon entrance was obtainable only by tickets (though these were never refused to anyone who asked politely for them).

Although the storm of the Revolution was gathering already, its shadow had not yet fallen upon Beaumarchais, who did not foresee either its fury or the extent of the devastation it was to carry in its train.

After the fall of the Bastille he had been appointed by the *Maire* of Paris to superintend the demolition of the structure so as to prevent damage to buildings in the neighborhood. Soon after he was named member of the Municipal Council, but, says Loménie, "denunciations soon began to rain upon him. All the adversaries of his numerous lawsuits and all those whom his riches irritated denounced him to the fury of the masses, as one who upheld authority, or who was hoarding wheat or arms. His house, situated at the very entrance to that terrible suburb, the center of the mob, presented itself as a sort of insolent provocation, which naturally called for the visits of the people." To rid himself of these dangerous visits became his constant preoccupation; first demanding official visits, then placarding about him the results of these visits, stating that nothing suspicious had been found in his possession, again distributing about him all the money possible, and suggesting to the municipality all sorts of charitable institutions, because "disorder and misery always march in company." Among the accusations persistently made against him was that he had enriched himself at the expense of the American people, and that he had sent them arms and munitions for which he charged them a hundred times their value. Stung to the quick by the falsehood of these accusations, coming as they did from his own countrymen, he made a ringing protest of self-defense to the commune of Paris in September, 1789, in which he said:

"You condemn me to speak well of myself by speaking so ill of me.... Attacked by furious enemies, I have gained, perhaps with too much brilliancy, all the lawsuits undertaken against me, because I never have brought an action against anyone, although for the greatest benefits I have received almost universally, I dare say it, unheard of and constant ingratitude....

"Since I have been attacked upon this point I am going to state before you all the unheard of labors, which a single man was able to accomplish in that great work. Frenchmen, you who pride yourselves to have drawn the desire and ardor of your liberty from the example of the Americans, learn that that nation owes me very largely her own. It is time that I should say it in the face of the universe, and if anyone pretends to contest what I say, let him rise and name himself; my proofs will reply to the imputations which I denounce....

"These accusations, as vague as despicable, relate to the Americans whom I served so generously; I, who would be reduced to the alms which I scatter, had not noble foreigners, taken in a free country, associated me with the gains of a vast commerce, while I associated them to my constant losses with America! I, who dared form all the plans of help necessary to that people, and offered them to our ministers; I, who dared blame their indecision, their weakness, and so loudly reproach them with it, in my proud reply to the English manifest by Gibbon; I, who dared promise a success which was very far from being generally admitted....

"All that I could obtain after a great deal of trouble ... was to be allowed to proceed on my own responsibility without the assistance of the government in any way, on condition of being stopped if the English made the least complaints, and of being punished if they produced proofs—which put so many hindrances in the way of my maritime operations, that to help the Americans, I was obliged to mask and to disguise my works in the interior; the expeditions, the ships, the manufactures of the contractors, and even to the reason of trade, which was a mask like the rest.

"Shall I say it, Frenchmen? The King alone had courage, and as for me I worked for his glory, wishing to make him the prop of a proud people who burned to be free; because I had an immense debt to fulfil towards that good king.... Yes, the King, Louis XVI, who assured to the Americans their liberty, who gives you yours, Frenchmen, gave back to me also my estate. Let his name be honored in all the centuries. Then, leaving aside the labors which I am ready to expose in a work where I will prove that I sent at my risks and perils, whatever could be had of the best in France, in munitions, arms, clothing, etc., to the insurgents who needed everything, on credit, at the cost price, leaving them masters to fix the commission which they would one day pay to their friend (for so they called me); and that after twelve years, I am still not paid. I declare that the measures which I am making at this moment before their new federal court, to obtain justice of them,—faithful report which a committee of the Treasury has just given of what is due me, is the last effort of a very generous creditor. But I will publish everything, and the universe shall judge us. Omitting, I say, all the details of my work, of my services towards that people, I will pass to the testimony which was given me by the agent, the minister of America, before he left France. His letter of March 18th, 1778, bears these words: 'After the perplexing and embarrassing scenes you have had to pass through, it must give you the most solid joy to see an armament going out to America.... I again congratulate you on this great and glorious event, to which you have contributed more than any other person.

'Silas Deane.'

"Alas, that was the last of my successes. A minister of the department to whom I showed that letter, alas, though up to that time he had treated me with the greatest kindness, suddenly changed his tone, and his style. I did my best to persuade him that I did not pretend in any way to appropriate to myself that glory, but to leave it entirely to him. The blow had carried, he had read the praise; I was lost in his favor. It was to take from him all idea of my ambition, to avert the storm, that I recommenced to amuse myself with frivolous theatrical plays, while keeping a

CHAPTER XXIV 143

profound silence upon my political actions. But that helped nothing. It is very true that a year later, the general Congress, having received my vivid complaints upon the delay of payment, wrote me the ... letter by the Honorable Mr. John Jay, their president, the 15th of Jan. 1779....

"If it was not money, it was at least gratitude. America, nearer the great services which I had rendered her, was not yet where she disputed her debts, fatiguing me with injustice, to wear out my life, if possible, and succeed in paying nothing. It is also true that the same year, the respectable Mr. Jefferson, to-day their minister in France, then Governor of Virginia, struck by the fearful losses which the depreciation of paper money would inflict upon me, wrote, to my general agent in America, M. de Francy, in these terms:

"'December 17, 1779.

"'Monsieur:

"'I am very much mortified that the depreciation of paper money, of which no one, I think, had the least idea at the time of the contract, passed between the supercargo of the *Fier Roderigue* (war vessel of mine, very richly charged, the cargo of which had been delivered on credit to Virginia, which state owes me still almost the whole, after more than twelve years have passed), and that state has enveloped in the general loss M. de Beaumarchais, who has merited so well of us, and who has excited our greatest veneration by his affection for the true rights of man, his genius, his literary reputation, etc.

Signed, "'Thomas Jefferson.'

"In the work, which I am going to publish, where I will show the proofs of the excellence of all my shipments to that people, after exact inspection which they themselves made, before the departure of my vessels, well attested by their ministers, and the excuses which he made me, of which I have all the originals, the surprise will be to see the patience with which I have supported all the invectives of my enemies. But it would have been to disgrace *the greatest act of my life*, the honorable part which I had in the liberty of America, if I had mingled it with the discussions of a vile law suit.... It was my scorn, my indignation, which made me keep silence. It is broken; I will hold my tongue no more on that great object, *the glory of my entire life*. They say that my sordid avarice has been the cause of the misfortunes of the American people. *My* avarice, mine, whose life is only a circle of generosity, of benevolence. I will not cease to prove it, since their savage libels have rendered so many men unjust. Not a single being, who went at that time from Europe to America, without having pecuniary obligations to me, of which nearly all are due me still; and no Frenchman has suffered in that country whom I have not aided with my purse. I invoke a witness, whom it does you honor to respect, the very valiant general of your troops. Ask him if my services did not hunt out unfortunate Frenchmen in every corner of America.

"Render justice to my good heart, noble Marquis de Lafayette; Your glorious youth, would it not have been ruined without my wise counsel and the advances of my money? You have very well repaid all that was loaned you by my orders; and I say it to your glory, you have added fifty louis more than were due to me, to join that money to the charitable institution which I was founding of the *pauvres mères nourrices*....

"And you, Baron von Steuben, Comtes Pulasky, Bienousky, you, Tronçon, Prudhomme, and a hundred others, who have never acquitted their debts to me, come out of your tombs and speak!

"Fifteen hundred thousand francs at least, of services rendered, fill a portfolio, which probably will never be acquitted by anyone, and more than a thousand unfortunates whose needs I have anticipated are ready to raise their voice in my favor.... The third of my fortune is in the hands of my debtors, and since I have aided the poor of Sainte-Marguerite, four hundred letters at least are on my desk from unfortunates, raising their hands to me.... My heart is torn, but I cannot reply to all.

"September 2, 1789."

But from the accusations of his enemies, and the pleadings of his own cause, let us turn, before worse calamities overtake him, to contemplate anew the charming picture, which the interior of his home presents.

It was in 1791 that he took his family to occupy the splendid new residence which we have just now mentioned. Its mistress Madame de Beaumarchais was a woman of rare intelligence and energy of character; "her physiognomy," says Bonneville, "offered an expression full of vivacity and intelligence. The eye is superb, tempered by long lashes, heightened by the daring arch of the brows; the mouth is admirably well formed; the chin full, the complexion brilliant.... The reputation for beauty of Madame de Beaumarchais was general. The public ratified on all occasions, the praise of her friends. It is traditional in her family that she rarely left her home without being recognized and followed at a distance by a cortège of admirers, drawn not only by the celebrity of the name she bore, but also by the prestige of her bearing. Often, even, she was obliged to gain her carriage to avoid the importunity of the too flattering attentions.

"Beaumarchais, as he confesses perhaps superfluously, was far from being a devotee; still he respected the beliefs of others; he had desired especially that his daughter should be brought up piously. Eugénie was at this moment a pupil at the convent of Bon Secours; her father often went there to visit her. The Superior, who had had proof of the generous and good heart of the father of her pupil, permitted herself to speak of one of the school-mates of Eugénie who was unable to pay the expenses of her education. The author of the *Mariage de Figaro* replied at once in the following delicate manner:

"'July 27, 1790.

"'I send you, Madame, a bill of 200 livres for your unfortunate pupil. This is for the year. I will have the honor of giving to you or to her, in money, the first time I go to the convent, three louis, which will make six francs a month for this year, the same as I give to my daughter; but I conjure you, Madame, that my help does not force or press her vocation. I should be distressed if she were in any way thwarted as to her future. I have not the honor of knowing her; it is the good which you have said of her which determined me. That she remains free, and less

CHAPTER XXIV

unhappy, this is all the thanks I ask; keep the secret for me. I am surrounded with virulent enemies.'

"One cannot," continues Bonneville, "hide oneself more gallantly, to do good.

"The prioress hastened to divulge the secret; and to the rough draft of the letter of Beaumarchais found among his papers, is attached a note in which his young protégée expressed with emotion all her gratitude to her benefactor."

The violences directed against the religious establishments soon forced Beaumarchais to bring his daughter home. It was about this time that we find a letter, addressed by the author of the *Mariage de Figaro*, to the Municipal officers of Paris, begging, with his characteristic energy, that the churches be opened, and more masses be said in the Quartier-Vieille-rue-du-Temple.

"In this letter," says Loménie, "it is the husband, the brother, but especially the father who speaks. The author of the *Mariage de Figaro* adored his only daughter, he had just brought her home from the convent, and if he went himself very little to mass, he was not sorry to have her go for him. It is this side of Beaumarchais, so good, so simple, so jovial, so gay, that makes us love him, and which comes out with special force in a song which he wrote to celebrate the young girl's return under her father's roof. This song has been classed as one of the best of the poetic inspirations of Beaumarchais. The turn *naïf* of the old popular songs is found in it, combined with a graceful mixture of friendliness, finesse and gaiety."

The charm of these verses, which it is impossible to render into English, gave the song a great popularity, and it circulated widely.

In it, there was question of the marriage of Mlle. Eugénie, where the father jestingly says: "My *gentilhomme*, is that all you are?

"Parchment and blazonry will never open my house.

> "*If someone really tender,*
> *Sings thee songs in the air,*
> *Let me hear them*
> *For thy Father sees clear*
> *And I will say if there is reason*
> *That he should enter here.*
>
> "*Should some excellent young man*
> *See heaven in thy eyes,*
> *Say to him 'Beautiful astronomer,*
> *Speak to that good old man,*
> *He is my father, and there is reason*
> *That he should choose his son-in-law.'*
>
> "*If he has some talent*
> *What matters his fortune?*
> *Judge, writer, soldier,*
> *Esprit, virtue, sweet reason —*
> *These are the titles valued here.*"

"The result of all this was that Beaumarchais was deluged," says Loménie, "with the most singular demands in marriage for his daughter. Here it is from a nobleman, but one who makes no point of his blazon, who despises the fortune which he has not, who esteems only virtue, and who aspires to marry Mlle. Eugénie and her dot; there, from a father, perfectly unknown to Beaumarchais, who begs him to keep the daughter for his son, still in college; farther on it is a captain, who has only his sword, but who is worthy of being a Marshal of France. Politely to turn aside this avalanche of virtuous and disinterested suitors, the father of Eugénie wrote a letter which, with slight modifications, serves him for all, and of which the following is a sample:

"Paris, May 21, 1791.

"Although your letter, Monsieur, appears to have its origin in a simple jest, since it is serious and honest, I owe you a reply.

"You have been deceived regarding my daughter. Scarcely fourteen years old, she is far from the time when I will allow her to choose a master, reserving for myself in this only, the right to advise. Perhaps you are quite ignorant of the exact situation. I have only lately taken my daughter from the convent; the joy of her return drew from my indolence a song, which after having been sung at my table, went the rounds. The tone *bonhomme* which I there took, joined to the jest of her future establishment, has made many persons think that I already thought of her settlement.

"But may I be preserved from engaging her before the time when her own heart will give her a consciousness of what it all means, and Monsieur, this will be an affair of years, not of months.

"What the song says jestingly, however, will certainly be my rule to enlighten her young heart. Fortune touches me less than talents and virtue, because I wish her to be happy....

"Beaumarchais."

But the young girl's presence under her father's roof was to be of short duration. Very soon, his anxiety for their safety led him to dispatch his family to Havre. For, says La Harpe,

"His house was placed at the entrance of that terrible faubourg like the Palace of Portici at the foot of Vesuvius.... The eruption of the volcano was as yet only at rare intervals; that of the faubourg was at every moment. It is inconceivable that under the lava always boiling, that house was not engulfed."

So it is here we will leave him to await alone,—except for his faithful Gudin—the coming of the storm, which his own writings had done so much to rouse, but which he neither desired, nor, to the end, comprehended.

HOUSE OF BEAUMARCHAIS

CHAPTER XXV

"I know very well to live is to combat, and perhaps I should be afflicted at this if I did not know that in return to combat is to live."

Caron de Beaumarchais.

"—Often broken-hearted, always consoled by the sublime principle of the compensation of good and evil—which was the ground of his optimism..."

Lintilhac in Beaumarchais et Ses Œuvres.

House of Beaumarchais Searched—The 10th of August—Letter to his Family in Havre—Letter of Eugénie to her Father—Commissioned to Buy Guns for the Government—Goes to Holland as Agent of *Comité de Salut Public*—Declared an Emigré—Confiscation of his Goods—Imprisonment of his Family—The Ninth Thermidor Comes to Save Them—Life During the Terror—Julie again in Evidence—Beaumarchais's Name Erased From List of Emigrés—Returns to France.

EARLY in 1792, Beaumarchais embarked in a new political and commercial operation which, says Loménie, "was destined to embarrass his fortune and to be the torment of his latter days. France was without arms and he undertook to procure them for her. It is difficult to understand that a man sixty years old, rich, fatigued by a most stormy existence, afflicted with increasing deafness, surrounded with enemies, and desirous only of repose should have allowed himself to be induced to attempt to bring into France sixty thousand guns detained in Holland under circumstances which rendered this operation as dangerous as it was difficult."

However, Gudin tells us, "he had only the choice of dangers. To have refused to procure the arms would have marked him for disfavor. He therefore chose the danger of being useful to his country. This resolution exposed him to the risk of being pillaged and assassinated, but in the end it saved his life.... During the days of frenzy which preceded the overthrowing of the throne, the most hostile menaces sounded around his house."

The populace insisted that he had stored it with wheat and guns. In vain Beaumarchais protested, in vain he placarded the walls of his garden with official state-

CHAPTER XXV

ments proving that the house had been searched and that nothing had been found. The fury of the mob was not to to be appeased. Finally on the 8th of August, the threatenings became so ominous that he was persuaded to spend the night in the home of a friend, who had sought safety outside Paris, leaving an old domestic alone in charge. Beaumarchais says:

"At midnight the valet, frightened, came to the room where I was, 'Monsieur,' he said to me, 'get up, the people are searching for you, they are beating the doors down, someone has turned traitor, the house will be pillaged.' ... The frightened man hid in a closet while the mob searched the house." When morning came, he returned to his own home, around which the threatenings still continued without ceasing.

Gudin says: "He received the most alarming notices, and the day after the imprisonment of the king, August 10th, a great multitude set out in the direction of his house, threatening to break down the iron gates if they were not immediately opened. I and two other persons were with him.

"At first his desire was to open the doors and to speak to the multitude. But persuaded that secret enemies conducted the crowd, and that he would be assassinated before he could open his mouth, we induced him to leave the house by a side entrance.... As we were but four we decided to separate in the hope of deceiving those who sought him....

"Whatever the cause, once admitted and masters of the situation, someone proposed to swear that they would destroy nothing. The populace swore and kept its word. Always extreme, it even swore to hang anyone who stole anything. It visited the whole house, the closets, the granaries, the cellars, and the apartments of the women and my own. They wished to hang my own domestic, who seeing the crowd, ran from room to room with some of my silver hidden in her pocket; they thought she was stealing, and she was forced to call in the other domestics as witnesses. They searched everywhere and found only the gun, hunting case, and sword of the master of the house, these they did not disturb.

"Thirsty from excitement and fatigue, that breathless troop, instead of opening a cask of wine, satisfied itself with water from the fountain. They even left the master's watch hanging at the head of his bed, and other articles of jewelry about the rooms.... A troup conducted by a magistrate would not have been more exact in its perquisition, or more circumspect in its conduct.

"Truth here resembles fable,—something extraordinary always mingled itself with the events which came to Beaumarchais. This conduct of the populace was the fruit of the benefits which he had poured upon the poor of his neighborhood. If he had not been loved, if he had not been dear to his domestics, all his goods would have been dissipated by pillage."

The next day Beaumarchais wrote to his daughter in Havre:

"August 12, 1792.

"... My thoughts turned upon thy mother, and thee and my poor sisters. I said with a sigh, 'My child is safe; my age is advanced; my life is worth very little and this would not accelerate the death by nature but by a few years. But my daughter! Her mother! They are safe? Tears flowed from my eyes. Consoled by this thought I occupied myself with the last term of life, believing it very near. Then, my head hollow through so much contending emotion, I tried to harden myself and to think of nothing. I watched mechanically the men come and go; I said, 'The moment approaches,' but I thought of it as a man exhausted, whose ideas begin to wander, because for four hours I had been standing in this state of violent emotion which changed into one like death. Then feeling faint, I seated myself on a bank and awaited my fate, without being otherwise alarmed."

"When the crowd had retired," says Gudin in his narrative, "Beaumarchais returned and dined in his home, more astonished to find all undisturbed than he would have been to have seen the whole devastated...."

"And so we continued to live alone in that great habitation, occupied in meditating on the misfortunes of the state and sometimes upon those which menaced us....

"On the 23rd of August, upon awakening I perceived armed men in the streets, sentinels at the doors and under the windows. I hastened to the apartment of my friend—I found him surrounded by sinister men occupied in searching his papers and putting his effects under seal. Tranquil in the midst of them, he directed their operations. When they were through, they took him with them and I was left alone in that vast palace, guarded by *sans culottes* whose aspect made me doubt whether they were there to conserve the property, or to give the signal for pillage."

Beaumarchais had been carried off to the *mairie* (police court) "where he defended himself so perfectly," continues Gudin, "that his denouncers were confounded and about to liberate him when Marat denounced him anew.... He was sent to l'Abbaye along with others whose virtues were a title of proscription.

"At the end of a week his name was called. General consternation in the prison.

"'You are called for.'

"'By whom?'

"'M. Manuel. Is he your enemy?'

"'I never saw him.' Beaumarchais went out. All the assembly sat silent.

"'Who is M. Manuel?' demanded Beaumarchais.

"'I am he. I come to save you. Your denouncer, Colmar, is declared culpable—he is in prison—you are free.'...

"Two days later came the September massacres. And thus a second time his life was saved. 'Long afterwards he learned that a woman to whom he had rendered an eminent service had solicited Manuel to obtain the liberty of her benefactor.'" (*Gudin*, p. 430.)

"It would seem natural," says M. de Loménie, "that in such a moment, the author of the *Mariage de Figaro* would consent to set aside the matter of the guns and occupy himself with his own personal safety."

He consented, however, to hide himself during the day outside Paris, but every night he returned on foot by byways and across ploughed fields, to urge the ministers to make good the promises of their predecessors and make it possible for him to obtain the sixty-thousand guns from Holland which he had promised the nation.

"The fact was," says Loménie, "that on the one hand, until those guns were delivered, he remained an object of suspicion to the people, while on the other he believed that the minister Lebrun was trying to exploit the matter to his own credit while leaving to Beaumarchais, if necessary, all the responsibility of failure. This was what rendered him so tenacious, that he tormented even Danton who, by the way, could not help laughing to see a man so badly compromised who should be thinking only of his safety, obstinately returning every night to demand the money which had been promised as a deposit, and to obtain a commission for Holland."

Finally Lebrun consented to give the author of the *Mariage de Figaro* a passport to Holland and promised to have the necessary money ready for him at Havre.

"He set out," says Lintilhac, "on the 22nd of September, 1792, with Gudin, directing himself toward Havre, where, after so many emotions, he wished to press his wife and his daughter in his arms. From there, he passed to England where he was arrested, imprisoned, then set free. As soon as Madame de Beaumarchais knew that her husband was safe, she returned to Paris to be nearer, so as to defend his interests. A noble task which she accomplished at the peril of her life.

"The departure of Beaumarchais, the motive of which remained a secret, emboldened his enemies who renewed their accusations. The 28th of November a second decree was rendered against him as suspected. Immediately seals were placed upon all the houses which he owned in Paris. Madame de Beaumarchais hastened to protest the accusations against her husband and against the placing of the seals. With great difficulty she finally obtained a decree dated February 10, 1793, which accorded to her husband a delay of two months to present his defense and at the same time the immediate removal of the seals. He wrote from London, December 9, 1792, to his family:

"'My poor wife and thou, my dear daughter. I do not know where you are, nor where to write to you, neither by whom to give you news. Still I learn by the gazette that seals have been placed for the third time on my property and that I am decreed, accused for this miserable affair of the guns of Holland.... Be calm, my wife and my sisters. Dry thy tears, my sweet and tender child! they trouble the tranquillity of which thy father has need to enlighten the National Convention upon grave subjects which it is important it should know.'"

Beaumarchais returned immediately to France, drew up a memoir for his justification, secured the removal of the seals at Paris; but the municipality of Strausborg maintained those which it had imposed. Beaumarchais grew impatient, addressed a petition to the minister of the interior who sent a dispatch to the administrator of that department of the Bas-Rhein. Again, the author of the *Mariage de Figaro* is vindicated and absolved.

The troubles of Beaumarchais showed no signs of diminishing either in number or perplexity. In the month of January, 1793, the English government, having joined the coalition against France, was on the point of herself taking possession of the sixty-thousand guns for which Beaumarchais had so long been negotiating.

"He, however," says Loménie, "did not lose his head, having already had wind of the project. At the very time when he was imprisoned in London he had induced an English merchant ... by means of a large commission ... to become the purchaser of those same guns and to maintain them in his name at Tervère as English property, until the real owner could dispose of them. But the fictitious owner could not hold them long, because the English ministers said to him, 'Either you are the real owner or you are not; if you are, we are ready to pay for them; if you are not, we intend to confiscate them.'...

"The English merchant remaining faithful to the engagement with Beaumarchais, resisted; affirmed the guns to be his property, invoked his right to dispose of them as he pleased, and this respect for law which distinguishes the English Government above all other governments, left the question undecided. The guns remained at Tervère under guard of an English battleship." (*Loménie*, Vol. II, p. 424.)

"Things were at this pass when the committee of public safety informed Beaumarchais that he must secure the arms, or else prevent their falling into the hands of the English; failing which his family and goods in default of his person would answer for the success of the operation." And so, early in June, 1793, again he left France on this most difficult mission.

"To enter into all the details of his interminable *tours et détours*, going from Amsterdam to Basle, from Basle to Hamburg, from Hamburg to London ... all which he directed like a very ingenious *intrigue de comédie* ... would be too long. He was able to keep the guns at Tervère and when the moment seemed to him favorable, he supplicated the committee of public safety with loud cries, to order the General Pichegru to come and carry off the guns; but the committee absorbed by a thousand things made no reply.... The only missive he ever received from them was the following, dated, *5 pluviose, An II* (January 26, 1794), written by Robert Lindet, 'You must be quick, do not await events. If you defer too long, your service will not be appreciated. Great returns are necessary and they must be prompt. It is of no use to calculate the difficulties, we consider only results and success.'"

"Not only," continues Loménie, "did the Committee abandon Beaumarchais to himself, but with a thoughtlessness which is another sign of the times, they allowed their agent to be put upon the lists as an *émigré*, which act entailed the confiscation of his property.

"Madame de Beaumarchais went at once to the committee of public safety, explained that her husband was *not* an *émigré*, since he had left the territory of the republic because of an official mission, and provided with a regular passport, and her proof in her hand, she succeeded in having the decree withdrawn and the seals removed from the property. Beaumarchais had at this time taken refuge in Hamburg.

"He found himself," says Loménie, "in the most cruel situation both materially and morally. He knew that the revolutionary tribunal was fixed permanently at

CHAPTER XXV

Paris, that it struck without pity mothers, wives, and daughters of the absent ones, and that the bloody knife never ceased to fall. The unfortunate man was in torture. Eugénie tried to comfort her father in the unconscious tranquillity of a young girl. Every precaution had been taken to hide from her the horrible tragedy which was being enacted about her; she presented a striking contrast with the terrible reality of the times.

"She walked alone and melancholy in the lovely garden, while the dismal car passed along the terrace perhaps. But in her sad dreaming, she did not turn her head; she admired the earliest advances of spring. On March 11th, she wrote to her father,

"'The verdure of our trees is beginning to appear, the leaves develop from day to day, and flowers already beautify thy garden. It would be very lovely, if we could walk here with thee. Thy presence would add a charm to everything which surrounds us. There is no happiness for me but what thou partakest in. We are only happy through thee, oh my tender father!'"

The very next day measures were taken which ended in the annulling of the decree rendered by the *comité de salut public* in which the *comité de sûreté générale*, which had taken its place, once more declared Beaumarchais to be an *émigré*, replaced the seals upon his property, confiscated his revenues and on the 5th of July, 1794, arrested his wife, his two sisters, and his daughter.

They were shut up in the convent of Port-Royal which had been changed into a prison and which, says Loménie, "by an atrocious irony was called *Port-Libre*, where they waited their turn to mount the fatal cart that should conduct them to the guillotine." The ninth *thermidore* came to put an end to these butcheries. Eleven days later, another decree of the *comité de sûreté générale*, again established, gave to the *Citoyennes* Caron their liberty.

During this frightful period of the terror, Beaumarchais, still at Hamburg, deprived of all communication with his family, was a prey to the most terrible mental agony. His correspondence shows that he had moments of the deepest despair when he asked himself if he were not losing his mind.

"Where shall I address thee?" he wrote his wife. "Under what name? What shall I call thee? Who are thy friends? Whom can I consider mine? Ah, without the hope of saving my daughter, the atrocious guillotine would be sweeter to me than my horrible condition."

It was at this period that the following address to the American people was written.

"Americans: Though I have served you with an indefatigable zeal, I have in my life received only bitterness for recompense, and I die your creditor. Permit then in dying that I will to my daughter the debt which you owe me. Perhaps after I am gone, other injustices, from which I cannot defend myself, will rob me of all I possess so nothing will be left for her, and perhaps Providence has ordained by your delay in paying me, that through you she will be spared absolute want. Adopt her as a worthy child of the state. Her mother, equally unfortunate, and my widow, will conduct her to you. Let her be looked upon as the daughter of a citizen! But if after these last efforts, if after all has been said, I must still feel that you will reject my demands—If I am to fear that you will refuse her arbitrators; at last, desperate, ruined in Europe as well as by you, your country being the only one in which I could beg without shame—what would remain for me to do, but to supplicate Heaven to give me the strength to take the voyage to America?

"Arrived in your midst, mind and body weakened, unable to maintain my rights, should I there be forced, my proofs in my hand, to have myself carried to the doors of your National Assembly, and, holding aloft the cap of liberty, with which I helped as much as anyone to adorn your heads—to cry out 'Give an alms to your friend, whose accumulated services have only had this recompense, *date obolum Belisario!'*

"Pierre-Augustin Caron Beaumarchais."

It was precisely to save her daughter, that Madame de Beaumarchais had broken all communication with her husband, retaken her family name and thought only of making herself forgotten.

"The Revolutionary laws," says Gudin, "ordained the divorce of the wives of *émigrés*, under pain of being suspected and of running the risk of death that could not be inflicted upon their husbands. Madame de Beaumarchais, worthy of the courageous man whose hand she had received, went to the Revolutionary Committee and with that firmness which inspired respect and that grace which embellished every action, said, 'Your decrees oblige me to demand a divorce. I obey, although my husband, charged with a commission is not an *émigré* and never had the thought: I attest it and I know his heart. He will justify himself of this accusation, as he has of all the rest, and I shall have the satisfaction of marrying him a second time, according to your new laws.'"

"Such was the effect of his destiny," observes this eighteenth century philosopher, "that he was obliged to renew the knot of his own marriage at the same time that he occupied himself with the marriage of his daughter."

The condition of the family of Beaumarchais when they found themselves once more free, was far from enviable. Their revenues had been seized and their beautiful home was ordered to be sold. Eugénie felt only horror for the place and persuaded her mother to live in a small house. Gudin had gone into the country and Julie, the faithful sister of Beaumarchais, went to live alone with an old servant in the deserted palace of her brother, which was now guarded by agents of the Republic and which bore written upon its walls, "*Propriété nationale.*"

"If, as I hope," says Loménie, "the reader has retained an agreeable impression of Julie, it will be a pleasure perhaps to see again that intelligent, merry, courageous face which neither age, privations, nor dangers had been able to change.

"A picture of the domestic and inner life of three women, once rich, forced to face the difficulties of a fearful epoch will give details of interest to that period which history itself cannot furnish.

"During the time when the head of the household was proscribed, it was Ma-

CHAPTER XXV

dame Beaumarchais, a person of rare merit who joined to all feminine graces a truly virile energy of character, who bore the weight of the situation and while working on one hand to prevent the sale of her husband's property, tried on the other, to have his name erased from the fatal list; and all the time was obliged to provide for her family with what she had been able to save from the wreck of their fortune. On her side Julie guarded the house of her brother, kept her sister-in-law in touch with events at the house, and urged her to resistance in the animated and original tone which characterised her.

"'Morbleu! my child,' she wrote her after the Terror, 'let us quickly get the decree suppressed. Even the fruits, the same as last year, are requisitioned; the cherries being ripe, they are to be picked to-morrow and sold, and the rest as it ripens, and then close the garden to the profane and the gluttons! Isn't it sweet to have lived here alone for six months, and only be allowed to eat the stones of the fruit? And even they are sold with the rest. It is for the birds that I am sorry ... nevertheless, it is a pity that the agency had to interfere this year;... See if thou cannot prevent this brigandage by a firm protest at the agency....

"'And here a pound of veal has been brought me which costs twenty-eight francs, and at even that it is a bargain, for it might sell for thirty. Rage! Fury! Malediction! One cannot even live by ruining oneself and devouring three times one's fortune. How happy those who have gone before! They feel neither the confusion in my head, nor my eye which weeps, nor the flame which devours me, nor my tooth which sharpens itself to eat twenty-eight francs worth of veal; they feel none of these evils.'

"Those twenty-eight francs worth of veal, which Julie consumed with humorous anger, bring us to say a word of the curious state of want which was produced by the constant depreciation of paper money after the Terror. It is still Julie who informs us how people lived at that time; her sister-in-law had just given her four thousand francs in paper money and she returned an account of the use to which she put them that December 1794.

"'When you gave me those four thousand francs, my good friend, my heart beat fast. I thought you suddenly had lost your reason to give me such a fortune; I slipped them quickly into my pocket and spoke of other things, so that you would forget them.

"'Returned home and quick, some wood, some provisions, before the prices go higher! And see Dupont (the old servant) who runs, exhausts herself! And lo, the scales fall from my eyes when I see the result of four thousand, two hundred, and seventy-five francs.

"'One load of wood	1,460 fr.
Nine pounds of candles	900
Four pounds of sugar	400
Three litrons (six qts.), of grain	120
Seven pounds of oil	700

A dozen wicks	60
A bushel and a half potatoes	300
Laundry bill for one month	215
One pound of powder for the hair	70
Three ounces of pomade (that used to be three sous)	50
	—————
	4,275 fr.
Over and above this is the provision for the month, butter, eggs, at 100 francs, as you know, and meat from 25 to 30 francs a pound and all else in proportion	576
Bread, there has been none for two days; we only get it every other day—for the last ten days I have only bought 4 pounds at 45 fr.	180
	—————
	5,022 fr.

"'When I think of this royal expenditure which costs me from eighteen to twenty thousand francs without allowing myself the least luxury, *J'envoie au diable le régime.*'

"Shortly after this the value of paper money decreased still more and the price of commodities increased in alarming proportion. In another letter to her sister-in-law Julie gave the following details:

"'Ten thousand francs which I have scattered in the last two weeks, give me such a fright, seize me with such pity that I no longer know how to count my income. In the last three days, wood has risen from 4,200 francs to 6,500 and all the costs of transporting and piling are in proportion, so that my load of wood has cost me 7,100 francs. Every week it costs from 700 to 800 francs for a *pot-au-feu*, and other meat without counting butter, eggs, and a thousand other details; laundry work has increased so that 8,000 francs are not enough for one month. All this makes me impatient and I solemnly affirm that I have not for two years allowed myself a luxury, or gratified a single whim, or made any other expenditures but for the house; nevertheless the needs I have are urgent enough to make me need potfulls of money.'

"But if the sister of Beaumarchais is at the point of famine, the wife and the daughter are no better off; I see in the correspondence of Madame de Beaumarchais that one of her friends went the rounds of the neighborhood to try to obtain some bread which was becoming rarer than diamonds; 'I am told,' she wrote, the 5th of June 1795, 'that at Briare, flour is to be had, if that is true I will make a bargain with some country man and send it direct to you by the barge which goes from Briare to Paris, but that will greatly increase the cost. Please tell me what you think, while waiting I still hope to get hold of a small loaf somewhere. Oh, if I had the gift of miracles, I would send you, not manna from heaven—but good bread and very white!'

"When Beaumarchais in exile, learned all the deprivations from which his family suffered he learned also that they had sufficient moral courage to support them. Gaiety had not wholly disappeared from that interior which used to be so joyous; even if exposed to starvation, the frightful guillotine no longer operated and one began to breathe more freely."

One of his old friends wrote to him, "See now the soup tureen of the family arrive, that is to say, upon the mahogany table (there is no such thing as a cloth) is a plate of beans, two potatoes, a carafe of wine, with very much water. Thy daughter asks for a white poodle to use as a napkin and clean the plates—but no matter, come, come; if we have nothing to eat we have plenty to laugh about. Come, I tell thee, for thy wife needs a miller since thy *salon* is decorated with a flour mill; while thy Eugénie charms thee upon her piano, thou wilt prepare her breakfast, while thy wife knits thy stockings, and thy future son-in-law turns baker; for here everyone has his trade and that is why our cows are so well guarded.

"It is too droll to see our women, without perruque in the morning, filling each one her occupation, because you must know that each one of us is at their service and because in our *régime*, if there are no masters, there are at least valets. This letter costs thee at least a hundred francs counting the paper, pens, the oil of the lamp, because for economy's sake I came to thy house to write it. We embrace thee with all our hearts."

And his faithful Gudin wrote him, though in much more somber strain, from his retreat in the country: "My most ardent desire, my friend, is to see you again and to press you to my heart; but circumstances are such that I had to leave Paris where I could no longer subsist. I have taken refuge in a little hamlet fifty miles away, where there are thirteen peasant cabins. The house which I inhabit was a tiny priory, occupied once by a single monk." And after a very long and profoundly pessimistic discourse upon the sad condition of affairs which he likens to the barbarity which formerly engulfed Greece and Egypt and Assyria, Sicily, and Italy, he terminates thus:

"Adieu my good friend, I would have wished to have talked to you of yourself, of your family, of those whom you love, the regrets which we feel to meet no more together. Our hearts like your own, are crushed with sorrow.... I embrace you and sigh for the happy moment that will unite us.

"Gudin."

Now that his anxieties for his family were allayed, Beaumarchais was not idle, for his stay in Hamburg was occupied in drawing up memoirs upon matters of public utility, in commercial negotiations, and in agreeable companionships with distinguished *émigrés* who like himself were anxiously awaiting the moment when they could return to France.

As for Beaumarchais, the affair of the 60,000 guns had ended, distressingly enough for his coffers, by the English carrying them off. They consented, however, at the urgent request of the merchant friend, to pay an arbitrary sum which was, however, far below their real value, but saved Beaumarchais from complete ruin. The affair ended, his only desire was to return home. This he was prevented from doing because of the proscription unjustly continued against him, which all the efforts of his friends and his family had been as yet unable to have removed.

MADAME DE BEAUMARCHAIS

Finally a member of the committee which he was serving, the same Robert Lindet before mentioned, wrote in his behalf to the minister of police, Cochon, the following letter:

"You have asked me to enlighten you regarding the second mission of Citizen Beaumarchais, and upon the exact time when that mission ended or should end.

"In charging the Citizen Beaumarchais with a mission, the committee of public safety proposed to itself two objects. The first was to procure the 60,000 guns deposited in the armory at Tervère, as objects of commerce; the second was to prevent these guns from falling into the power of the enemy.

"The Committee was obliged to pay for them only at the agreed price on con-

CHAPTER XXV

dition that they should be delivered and placed at their disposition in one of the ports of the Republic, within five or six months, The negotiation might take longer, but these terms were used to excite the zeal of the Citizen Beaumarchais.

"Before the expiration of the term he sent from Holland to Paris, the Citizen Durand, his friend, who had accompanied him on his journey, to give an account of the obstacles which delayed the execution of the enterprise and to propose measures which he thought were needful.

"Citizen Durand was sent back to Citizen Beaumarchais with a revised passport, which ran thus; 'to conduct him to his destination and to continue his mission;' because it seemed important to procure the guns for the government at whatever time that should be found possible, and also that the enemy should be prevented from seizing and distributing them in Belgium among the partisans of the house of Austria.

"The department of Paris placed the Citizen Beaumarchais upon the list of *émigrés* and placed seals upon his property.

"The committee decreed that since the Citizen Beaumarchais was on a mission he should not be treated as an *émigré*, because he was absent on a mission for the government. The department removed the seals.

"Some time after, the citizen Beaumarchais was replaced on the list of *émigrés*. There had been no new motive. The mission was not finished, his negotiations continued to be useful, he had not been recalled.... However, they persisted in considering him an *émigré*! ... the presence of citizen Beaumarchais in a foreign country was necessary up to the moment when the secret of his mission having been divulged, the English carried off the guns from the armory at Tervère to their ports, which they did last year.

"Nothing would then have prevented citizen Beaumarchais from returning to France because he could no longer hope to be able to fulfil his mission; but his name still rested on the list of *émigrés* and he could not return until it was erased.

"It was an injustice ever to have placed it upon the list of *émigrés*, since he was absent for the service of the Republic.

"Robert Lindet."

"To the Minister of Police."

This letter and the ardent solicitations of the wife and friends of the proscribed man, finally induced the committee to have his name erased from the list of *émigrés*, and so after three years of absence the author of the *Mariage de Figaro* was able to return to his native land.

CHAPTER XXVI

> *"Qu'étais'je donc? Je n'étais que moi, et moi tel que je suis resté, libre au milieu des fers, serein dans les plus grands dangers, faisant tête a tous les orages, menant les affaires d'une main et la guerre de l'autre, paresseux comme un âne et travaillant toujours, en butte à mille calomnies, mais, heureux dans mon intérieur, n'ayant jamais été d'aucune coterie, ni litéraire, ni politique, ni mystique, n'ayant fait de cour à personne, et partout repoussé de tous.... C'est le mystère de ma vie, en vain j'essaie de le résoudre."*

Beaumarchais After His Return from Exile—Takes Up All His Business Activities—Marriage of Eugénie—Her Portrait Drawn by Julie—Beaumarchais's Varied Interests—Correspondence with Bonaparte—Pleads for Lafayette Imprisoned—Death of Beaumarchais—Conclusion.

On his return to Paris, July 5th, 1796, "Beaumarchais," says Loménie, "found himself faced with a fortune ruined, not alone as so many others had been in the general crisis, but still more, by the confiscation of his revenues, the disappearance of his papers, and of the debts owing to him. His beautiful house was going to destruction, his garden torn up. While on one hand his debtors had disembarrassed themselves of their obligations by settling with the state in paper money, his creditors were waiting to seize him by the throat. He had accounts to give to, and to demand of the State, who, after confiscating his fortune, held still 745,000 francs deposited by him when he undertook the mission to secure the 60,000 guns...."

Not to go into all the perplexing details of the decisions and counter decisions rendered by the State, the anxieties, the almost insuperable difficulties that surrounded him on every side, let it suffice to say that with old age advancing apace, he still retained almost the same vigor, the same tenacity of purpose, the same indefatigable energy that have characterized him through life. Without ceasing, he drew up memoirs, conferred with the ministers, worked day and night to re-establish his fortune, so that those dear to him might not be left in want.

That he eventually succeeded in this may be judged by the fact that his family continued to inhabit their splendid residence until 1818, when the French government under the Restoration bought it for purposes of public utility. Moreover, the report rendered after his death by his bookkeeper, shows that the fortune which he was able to will his family rose very near the million mark, and this, not counting the debts owing him and lawsuits still pending, notably that with the United States.

But at the moment of his return to France it was not simply with his shattered fortune that Beaumarchais's mind was occupied. During their sojourn at Havre in 1792, the wife and daughter of Beaumarchais had made the acquaintance, says Bonneville, "of a young man of distinguished family, Louis André Toussaint Delarue, whose sister, a woman of remarkable intelligence, had married M. Mathias Dumas, a soldier with a very great future, who, after having taken part brilliantly in the war of American Independence as aide-de-camp of Rochambeau, was now Adjutant General of the Army under the orders of Lafayette, and had attached to him his young brother-in-law as *officier d'ordonnance*.... In 1792 they all found themselves waiting in Havre for an opportunity to escape into England."

It was there that M. Delarue met Mlle. Eugénie.... The two young people coming together under these unusual circumstances soon learned to love one another. His determination to obtain her hand in marriage was not at all affected by the fact that at that moment the entire possessions of her father were lost. Beaumarchais on his return to France, touched by so much constancy and devotion, hastened to assure the happiness of the young people. "Five days after my arrival," he wrote to a friend, "I made him the beautiful present.... They will at least have bread, but that is all, unless America discharges her debt to me, after twenty years of ingratitude."

They were married June 15th, 1796, Eugénie being nineteen, and her husband twenty-eight years of age. On the eve of her marriage, the Aunt Julie sketches for a friend the portrait of the young girl, in which she shows her as one in every way worthy of her father's affection—and with a character which, while indicating many contradictory possibilities, had, nevertheless, great charm and lovableness as well as intellectual force. It shows, too, that the terrible experiences through which she had passed, had left their trace upon her. Time, however, softened this very complex and somewhat formal young lady. "Dying in 1820 the daughter of the author of the *Mariage de Figaro*," says Loménie, "left in the hearts of all who knew her, the memory of a person of charming vivacity, of *finesse* and goodness; loving and cultivating the arts with passion, an excellent musician, woman of the world, and at the same time an accomplished mother."

The young man whom she married proved himself in every way worthy of her. In 1789 he was aide-de-camp of General Lafayette, and later held honorable official positions under the empire, the Restoration, and the government of July. In 1840 he was made *maréchal de camp de la garde nationale*, which post he held until 1848 when he resigned, at the age of eighty-four years. "In 1854," writes Loménie, "he still lives, surrounded in his flourishing old age by the respectful affection of all those who know how to appreciate the noble qualities of his heart and his character."

But to return to Beaumarchais; hardly had he found himself reunited to his family than he wrote to his faithful Gudin, bidding him return. The Revolution, however, had left this good man so destitute that he was obliged to request a loan in order to make the journey. This was at once promised. He wrote, August 26, 1796, "I start as soon as I shall have received the ten louis.... My whole heart glows at the thought of finding myself again under the roof with your happy family. And Oh, I shall see you again! How I regret that aerostatic machines are not already perfected.... But any conveyance is good, if it only conducts me to you. Adieu my good friend; keep well. I will write you the moment of my setting out."

Of their meeting, he writes later, "I came from the depths of my retreat to embrace my friend. Meeting after so many years, after so many atrocious events, was it not to be saved from the dangers of shipwreck and to find ourselves upon the rocks? It was in a way like escaping from the tomb, to embrace each other among the dead, after an unhoped for resurrection."

Beaumarchais's activities of this period continued to be the most varied. He entered with interest into the changing fortunes of the republic—which he accepted and over whose future he tried at times to become enthusiastic. In March, 1797, he had written to a friend:

"Yesterday's dinner, my dear Charles, is one that will long remain in my memory because of the precious choice of *convives* which our friend Dumas [General Mathieu-Dumas, brother-in-law of M. Delarue] had assembled at the house of his brother. On former occasions when I dined with the great ones of the State, I have been shocked at the assemblage of so many whose birth alone allowed them to be admitted. *Des sots de qualité, des imbéciles en place, des hommes vains de leurs richesses, des jeunes impudents, des coquettes,* etc. If it was not the ark of Noah, it was at least the court of the *Roi Petaut*; but yesterday out of twenty-four persons at table, there was not one whose great personal merit would not have given him a right to his place. It was, I might say, an excellent *extrait* of the French Republic, and I, who sat silent, regarding them, applied to each the great merit which distinguished him. Here are their names:" And then, after making the inventory, he terminates thus:

"The dinner was instructive, in no way noisy, very agreeable, in a word such as I do not remember to have ever before experienced.

"Caron Beaumarchais."

"Four months later," says Loménie, "*un coup d'état* had proscribed nearly every one of those twenty-four *convives*."

"The deputies of the people," says Gudin, "were taken from their sacred seats, locked up in portable cages like wild beasts, tossed on board vessels and transported to Guyan." This *coup d'état* cooled very considerably the republican ardor of Beaumarchais; "He was totally at a loss," continues Gudin, "to understand either the men or their doings; he failed to comprehend anything relative to the forms or the means employed in those times without rule or principle. He called upon reason, which had helped him triumph so many times; reason had become a stranger, she was, if we dare say it, a species of *émigrée* whose name rendered suspicious anyone who invoqued her."

But though Beaumarchais was forced to leave the political revolution to take

CHAPTER XXVI 163

its course without attempting to change it, his mind ever alert, found innumerable points of contact with the age in which he lived. "Although afflicted with almost complete deafness we see him," says Loménie, "rising above his personal preoccupations and the sorrows that assailed him, to apply his mind with the whole force of his indefatigable ardor to questions of public utility, to literary affairs, and a thousand other incidents foreign to his own interests. Now he points out with indignation, in the journals of the times, the unbelievable negligence which permits the body of Turenne, rescued from the vandalism of the Terror, to remain forgotten and exposed among skeletons of animals in the *Jardin des Plantes*, until he finally brings about a decree of the Directory which puts an end to this scandal; again he writes letters and memoirs upon all subjects of public interest ... now to the government, now to such deputies as Baudin des Ardennes, who represent ideas of moderation and legality.

"He bestirred himself for the agents of rapid locomotion, aided Mr. Scott in the development of aerostatic machines; celebrated in verse a motor called the *velocifère*, talked literature and the theatre with amiable Collin d'Harleville, or pleaded still with the Minister of the Interior for the rights of dramatic authors against the actors, ... and occupied himself at the same time with having his drama *La Mère Coupable* brought again before the public."

This drama which had been written immediately preceding the outbreak of the Revolution, had been read and accepted by the Théâtre Français in 1791, but following this, Beaumarchais had been chosen by the Assembly of Dramatic Authors to represent their interests before the *corps législatif*, which was about to pronounce judgment, and he had acquitted himself with so much ardor that a rupture had followed between himself and the Théâtre Français. Another troupe of the neighborhood demanded the play with so much insistence that he allowed them to produce it upon their new theatre; here it was performed for the first time in June, 1792. But the piece was so poorly played that its success was indifferent. During the time of the Revolution its performance was not to be thought of, but it will not be considered surprising that one of Beaumarchais's first concerns, after the settlement of the most pressing of his family affairs, was to have the piece brought again before the public and played at the Comédie Française. This was effected in May, 1797. Its complete success brought a great happiness to his declining years.

The characters of *La Mère Coupable* are the same as those of *Le Barbier*, and *Le Mariage de Figaro*—although from a literary point-of-view it is very far from rivaling the two earlier productions, "the subject," says Loménie, "taken in itself, is at the same time, very dramatic and of an incontestable morality."

Among the numerous letters, written or received by Beaumarchais in regard to this drama, is one addressed by him to the widow of the last of the Stuarts, the Countess of Albany, who happening to be in Paris in 1791 had begged Beaumarchais to give a reading of *La Mère Coupable*, in her salon. He replied:

"Paris, 5th February, 1791.

"Madame la Comtesse:

"Since you insist absolutely upon hearing my very severe work, I cannot refuse you. But observe that when I wish to laugh, it is *aux éclats*; if I must weep, it is *aux sanglots*. I know nothing between but *l'ennui*. Admit then, anyone you wish Tuesday, only keep away those whose hearts are hard, whose souls are dried, and who feel pity for the sorrows that we find so delicious.... Have a few tender women, some men for whom the heart is not a chimera, and who are not ashamed to weep. I promise you that painful pleasure, and am with respect, Madame la Comtesse, etc.,

"Beaumarchais."

But from his own interests let us turn with him again to those of national importance.

"As ardent an imagination as that of Beaumarchais," says Loménie, "could not be expected to remain a stranger to the universal enthusiasm which in 1797 was inspired by the youthful conqueror of Italy."

Through the intervention of the General Desaix, Beaumarchais who had celebrated in prose and verse the movements of the young conqueror across the Alps, was able to address a letter to him directly, to which he received the following concise reply:

"Paris, the 11 *germinal* An VI,

March, 1798.

"General Desaix has handed me, citizen, your amiable letter of the 25 *ventose*. I thank you for it. I shall seize with pleasure, any circumstance which presents itself, to form the acquaintance of the author of *La Mère Coupable*.

"I salute you,

"Bonaparte."

"Thus," says Loménie, "for the General Bonaparte, Beaumarchais is above all else, the author of *La Mère Coupable*. Can this be an indication of a literary preference for this drama, or a certain political repugnance for the *Mariage de Figaro*, or simply the result of the fact that *La Mère Coupable* had recently been placed upon the stage? This is a question that seems difficult to answer.

"I find," continues Loménie, "among the papers confided to me by the family of Beaumarchais, another letter of Bonaparte, at that time first Consul, addressed to Mme. de Beaumarchais after the death of her husband, which is a reply to a petition. It reads:

"Paris, *vendémiaire* An IX.

"Madame:

"I have received your letter. I will bring into this matter all the interest which the memory of a justly celebrated man merits, and that yourself inspires.

"Bonaparte."

In one of the *mauvais vers* (from a literary viewpoint) with which Beaumarchais in his old age commented upon the career of the great general, is one which,

CHAPTER XXVI

says Loménie, "honors his sensibility." It was written in 1797, and runs thus:

> "Young Bonaparte, from victory to victory,
> Thou givest us peace, and our hearts are moved;
> But dost thou wish to conquer every form of glory?
> Then think of our prisoners of l'Olmutz."

The allusion in the verse was to Lafayette and his fellow-prisoners, who for five years had been detained, first in a prison in Prussia, and later in the Austrian fortress of Olmutz. In 1792, Lafayette had been declared a traitor by the National Assembly after the fateful tenth of August, and been forced to cross the frontier and give himself up to the Austrians, who were then fighting against France. He was held as a prisoner of State. His wife and family, having been unable to secure his release, were permitted to share his captivity with him. Napoleon, who never had entertained a very high opinion of the military capacity of Lafayette, nevertheless stipulated for his release and for that of his fellow-prisoners in the treaty of Campo Formio, which was signed during the year 1797.

But to return to the private life of Beaumarchais. Gudin, after visiting his friend, had not consented to remain under his roof, feeling that now he would be a burden and so had returned to his country retreat to await events. It was there that he learned of the joy that was about to crown the old age of his friend. He wrote to Beaumarchais:

"I remember the songs you made for Eugénie, when you cradled her on your knees, and it seems to me that I can hear you sing others for her child. Kiss her for me, my dear friend, compliment her for me, and all of you rejoice over your domestic happiness; it is the sweetest of all, the most real perhaps."

For Beaumarchais, this was indeed the crowning blessing of this life. On January 5th, 1798, Madame Delarue gave birth to a daughter, Palmyr, as they called her. This event caused her grandfather to give way to "transports of joy," though at first his only thought was "for his beloved Eugénie."

With the reëstablishment of Beaumarchais's fortune, Gudin, who had in the meantime settled his own affairs, returned to live with his friend.

"I came again," he says, "to my native city, delighted to see my friend, and to find his family augmented. We tasted the sweetness of friendship the most intimate. I saw him abandon himself in our conversations to the most vivid hope for the prosperity of the state and of our arms.

"Beaumarchais, at this time, was full of force and of health. Never were his days devoured by so many plans, projects, labors and enterprises.... His age allowed us to hope that we might retain him a long while.

"We had spent the day together in the midst of his family, with one of his oldest friends. He had been very gay and had recalled in the conversation several events of his youth, which he recounted with a charming complacency.... I did not leave him until ten o'clock; he retired at eleven, after embracing his wife. She was slightly indisposed; he recommended her to take some precautions for her health,—his own seemed perfect. He went to bed as usual, and wakened early.

He went to sleep again and wakened no more. He was found next morning in the same attitude in which he placed himself on going to bed."

An attack of *apoplexie foudroyante* had carried him off at the age of sixty-seven years and three months. This was on the 18th of May, 1799.

The suddenness of the death of Beaumarchais caused, as may be imagined, the most profound sorrow to his family and friends.

Madame de Beaumarchais wrote a few days after his death:

"Our loss is irreparable. The companion of twenty-five years of my life has disappeared, leaving me only useless regrets, a frightful solicitude and memories that nothing can efface.... He forgave easily, he willingly forgot injuries.... He was a good father, zealous friend, defender of the absent who were attacked before him. Superior to petty jealousies, so common among men of letters, he counselled, encouraged all, and aided them with his purse and his advice.

"To the philosophic eye, his end should be regarded as a favor. He left this life, or rather, it left him, without struggle, without pain, or any of those rendings inevitable in the frightful separation from all those dear to him. He went out of life as unconsciously as he entered it."

"The inventory," says Gudin in his narrative, "which is made at a man's death, often reveals the secrets of his life. That of Beaumarchais showed us that to succor families in distress, artists, men of letters, men of quality, he had advanced more than 900,000 francs without hope that these sums ever should be repaid. If one adds to these, sums that he had lavished without leaving the least trace, one would be convinced that he had expended more than 2,000,000 in benevolences."

The mortal remains of Beaumarchais were laid to rest in a sombre avenue of his garden which he himself had prepared. "In planting his garden," says Gudin, "he had consecrated a spot for his eternal rest.... It was there that we placed him. It was there that his son-in-law, his relatives, his friends, a few men of letters, paid him their last respects, and that Collin d'Harleville read a discourse which I had composed in the overflowing of my sorrow, but which I was not in a condition to pronounce."

"A beautiful copy of the Fighting Gladiator," says Lintilhac, "decorated the entrance to the ostentatious mansion where camped *la vieillesse militante* of Beaumarchais. The posture of the combat, like the face of the gladiator, betrayed a manly agony. What expressive symbol of his life and work!"

In pausing now to cast a backward glance over the achievements of this one man, we scarcely can fail to admit with Lintilhac that Beaumarchais was not boasting when he wrote toward the end of his life: "I am the only Frenchman, perhaps, who never has demanded anything of anyone, and nevertheless, among my great labors, I count with pride, to have contributed more than any other European towards rendering America free."

That he ever looked upon his work in the cause of American Independence, as his strongest claim to immortality among men, can be judged from his constant return to the subject and especially from what he says in his memoir of self-justification delivered before the Commune of Paris in September, 1789. (Given in Chapter XI.) It may be said that the very persistence of his reclamations in this regard was responsible for the indifference with which they were universally received. A man so rich, so happy, so prosperous, so gay, so universally successful in all his undertakings, could not expect to be taken seriously when he loudly decried the universal ingratitude of mankind, even though his accusations might be just. What Beaumarchais essentially lacked, as La Harpe has pointed out, was above everything else, *measure* and *good taste*. He was too ostentatious, too expansive, talked too much of himself, pushed himself forward with too much noise, was too brilliant, too daring, too successful; and yet, as M. de Loménie has said in the remarkable résumé of the character of Beaumarchais given at the end of his work: "It does not seem to us possible to contest the fact that Beaumarchais is one of those men who gains the most by being seen at close range and that he is worth infinitely more than his reputation." And the same author continues:

"Beaumarchais had implacable enemies; but one very important point is to be noted, namely that all those who attacked him with fury either knew him very little, or did not know him at all; while those who lived intimately with him loved him passionately. All the literary men who knew him in life, and who spoke of him after his death, have spoken with affection and esteem. Two minds as different as those of La Harpe and Arnault meet, in regard to him, with the same expressions of sympathy, and I have not found a trace in all the papers left after his death of a single man who, after knowing him intimately, became his enemy. On the contrary, I constantly have found testimonials of attachment that are far from common. I have found that friendships, begun in his youth, when he was a simple watchmaker, or *contrôleur* of the house of the king, follow him for thirty or forty years without ever changing or weakening, but on the contrary, redouble in intensity and manifest themselves in the greatest tenderness, and in the most disinterested ways....

"The goodness of the author of the *Mariage de Figaro*, extended not only to those about him. Gudin affirms that M. Goëzman fallen into misery was succored by him; that Baculard was on his register for 3,600 frs. which were never returned.

"A charming trait of his character often has been remarked, in relation to the inscription engraved upon the collar of his little dog, which was as follows:—'I am Mlle. Follette; Beaumarchais belongs to me. We live on the Boulevard.'

"We can therefore say with La Harpe and Arnault who knew him, that although the author of the *Mariage de Figaro*, was followed all his life by black calumnies, he resembled in nothing the portrait which his enemies have left us of him. It is true that his good qualities are often somewhat veiled by *légèreté d'esprit* and *défaut de tenue*. His friend d'Atilly painted him to nature, when he said, '*he has the heart of an honest man*, but he often has *the tone of a bohemian.*' The frivolity of the century in which he lived had too much colored his ideas ... and indeed equitably to judge the character of the man in its entirety, one must not forget either the situation in which he found himself, or the century in which he lived."

Louis de Loménie wrote in 1854, more than half a century after the death of

Beaumarchais. Since the appearance of his work, many others have taken up the pen to discuss the pros and cons of this many-sided character. The last of these, M. Eugène Lintilhac, calls attention to the crowd of obliges from the scepter to the shepherd's crook. "What man in need," he says, "great lord or modest author, ever came and knocked at his door, without carrying away consolation in words and species? To how many oppressed, mulattos, slaves, Jews, protestants has he not held the hand?"

Sainte-Beuve says somewhere, that the Society of Dramatic Authors should never assemble without saluting the bust of Beaumarchais. It can do so henceforward because they have placed in the hall where their meetings are held, a marble bust of its founder.

On the one hundredth anniversary of the first production of the *Mariage de Figaro*, on April 27, 1884, the play was performed again at the Théâtre Français. At the close of the performance the bust of Beaumarchais was brought forward, and crowned while Coquelin recited verses to his praise written for the occasion by M. Paul Delair.

Thus to have survived a veritable death from oblivion, and to have come after a century of neglect into a resurrection of honor and fame, is sufficient proof of the real greatness of the literary genius of Beaumarchais to convince all unbelievers. This has been the act of reparation accorded him by France. The debt of gratitude owed him by America is still unpaid. It remains to be seen whether the same resurrection of honor awaits him among us.

This book is a first attempt to state fully the facts of the life of Beaumarchais for the American people, so that they may know the man who was their friend, even before they came into existence as a nation, and it is put out in the hope that they may share the sentiment renewed in M. Eugène Lintilhac and so forcibly expressed by Gudin—"I soon found that I could not love him moderately when I came to know him in his home."

And so with this expression of a friend's esteem, let us leave Beaumarchais in company with his faithful Gudin, Gudin, "whose great work," says Lintilhac, "*the History of France*, still sleeps in the *Bibliotèque Nationale*, ... but whose author has found a surer path to glory in taking the first place in the cortège of his illustrious friend,—Beaumarchais."

Although America has been slow to recognize the claims of Beaumarchais to her gratitude, yet Time, the great leveler, is restoring all things to their place; and to-day, if our "friend" is cognizant of what history is doing, he realizes that this same United States, which his services did so much to found, is repaying this debt with interest so far as money goes, but still more with warm affection and heartiest friendship cemented by the life blood of both nations—and to-day he repeats what he wrote in December, 1779—"As for me, whose interests lose themselves before such grand interests; I, private individual, but good Frenchman, and sincere friend of the brave people who have just conquered their liberty; if one is astonished that my feeble voice should have mingled with the mouths of thunder which plead this great cause, I will reply that one is always strong enough when one has right

CHAPTER XXVI

on his side....

"I have had great losses. They have rendered my labors less fruitful than I hoped for my independent friends, but as it is less by my success than by my efforts that I should be judged, I still dare to pretend to the noble reward which I promised myself; the esteem of three great nations; France, America, and even England.

"Caron de Beaumarchais."

BIBLIOGRAPHY

Beaumarchais et son Temps par Louis de Loménie, Paris, 1850. Translated by H. S. Edwards. N. Y. 1857

Histoire de Beaumarchais, Gudin de la Brenellerie. Edited by Maurice Tourneux, 1888

Œvres Complètes, précédées d'une notice sur sa vie et ses ouvrages par Saint Marc Gerardin, 1828, 6 tomes

Nouvelle Edition Augmentée de quatre pièces de Théâtre et des documents divers inédits avec une introduction par M. E. Fournier, ornée de vingt portraits, etc. 1876

H. Doniol—*Histoire de la Participation de la France dans l'établissement des Etats-Unis*, 5 tomes. Paris, 1886-1892

E. Lintilhac—*Beaumarchais et ses œuvres; précis de sa vie et histoire de son esprit, etc.* Paris, 1887

Beaumarchais the Merchant. Hon. John Bigelow in *Hours at Home*, June 1870

Marie Thérèse Amélie Caron de Beaumarchais d'après sa correspondence inédite par Bonneville de Marsangy, 1890

Bibliographic des œuvres de Beaumarchais. H. Cordier, 1883

Beaumarchais: eine Biographie. A. Bettleheim, 1886

Mémoires sur le Chevalier d'Eon, suivis de douze lettres inédites de Beaumarchais. F. Gaillardet, 1866

New Material for the History of the American Revolution. J. Durand, 1889

Diplomatic Correspondence. Francis Wharton

Diplomatic Correspondence of the American Revolution. J. Sparks, 1829-1830

Life and Times of Benjamin Franklin. James Parton, 1864

Deane Papers, (6 vols.). 1887

A Vindication of Arthur Lee, designed as a refutation of the charges found in the writings of Benjamin Franklin, as exhibited by Jared Sparks, etc. 1894

Beaumarchais: étude par P. Bonnefon, 1887

BIBLIOGRAPHY

Beaumarchais and Sonnenfels. A. von Arnett

Mémoires de Beaumarchais. Nouveile édition, précédée d'une appréciation tirée des Causeries du Lundi par M. Sainte-Beuve, 1878

Cours de Littérature ancienne et moderne par La Harpe, 1799-1803

A History of England, in the 18th Century. By W. E. H. Lecky (4 Vols.) 1887

Correspondence and Public Papers of John Jay, 1890-93

Judgement—qu'approuve le nouvel échappement de montres du Sieur Caron, 1754

Claims of the Heirs of Beaumarchais Against the United States. House Documents

Report of the Committee of Claims on the Petition of the Heirs of Beaumarchais. 1812-1817

Le Barbier de Séville. 1902. 20th Century Text-Books

Life of F. W. von Steuben, with an Introduction by George Bancroft, 1859, by F. Kapp

Beaumarchais. Vortrag von Dr. S. Born, 1881

Beaumarchais. A. Hallays, 1897

La Fin de l'ancien Régime. 1879. Imbert de St. Amand.

Les Femmes de la cour de Louis XV. 1876. Imbert de St. Amand

Les beaux jours de Marie Antoinette, Imbert de St. Amand

The Lost Million. Charles J. Stillé

Silas Deane. Paper read before the American Historical Association of Boston and Cambridge, 1887, by Charles Islam

The Marquis de La Fayette in the American Revolution. Charlemagne Tower, 1895

The American Revolution. 2 vols. John Fiske, 1891

House Documents, Vol. 9. Report 111. Fifteenth Congress, First Session.

INDEX

A

Admiral D'estaing *136*
After The Terror *155*
Ammunition *34, 86, 91*
Archbishop Of Lyon *130*
Armament *104, 108, 111, 112, 135, 142*
Arthur Lee *12, 27, 33, 34, 45, 46, 47, 58, 63, 87, 88, 96, 104, 109, 115, 116, 170*
Assumed Name *62*
Attitude Of France *14*
August 10Th *149*

B

Barbeu Dubourg *43*
Baron Von Steuben *69, 77, 78, 79, 85, 112, 144*
Bastille *122, 131, 140, 141*
Beaumarchais Et Ses Œuvres *148, 170*
Beauty Of Madame De Beaumarchais *144*
Benjamin Franklin *63, 170*
Bon Secours *144*
Bonvouloir *12, 15*
Buchot *116*
Burgoyne *76, 82, 86*

C

Calumny *3, 115*
Canada *15, 37*
Cape Francis *41, 42, 76, 90*
Caron De Beaumarchais *Iv, 19, 22, 24, 30, 32, 42, 90, 91, 108, 113, 115, 121, 136, 139, 148, 169, 170*
Carried In Triumph *53*
Cause Of America *26, 30, 56, 57, 76, 85, 135*
Chenu *131, 132*
Chevalier D'eon *Vi, 1, 2, 4, 6, 9, 11, 12, 13, 16, 23, 170*
Colonists *13, 15, 20, 63, 74, 94, 100, 114*
Comédie Française *128, 130, 163*

INDEX

Commercial House Of Roderigue Hortalès Et Cie *67*
Comte De Guerchy *2, 3, 6*
Comte De La Blache *53, 54, 97, 98*
Comte De Vergennes *25, 42, 43, 44, 45, 65, 82, 84, 106, 107*
Continental Congress *55, 76, 94, 109*
Court Of Versailles *111, 123*
Creation Of Figaro *128*

D

Daughter Of Beaumarchais *161*
Dauphin *70*
Des Epinières *69, 78*
Doniol *13, 16, 17, 24, 30, 32, 35, 39, 43, 44, 50, 52, 57, 60, 61, 62, 63, 64, 65, 66, 69, 74, 75, 76, 79, 80, 82, 83, 85, 105, 170*
Dramatic Authors *53, 163, 168*
Duc De Fronsac *122, 123, 124*
Du Verney *39, 97*

E

English Government *3, 15, 63, 69, 82, 102, 152*
Eugène Lintilhac *168*
Eugénie *135, 144, 146, 148, 153, 154, 157, 160, 161, 165*

F

Fall Of New York *61*
Famous Receipt *42, 116*
Figaro *1, 32, 121, 122, 123, 124, 127, 128, 129, 130, 131, 132, 133, 144, 145, 150, 151, 159, 161, 164, 167, 168*
Flanders *12, 13*
Friend Of Franklin *43*

G

Gaillardet *Vi, 2, 3, 4, 6, 8, 13, 15, 36, 37, 138, 170*
Gérard De Rayneval *110*
Good Officer *65*
Government Of France *12*
Grennevilliers *121, 123, 124, 125*
Gudin De La Brenellerie *69, 100, 170*

H

Hamburg *31, 116, 152, 153, 157*
Havre *62, 66, 74, 87, 146, 148, 149, 151, 161*
Heirs Of Beaumarchais *104, 117, 120, 141, 171*
Holland *13, 36, 41, 114, 148, 151, 159*

Hon. John Bigelow *76, 86, 170*
Horatio Gates *109*
Hotel Boulevard *139*

I

Imbert De Saint-Amand *128*
Indiscretion Of *62, 71, 83*
In London *2, 7, 12, 13, 15, 16, 17, 19, 27, 30, 31, 34, 47, 63, 69, 75, 81, 95, 99, 100, 104, 152*
Institut De Bienfaisance *130, 131*

J

Jefferson *63, 118, 143*
John Jay *59, 60, 96, 105, 118, 126, 137, 143, 171*

L

La Harpe *122, 146, 167, 171*
La Mère Coupable *163, 164*
La Victoire *74*
Lawsuit *52, 107*
Le Barbier De Séville *62, 133, 171*
Lebrun *151*
Le Comte De Maurepas *70, 82, 83, 84, 107*
Le Fier Roderigue *90, 104, 111, 112, 135, 136, 138*
Le Mariage De Figaro *1, 126, 163*
Le Point Jaloux *15*
Living *2, 3*
Lord Ferrers *4, 6, 8*
Lord Mayor Wilkes *4*
Lord Rochford *27, 30, 32, 33*
Louis De Loménie *167, 170*

M

Madame De Beaumarchais *135, 139, 144, 151, 152, 154, 156, 158, 166*
Manly Firmness Of *73*
M. Arnault *132*
Marquis De Lafayette *87, 90, 143*
Maupeou *52, 53, 97, 99*
Maurice Tourneux *170*
M. De Breteuil *124, 125*
M. De Sartine *5, 12, 16, 17, 18, 30, 33, 53, 65, 66, 71, 107, 135*
M. De Vaudreuil *123, 125, 133*
Metz *57, 65, 74*
M. Grand *81*

INDEX

Miss Margaret Shippen *109*
Mlle. Eugénie *145, 146, 161*
Mlle. Follette *167*
Mr. Tucker *104, 118*

N

Nephew Of Beaumarchais *59, 78*

P

Papers Of *4, 7, 60, 124, 171*
Parliaments *70*
Parties In England *12*
Passy *64, 77, 80, 81, 82, 86, 88, 89, 104, 112*
Philadelphia *18, 36, 46, 58, 104, 109, 110, 111, 137*
Pleads For Lafayette Imprisoned *160*
Poland *22*
Port-Libre *153*
Private Character *44, 94*
Private Life *165*

R

Recommendations For Aix *32*
Returns To France *148*
Rights Of Dramatic Authors *163*
Robert Lindet *152, 158, 159*
Robert Morris *93, 95*
Roderigue Hortalès Et Cie *39, 41, 43, 49, 56, 58, 67, 79, 86, 90, 91, 92, 95, 108, 110*

S

Saratoga *80, 109*
Secret Aid *28, 114*
Silas Deane *34, 39, 40, 43, 44, 45, 46, 47, 48, 56, 57, 58, 59, 63, 65, 69, 74, 87, 88, 89, 91, 96, 104, 108, 109, 110, 113, 142, 171*
Sister Of Beaumarchais *154, 156*
Spain *13, 19, 28, 39, 42, 43, 59, 76, 79, 82, 87*
St. Petersburg *2*
Sully *70*
Surrender Of Burgoyne *69, 80, 109*

T

Théâtre Français *163, 168*
The Opposition *14, 16, 27, 28, 29, 36, 54, 89, 104*
The Parliament *2, 28, 51, 52, 53, 97*
Theveneau De Francy *69, 77, 78, 86, 91, 92, 116*

Thrown Into Prison *116*
Toryism *109*
Treaty Of Campo Formio *165*

V

Versailles *5, 7, 8, 12, 16, 17, 20, 27, 33, 46, 51, 52, 62, 64, 65, 76, 77, 78, 107, 122, 123*
Vessel Of Beaumarchais *136*
Voltaire *2, 69, 88, 99, 102*

Lector House believes that a society develops through a two-fold approach of continuous learning and adaptation, which is derived from the study of classic literary works spread across the historic timeline of literature records. Therefore, we aim at reviving, repairing and redeveloping all those inaccessible or damaged but historically as well as culturally important literature across subjects so that the future generations may have an opportunity to study and learn from past works to embark upon a journey of creating a better future.

This book is a result of an effort made by Lector House towards making a contribution to the preservation and repair of original ancient works which might hold historical significance to the approach of continuous learning across subjects.

HAPPY READING & LEARNING!

LECTOR HOUSE LLP
E-MAIL: lectorpublishing@gmail.com

Lightning Source UK Ltd.
Milton Keynes UK
UKHW010646090820
367908UK00002B/433